D0031279

THE GOOD OF AFFLUENCE

THE GOOD OF AFFLUENCE

Seeking God in a Culture of Wealth

JOHN R. SCHNEIDER

WILLIAM B. EERDMANS PUBLISHING COMPANY
GRAND RAPIDS, MICHIGAN / CAMBRIDGE, U.K.

HOUSTON PUBLIC LIBRARY

R01246 00136

© 2002 Wm. B. Eerdmans Publishing Co.

All rights reserved

Wm. B. Eerdmans Publishing Co.

255 Jefferson Ave. S.E., Grand Rapids, Michigan 49503 /

P.O. Box 163, Cambridge CB3 9PU U.K.

Printed in the United States of America

06 05 04 03 02   7 6 5 4 3 2 1

Library of Congress Cataloging-in-Publication Data

Schneider, John R.

The good of affluence : a theology for people seeking God

in a culture of modern capitalism / John R. Schneider.

p.   cm.

Includes bibilographical references.

ISBN 0-8028-4799-4 (cloth: alk. paper)

1. Wealth — Religious aspects — Christianity.

2. Wealth — Biblical teaching

3. Capitalism — Religious aspects — Christianity.

I. Title.

BR115. W4 S37 2002

261.8'5 — dc21

2002024469

www.eerdmans.com

To my mother
Jean Schneider
and my father
Robert "Bob" Schneider
(1928-2001),
who taught me by example
that in every passing moment
there is eternity

Contents

Preface

This book was supposed to be a revised edition of my earlier book, *Godly Materialism: Rethinking Money and Possessions,* but it grew into what really amounts to a new work on Christian faith and wealth. The extended introduction and first chapter are completely new. The argument adopts the form and method of a Christian theology more explicitly than the older one did. And while the major thesis remains pretty much the same, the argumentation stands more solidly and conspicuously upon well-established scholarship. Almost every point of argument has been sharpened and, in many instances, elaborated in greater analytical detail. And I would like to think that the argument of the work as a whole is thereby considerably stronger than in the previous version. Of course the discussion has also been brought up to date by the inclusion and engagement of important works that have been published since 1995. In the end, everyone involved with this project agreed that publication under a new title was very much in order. And so it has one, *The Good of Affluence: Seeking God in a Culture of Wealth.* I will let the explanation of its sense emerge in the discussion that follows.

I must take time to thank the academic administration of Calvin College for approving the recommendation by the Committee on Scholarship to grant a Calvin Summer Research fellowship to support me in this work. The grant was of considerable help and an encouragement to finish the manuscript on schedule. I must also thank the staff at Eerdmans Publishing Company for its kind cooperation in moving the book so quickly into production. I especially thank Andrew Hoogheem, my editor, and also

Pat Sturgeon, formerly my secretary and still my friend, who prepared the bibliography. Of course any and all errors are my responsibility.

I am also indebted to several colleagues around the country for their unrelenting insistence that this book — or one like it — needed to be in print. There are too many such colleagues to name here without fear of leaving one or more of them out. One in particular, New Testament expert Kenneth Pomykala of the Religion Department at Calvin College, deserves special mention for steering me toward works of social history that were of inestimable help in writing Chapter 5.

I want to thank, too, various people in the world of business for their encouragement, most especially Ms. Janet Wills, CEO of the Wills Corporation. It is good to know that reflective people who really live and move and have their being in that world find that the contents of the book ring true and challenge them in a way that those of a great many scholarly writings on the subject do not.

Unfortunately, I had to complete this book during what my family and I knew were my father's last days. He died on September 10, just a few days after I submitted the manuscript to the publisher. I wrote most of it during early mornings in his home in York, Nebraska, the town where I was born. I told him I would dedicate the book to him and to my mother, which brought tears to his eyes (definitely not his style). Not being a scholar in any sense, he would find it perplexing, and perhaps even annoying, were I able to tell him that by example — one that was by no means obviously or deliberately Christian — he and my mother taught me a truth that few but the great Kierkegaard have understood well enough to express in language. I think it sad that so few Christians, conservative or liberal, seem to understand it very well now. I have thus expressed it in the one sentence of dedication, and readers should ponder it, for it is a key to the deeper meaning I am after in this book. I believe it is a key to the true Christian life of faith, as distinct from life lived under mere Christian belief and ethical duty. Whether this book achieves anything like what that dedication means to express is something readers will have to judge for themselves.

Seeking God in a Culture of Wealth

We are going to see a revival in this country, and it's going to be led by rich people.

MICHAEL NOVAK[1]

This is a book of Christian theology written to help people seeking God in the culture that has grown from modern capitalism. The people I have in mind are probably in some form of business. They are corporate professionals, entrepreneurs and high-level employees, who spend the better part of their days producing goods and services in the context of making money. Of course, every member of an advanced society (including even the scholar) is immersed in its economy — sometimes more than she knows, or wishes to admit. We are all consumers who help compose innumerable markets for which businesses compete. And it is very important to stress that all of us who live in so-called advanced societies are quite rich. If we do not think so, we need only ask the people living elsewhere, on the outside.

There are today twenty-five societies that have successfully deployed capitalism. These societies have prospered, and as they have done so, they have also developed distinctive cultures — cultures of capitalism. They are

1. Michael Novak quoted in Dinesh D'Souza, *The Virtue of Prosperity: Finding Values in an Age of Techno-Affluence* (New York: Free Press, 2000), p. 143.

1

cultures of a sort that never existed before on the planet. The astonishing thing about them is not that they contain a lot of affluence, but that they are *cultures* of affluence.

There have always been rich people in the world, and in the church there have always been rich Christian people. But human history has never before known circumstances in which entire societies were affluent and engaged in this sort of constant economic activity. For most of human history, almost everyone was poor; only a few were rich. And for the most part the vast majority of Christians were poor. The spiritual and moral traditions of the church in its teachings on wealth and poverty (going back to the New Testament) thus emerged from economic circumstances that could not be more different from ours in the West. In ancient cultures, where poverty was widespread, theologians naturally stressed the questions that arose when people had to deal with poverty. But we do not inherit a similarly advanced tradition on what it means to be rich. And what sparse teaching we do have is very much the product of ancient economic times. We desperately need integrated Christian spiritual and moral theology on what being affluent means in our time.

There is no short supply of scholarship and preaching from Christian leaders on the subject. The trouble is — and this is a strong assumption of my book — that the majority of writers interpret capitalism and the unique culture to which it gives rise in terms that are quite antiquated. These are largely the terms received from social theorists Karl Marx and Max Weber (more on them in due course). And furthermore, Christian tradition going back to very ancient times has been mainly negative in its judgments on the morality of affluence. We shall see why that is in the next chapter. But what it means is that Christian tradition only disposes Christian theorists to accept the negative social analysis of capitalism and its manner of life. The underlying thesis of this book is that both these common perspectives — the cultural and the biblical — on faith and wealth have to be renovated in the light of fresh evidence and theory.

With the help of others (particularly Michael Novak) I have come to believe it is mistaken — grievously so — to interpret the workings of capitalism in terms of exploitation, class warfare, and oppression (as Marx does), and its human vision and habits of economic life as incompatible with true Christianity (as Weber does). As will be clear, I have come to believe (in the light of fresh theory) that capitalism (for all its problems) is not just the greatest liberating power in human history, but also that its cultural workings provide an unusually good opportunity for the expression of true Christian faith and virtue. Of course the truth of these claims also depends on our interpretation of Scripture, and on what we believe true Christian faith and virtue to be.

The main body of this book, then, is a theological interpretation of sacred Scripture on the place of material affluence. Obviously, if the weight of ancient Christian tradition prevails, and the proper Christian view of affluence must be negative, then our view of capitalism and its culture of affluence must be negative, too. But in spite of its time-honored status, I do not think our scriptures on the whole support that tradition. I believe that historic Christian teaching on wealth and poverty is as much a product of ancient economic times as it is of the full biblical narrative.

It is very widely presumed in Christian theology today that the economic condition of affluence is not a very good one for Christians to be in. It is widely presumed that this condition is almost inherently a bad one for hearing and responding with faith and integrity to the Gospel of Jesus Christ. In the main body of this book, I will seek to show that this wealth-negative assumption is mistaken. For it oversimplifies the truth that there is a way — an all too common way — to be rich that is evil in God's sight. That truth is as clear as can be in the Law, the Prophets, and in the teachings of Jesus. However, it also seems clear in the Bible, from beginning to end, that there is a way to be affluent that is good. In fact, as I will seek to show, it is a fundamental biblical theme that material prosperity (rightly understood) is the condition that God envisions for all human beings. It describes the condition that God desired for human beings when he created the world. It describes the condition that God has in view for human beings in eternity. And it describes the condition that God (circumstances being right) desires for human beings now. In my view, being affluent in a certain way — I call it "delight" — indeed reflects the good created order of God. That is what I mean in the title by "the good of affluence." Properly understood, the condition of affluence in advanced societies is good in the same way that conditions in Eden, the Promised land, and the Messianic Banquet are said to be good. They are good in the potential they have for human flourishing and, through it, the flourishing of the cosmos as God wills it to be.

It is my experience that a good many wealthy Christian people are seriously looking for ways to cultivate the good of affluence, but they are not sure how. Like the chief tax collector Zacchaeus, they are seeking to find the light and order of God in an economic world that they know (we do not have to tell them) is too often dark and full of chaos. In his most recent book, *The Virtue of Prosperity,* American Enterprise Fellow Dinesh D'Souza quotes from an interview he conducted with influential Christian social theologian Michael Novak.

> We are going to see a spiritual revival in this country, and it's going to be led by rich people. I realize that sounds odd, but it really isn't. The Bible tells us that man cannot live by bread alone. But you have to have bread to realize that. Rich people are finding that wealth by itself does not bring meaning and fulfillment, and they are starting to search for answers. In the past people came to God because they were suffering, because they were broken. But increasingly, in the West, it's going to be affluence that leads people to God.[2]

In this quote, Novak is describing people I know. I think of people like Janet Wills, who is CEO of the Wills Corporation, a firm that manages large investment portfolios held mainly by Christians. In telephone conversations, she has spoken at length and with obvious passion about her clients who have become wealthy beyond their imaginings during the last decade of growth in the stock market. She tells me that these people are almost invariably moved by their good fortune, and deeply troubled by it at the same time. Unlike the rich rulers of the prophet Amos's time (we will examine them in due course), the instinct of these wealthy people is most often to wonder what it all means. And they look to the intellectual leadership in the church for direction. My primary aim in this book is to do my best as a Christian theologian to give it to them.

Before going to the first chapter, though, I want to make one last brief point. It is that, while I do not accept the major wealth-negative premise of "radical Christianity," as it is often called, I do not wish my approach to be confused with that of the "Prosperity Gospel," either. Contrary to the radicals, the basic assumption of this more popular Christian view is that the condition of economic affluence is God's will for every faithful Christian. So they infer that, if one is faithful, one will thus prosper. The trouble (again) is not that the assumption has no truth in it — Scripture clearly shows (in my view) that God's primary will is that his human creatures should flourish materially. And these Christians are right (even if unso-

---

2. D'Souza, *Virtue of Prosperity,* pp. 143-44.

4

phisticated) in berating scholars for almost completely ignoring (or rewriting) these texts. But the mistake is in an unstated premise that the inference requires. It is that there are no times or circumstances in this world in which God would, on balance, prefer someone to be poor. And Scripture makes very clear that such times and circumstances often do exist. If the radical Christians and those who are sympathetic with their approach oversimplify the moral relationship in Scripture between affluence and evil, then advocates of the Prosperity Gospel oversimplify the relationship between affluence and the moral good. As we shall see, they both greatly oversimplify the teachings of Scripture and underestimate the role of culture in making wealth possible.

THEOLOGY AND METHOD

Some readers may wish to skip over this part of my introduction: those who do not particularly care about the assumptions of my theology, or about my approach to theological method in using Scripture. They will care more about the theology itself, as applied to faith and life under capitalism. And they will want to begin reading that theology straightaway. I see no reason for them not to do so, and to go directly to the first chapter of the book. (I do, however, recommend that they read the brief summary of the book's arrangement and argument at the very end of this section.) Other readers — usually fellow scholars — care a lot about the assumptions of theology and the approach to method. And they will wish to take time to read what follows.

The first thing I want to make clear is that my assumptions in writing theology are classical and orthodox in nature. This means that I bring beliefs to Christian theology that modern theologians widely presume to be discredited in our time. I affirm, for instance, the classical idea of divine revelation, and the beliefs about God and his relationship with the world that come with it. They are that the word "God" is not a merely human construction but refers to an objectively real, person-like First Being who created everything from nothing, who is all-powerful, perfectly good, and consists of three personal agencies — Father, Son, and Holy Spirit. They are also that this God has at key times intervened decisively in human history both to reveal truth about himself to selected people and to redeem them. The most important of these acts of revelation and redemption is

5

the Incarnation of the divine Son of God in the human being known as Jesus of Nazareth. In sum, I believe that Jesus was no mere teacher of religious truth, nor merely the "Christ" or Messiah of the world, but the divine Son of God incarnate. I believe that, as God in human flesh, he lived among us, was crucified, died, and was buried; and that on the third day following his execution God the Father raised him from the dead for our justification, and to exalt him to his own right hand as the measure, lord, and judge of human history.

All these claims are controversial, to say the least. But in this book I offer no defense of my belief that they are true. I simply assume that they are. I believe that there are good defenses in print, and I believe the reasons for giving away these traditional beliefs are vastly overrated. But in this book I will freely make the assumption that they are true without explanation. If by chance some of my readers have doubts, though, I urge them to investigate for themselves by reading the most rigorous Christian writers who do defend them.[3]

In addition to the beliefs just noted, I also accept as true the traditional claim that the writings of the Old and New Testaments are inspired by God. Of course, people understand this claim in quite diverse ways. I understand it to mean, at very least, that these writings are not merely human deposits of traditions. They are human literary deposits of tradition — tradition that developed remarkably during the ancient history of Israel and the early Christian church. But the doctrine of inspiration (whatever else it might mean) means that they are not *merely* human in origin, composition, and function in the canon and community. This doctrine enshrines the view that on all these levels the writings of Scripture are the outcome of divine purpose in a way that other human writings are not. I presume that to affirm the inspiration of the Bible is to affirm that God took special care (exactly how we do not know) to make sure that the essential meaning of his doings in history would be preserved in a text and

---

3. Three books occur to me as particularly good, if very difficult for readers who are not professional scholars. They are Richard Swinburne, *The Coherence of Theism* (Oxford: Clarendon, 1977); William J. Abraham, *Divine Revelation and the Limits of Historical Criticism* (Oxford: Oxford University Press, 1982); and Alvin Plantinga, *Warranted Christian Belief* (Oxford: Oxford University Press, 2000). Anyone who reads and grasps the arguments of these three books will have great difficulty denying that the historic Christian faith is essentially rational (if not provably true) in the quality of its beliefs.

thus available to his people for all time. In this book I simply treat the writings of Scripture as inspired by God in that sense for this purpose.

These assumptions of my theology about God, God's actions, and the status of Scripture do have a deciding effect upon my method in using the Bible to write theology. For one thing, I presume that if God was interested in having a written text that enshrined the essential meaning of what he took trouble to reveal, then people should be able to get at that meaning without first earning advanced graduate degrees in the technical science of critical history. Indeed, they should be able to do a fair job of getting at that meaning without having to rely entirely on the few elite scholars who do have degrees in those studies.

Partly for this reason Christian philosopher Peter Van Inwagen argues forcefully that the "historical-critical method" is of no use at all in our effort to establish any important truth about the Bible.[4] That is not to say that it is of no importance or use at all to anything, nor is it to deny that its speculations are not endlessly interesting, which I think they are. But in this book I have tried to be very careful to make minimal use of scholarly reconstructions of the history "behind" the text. I have done so only in instances where the evidence produces consensus (or nearly does so) and when that history really does illuminate and deepen our sense of what the text means.

For me, the most useful methods that have turned up in recent scholarship for getting the core meaning of Scripture are the ones we associate with the narrative school of interpretation. In this school, many biblical texts — especially the so-called historical books — are presumed to be carefully crafted stories. And there is a creative art to reading and getting the full meaning of such stories, owing not least to their antiquity. The average person has not learned this art in school, no doubt. But when the trained person offers a narrative interpretation, the average reader can rather easily compare it with the text, and then make an informed judgment regarding its truth. The idea of narrative is entirely consistent with that of Bible study among congregations, and I hope that this book is useful to Christians in that context.[5]

---

4. Peter Van Inwagen, "Critical Studies of the New Testament and the User of the New Testament," in *God, Knowledge and Mystery: Essays in Philosophical Theology* (Ithaca: Cornell University Press, 1995), pp. 163-90.

5. For a very good introduction to narrative theology, see Stanley Hauerwas and

Furthermore, the doctrine of inspiration very strongly suggests something else that professional biblical scholars routinely deny. This is that the Bible hangs together as an integrated theological whole. The most common view is rather that the Bible consists of a plurality of theologies, and that the "meaning" of the Bible emerges somehow in the conflict between them. The idea is that if we could get the writers of Genesis, Isaiah, Proverbs, Matthew, Mark, and John, for instance, together in one room, they would debate almost everything. Now, I do not deny that these writers were human, and that as individuals they would certainly have had their differences and disagreements. (Would that we could get them here and listen in!) But the teaching of inspiration makes me think that biblical scholars have vastly overstated this point. I prefer to think that these ancient writers, given the opportunity and time, on the really big issues, would find ways to agree. I doubt, for instance, that any of them would affirm the impersonal or immoral character of God, or that the world is divine, or that the body is evil, or that human beings are not fallen, or that God has not managed to reconcile the world to himself in and through Jesus Christ. And so I prefer to think it is reasonable, at least, to look for unified pictures, to seek a "biblical" vision on any given topic that really does come forth from the Bible as a whole. That is what I will seek to do in this book, and in the end I believe I have done so. I am convinced that the Bible gives forth an integrated vision for the theology that wealthy people in our own day need. My readers will at least have a text (their own Bibles) before them as a standard for agreement or disagreement.

This intuition of unity also encourages me to think that it is all right to build a theology from selected texts rather than try to cover them all. I presume, for instance, that the prophet Amos is in essentials representative of what the prophets generally have to say on the subject of God and wealth. And I presume that Luke, who stresses the topic more than do the other Gospel writers, does not give us a spiritual and moral perspective that Matthew, Mark, or John would flatly contradict. I presume, for instance, that when Luke writes that Jesus said, "Blessed are you poor" (Luke 6:20), his meaning was not in logical conflict with Matthew's more qualified version, "Blessed are the poor in spirit" (Matt. 5:3). To be clear, I do not claim that there are no conflicts at all between the assertions of biblical writers on any

L. Gregory Jones, eds., *Why Narrative? Readings in Narrative Theology* (Grand Rapids: Eerdmans, 1989).

subject. I do not think that the doctrine of biblical inerrancy follows from the most conceptually proper doctrine of inspiration. I accept the arguments of William Abraham on this subject, whose book I recommend that every interested person read.[6] Nevertheless, given the doctrine of inspiration, I do think it unlikely that two writers (like Matthew and Luke) in such close proximity to each other in the development of tradition would contradict each other on a matter of such deep importance to the core of Christian faith and life. If they are in flat disagreement on the matter of whether Christians might have adequate possessions, then they are very close to disagreeing in a very basic way about what Christianity is in the first place. That is of course possible, but unless we abandon our orthodox assumptions about Christian tradition and the place of Scripture within it, this judgment will seem improbable.

That is all I have to say here about my theology and method. I will thus bring this introduction to a close simply by giving a brief outline of the book and the plan of its argument.

SUMMARY OF THE BOOK'S ARRANGEMENT AND ARGUMENT

As I stated, one of this book's premises is that the distinctly modern nature of affluence in the West poses new cultural questions. In short, our topic of faith and wealth is not just a matter of interpreting Scripture. It is at least in part also a matter of interpreting the economic culture. To use the famous terms of H. Richard Niebuhr, our topic is one of those perennial problems of "Christ and culture."[7] In the first chapter, then, I seek to provide a framework for understanding the workings of modern capitalism in spiritual and moral terms. My conclusion is that the workings of modern capitalism (in contrast to older forms) are unusually well suited to the expression of an integrated Christian faith and life. In my view, Christians ought to have a view of modern capitalism that is "world affirmative" and "world formative" rather than mainly negative and prone to strategies of separation and withdrawal.

The remaining chapters are devoted to understanding "Christ" in the

---

6. William J. Abraham, *The Divine Inspiration of Holy Scripture* (Oxford: Oxford University Press, 1981). This is the very best essay I know on the subject of biblical inspiration.

7. H. Richard Niebuhr, *Christ and Culture* (New York: Harper, 1951).

context of our culture. This requires a theological exploration of sacred Scripture. I have chosen to arrange the investigation in a canonical manner. The second chapter thus handles narratives of creation. The third handles the narrative of the exodus; the fourth narratives of the exile (that is, the Prophets and Wisdom). In examining these Old Testament writings, I conclude that the narratives of creation establish a cosmic vision that includes a divinely ordered vision for humankind. And at its core is God's deliberate institution of material prosperity and flourishing as the proper condition for human beings in the world and before God. As noted before, I call this condition "delight," and I believe it endures throughout the biblical story as the vision that God has for all human beings. That is clearly so in the narratives of the exodus and the exile, as we shall see. In discussing those texts, I shall seek to show that the pervasive spiritual and moral directives they contain all follow from the affirmation of affluence, not, as is commonly claimed, from its negation. I also seek to show precisely what those directives are, to show what obligations follow from them, and to offer fresh perspectives on the "prophetic" morality of wealth and poverty for rich Christians of our day.

We then make the transition into the writings of the New Testament. The fifth chapter is about the social and economic world of Jesus and his followers. In this chapter I argue, with the support of a great deal of primary literature, that Jesus' incarnational identity was not one of poverty in its literal economic sense. Nor is it accurate to assert (as is commonly done) that in his earthly form he identified with the economic poor more directly and intensely than he did with other classes of people. I argue that he identified remarkably with every such grouping, but in different ways, and with extraordinary creativity of purpose. I argue that his manner of identifying with comparatively affluent people in the working and business classes has important bearing on the identification claims we ought to make about him in our day.

In the sixth chapter, the focus shifts to the manner of economic life that Jesus adopted, and directed his disciples to adopt, during his public ministry. In the light of selected works of New Testament scholarship, especially on Luke's Gospel, I argue that Jesus did not adopt a life of poverty, but rather called his disciples out of the ordinary world and into a community of celebration. It was a form of celebration that deliberately enacted the messianic feast of his vision, and it thus re-instituted the proper form of affluence — that is, delight. In the seventh chapter, I examine four parables of Jesus in Luke's Gospel. These parables, I contend, call Christians not to become poor (as is commonly thought), but to be wealthy in the right way.

In the eighth chapter we turn to Luke's narrative in the book of Acts, and the focus is upon his key "summaries" of what economic life was like following Pentecost. The scenes that he depicts are controversial — they are difficult to interpret, much less to apply to economic circumstances today. I argue (with others) that Luke has given a picture that, while it is rooted in real events, functions as a narrative ideal that grows from prophetic tradition. In Pentecost, God has at last created a New Israel, a people who have the law in their hearts, and among whom none is poor. I seek to discern what enduring norms emerge from this ideal, and to show that their spiritual and moral demands can be met in social and economic structures other than communalism. I also seek to show that they are norms for true delight rather than some other ideal (such as poverty, or lifestyles of moderation).

In the last part of the chapter, my focus is upon key texts in the writings of Paul and James. I mainly discuss Paul's famous Great Collection, and I seek to identify the nature of his appeal for funds to support the impoverished church in Jerusalem. I argue that this appeal is exceptional, and that his moral arguments must be used very cautiously in our day. Contrary to a judgment that is very common, in my view they do not provide a normative framework for spiritual and moral teaching in our day. Likewise the epistle of James. I believe it is most reasonable to place James, as many scholars do, in the tradition of the prophets and biblical Wisdom. It is most reasonable, then, to understand his very severe moral judgments against the rich in those terms, and thus not as a counsel of divestment and a model of poverty as a virtue.

Finally, I offer an epilogue on the issue of global poverty in the context of modern globalism. In this brief section, I seek to apply the principle of "moral proximity" (which I believe gave shape to the social ethics of Israel, Jesus, and the early church) to the ethics of world poverty. I strongly challenge the widely held belief that the world-shrinking effects of globalism generate strong obligations for any wealthy person in an advanced society to any poor person in an undeveloped one. The mere fact that any such wealthy person has, because of globalism, the technical ability to reach and thus to help any such poor person is not by itself enough to create the very strong obligation to do so that Christian writers commonly claim it does.

In my view, globalism does create obligations of some kind, but not of that kind. I conclude with a general framework for working out, individually, what kind of worldwide obligations rich Christians do have in an age of hunger.

I should probably add (to explain the many references to his views) that in the course of the book I have included a running debate with Ronald J. Sider, mainly in the context of his very influential work *Rich Christians in an Age of Hunger*.[8] I have done so for the main reason that teachers and students often read our works together and compare our arguments, and so I believe the direct engagement of his view by me will be useful to them. Moreover, I believe that (while it is in many ways a monument to good Christian social ethics) his work is very influential at points where it is mistaken, and so my purpose is to offer what I think are important criticisms of his work at those key points. Readers of course will judge for themselves whether the criticisms are on the mark.

8. Ronald J. Sider, *Rich Christians in an Age of Hunger*, 20th Anniversary Revision (Dallas: Word, 1997).

CHAPTER ONE

The "New" Culture of Capitalism

> *Democratic capitalism is not just a system but a way of life.*
>
> MICHAEL NOVAK[1]

"OF THINGS NEW"

In 1891 Pope Leo XIII published an official letter named simply *Rerum Novarum*, "Of Things New."[2] Its reference was to the breathtaking changes that had come over the Western world in the previous century: the great revolutions in democracy and science that had spread to all parts and been midwives to the birth of modernity. But the focus of the letter was most directly on the "new things" that came with the new economic order of capitalism. For this new economic order — still in its awkward adolescence — had already begun to raise a legion of new challenges for Christians.

Of course the problem of "God and mammon" is not new. It is as old as Christianity itself. H. Richard Niebuhr observed over half a century ago in his classic book *Christ and Culture,* that it is one of those perennial

---

1. Michael Novak, *The Spirit of Democratic Capitalism* (New York: Simon & Schuster, 1982), p. 29.
2. Leo XIII, *Rerum Novarum* (Vatican City: Democrazia Christiana, Direzione Nazionale, Dipartmento Formazione, 1991).

problems that every generation of Christians must face in one form or another.[3] But the forms of culture do change, and the things of capitalism were in that sense of the word new. They were new incarnations of very old questions about our treasure on earth. They were like the new wine in Jesus' simile, and the old leathers of tradition were already cracking from the fermentation. The church urgently needed new wineskins, lest all authority be lost, and Leo XIII knew it — hence *Rerum Novarum.*

The need for new teaching on capitalism was clear and urgent enough. But what should be the answers to the questions it posed was anything but clear. Not a few Christian theologians had come to believe that capitalism was a great, seductive evil, a harlot on seven hills that could deceive even the very elect. They believed that good Christians should do everything they could to defeat it. They had read the revolutionary writings of Marx. They observed the widespread exploitation of labor, the opulence of the few, and the widening chasm between rich and poor. And in that grim light, they had also read their scriptures with fresh eyes and awakened hearts, and they did not find a very great difference between what they found in the Law and the Prophets and the vision of socialism put forth by Marx. They judged that he was right about the moral nature and future of any society shaped by the order of capitalism. They believed that at the end of its evil was a grand triumph of irony: that capitalists would indeed manufacture the very noose by which powers of justice would hang them on the gallows of history. And the swelling ranks of Christian socialists seriously believed (as many have done until quite recently) that state socialism was the best framework for building a society that embodied the virtues of Christ and the Gospel.[4]

Leo did not agree — not entirely, anyway. His letter was no sterling defense of capitalism (as none of the great encyclicals have been).[5] The burn of his rather plain text is slow enough, but its sacred rage comes through nonetheless. Its main focus is on evils done to this new class of workers — "labor" — in the name of this new form of property — "capital." But in response to the new troubles and this newly proposed alternative to capitalism, Leo XIII did something that now seems very remarkable. For while

3. H. Richard Niebuhr, *Christ and Culture* (New York: Harper, 1951).

4. On the rise, appeal, and spread of Christian socialism among influential Christian theologians in the 20th century, see Richard John Neuhaus, *Doing Well and Doing Good: The Challenge to the Christian Capitalist* (New York: Doubleday, 1992), pp. 46-49.

5. See Neuhaus, *Doing Well,* pp. 30-32.

the letter is indeed about the new social evils of capitalism, unlike the Christian socialists, he did not understand the *essence* of capitalism in those terms. Instead, he looked into its deeper parts. And what he saw was an order of economic life that was, in its core, the embodiment of certain eternal truths and virtues (both natural and distinctly Christian). These included the validity of private property, the primacy of the individual, the importance and dignity of work, and the basic character of freedom — which Christians must take care always to link with the distinctly Christian truth about human beings as both created and fallen.[6]

In sum, Leo XIII understood early that the evils growing from the system were not the marks of its true essence. He understood that they were unnecessary and ironic indications of capitalism's strength. He understood that they grew from the distortion of something very good: that is, the newly won condition of freedom. It was the basic condition of freedom that allowed people to pursue material happiness in this world in ways that had never been possible before — not ever. So (and this is often forgotten) his powerful critique of capitalists in his day was also an implied affirmation of the basic principles in the foundations of the very system that they abused.

Leo XIII thus understood capitalism in much the way that the church had learned (tortuously) to understand the other new orders of the revolution — democracy and free intellectual inquiry (science). The church had learned with no little difficulty to affirm these orders for the goods and truths that they embodied rather than to renounce them for the dangers that they, as orders of freedom, naturally carried with them. And it was crucial that Christians give freedom the moral and spiritual direction it needed. By the same reasoning, Leo XIII also presciently denounced socialism, alienated as it was from those key natural and Christian truths of human existence. With that in mind he intuited its potential for evil, if not its sure demise. And his Christian sensibilities led him to believe that the Marxist order, no matter how appealing its rhetoric of justice, was completely unfit in its metaphysics as a cultural environment for the expression of even that basic social virtue.

Leo's encyclical is today a standard point of reference for official Catholic moral theology on modern economic life. As Pope John Paul II ob-

---

6. See John Paul II, *On the Hundredth Anniversary of "Rerum Novarum"* (Boston: St. Paul, 1991), p. 14.

served on the one-hundredth anniversary of Leo's writing, it is indeed an "immortal document."[7] But as he also pointed out, it is not immortal in the sense that Christians can simply take its answers as given in 1891 to be answers for all the questions about capitalism we have now. For the capitalism that exists now bears almost no visible resemblance to capitalism as it was known then.[8] Indeed, capitalism in 2002 looks significantly different from the way it did even half a century ago. Neither Marx nor Leo XIII nor even John Maynard Keynes could have begun to imagine the global, high-tech economy of our day, with its divisions of labor, its engines of investment and credit, its astonishing distribution of capital and affluence — and the really new challenges it poses. As John Paul II implied, *Rerum Novarum* provides but a framework for the theology and ethics that we need for coping with the new things of life under capitalism in our day. But at very least, it stands as a monument to that most basic wisdom of all — the good sense to know which end of the stick to pick up.

Christian intellectuals have made great strides in contending theologically with the modern orders of democracy and science. But when it comes to capitalism, for some reason we are still in the beginning stage. With rare exceptions, Christian intellectuals (as Western intellectuals generally) have not offered systematic spiritual and moral guidance for living *within* capitalism. In contrast, we are long in supply of theologies that teach us how to be good socialists — the entire movement known as liberation theology is a composite of various advocacies for Christian socialism. But the stunning collapse of socialistic regimes in 1989 redoubles the truth of Novak's earlier observation that "Latin American liberation theology exists at present [1986] much more powerfully in books than in reality."[9] On the other hand, "For two centuries democratic capitalism has been more a matter of practice than theory."[10] It exists almost exclusively in reality, and almost not at all in the theories of books. While it has grown to dominate the real

7. John Paul II, *On the Hundredth Anniversary,* p. 4, citing Pius XI.

8. I gladly accept Neuhaus's distinction between the "Old Capitalism" and the "New Capitalism" of today. Christians who affirm "market systems" today affirm the second form of capitalism with its integrated system of laws and regulations for linking freedom with truth and dignity. See *Doing Well,* pp. 54-56.

9. Michael Novak, *Will It Liberate? Questions about Liberation Theology* (New York: Paulist, 1986), p. 3.

10. Novak, *Democratic Capitalism,* p. 19.

world, "theologians . . . have, however, failed to articulate a theology commensurate with the novelty of the new world."[11]

As Novak points out, one reason for this was the deliberate avoidance of ideological disputation on the parts of war-weary European thinkers. Another is the unfortunate attraction that theories of anti-capitalism held (and continue to hold) for European and even North American intellectuals.[12] But especially considering the events that came upon us so suddenly in 1989 — the fall of the Berlin Wall and with it any hope that national socialism might ultimately liberate the poor of the earth — this inattention to theory for people living almost by default under the regime of capitalism is even more intolerable than it was in 1982, when Novak made his appeal to Western intellectuals to get cracking. In his words: "Inattention to theory weakens the life of the spirit and injures the capacity of the young to dream of noble purposes."[13]

Indeed, countless people in the field we broadly know as business need the sort of distinctly Christian theory that Novak (who for quite awhile soldiered on almost literally as an army of one) has brilliantly begun to frame.[14] And it is an irony getting dangerously close to intolerable that we intellectuals, too, need that kind of carefully constructed theory for life under capitalism. For like it or not, our universities and colleges and various other educational institutions are corporations of one sort or another. It will not do anymore to tolerate that sad spectacle of the scholar who goes around decrying things like "materialism," "consumerism," and "individualism" in ways that shamelessly expose her own behavior, too, as ludicrously immoral. It is time for Christian intellectuals to understand that we are all in this boat together, and that the church needs our help in knowing how to go about navigating it the right way through very new waters.

11. Novak, *Will It Liberate?* p. 3.

12. Novak, *Will It Liberate?* pp. 19-20.

13. Novak, *Will It Liberate?* p. 20.

14. Neuhaus observes that even in 1982, when Novak wrote *The Spirit of Democratic Capitalism,* "almost the entire Christian intellectual establishment, Catholic and Protestant, got out bell, book and candle to banish the heretic from their midst." *Doing Well,* p. 49. For an exceptional treatment of business ethics in the aftermath of socialism's downfall, see Max L. Stackhouse and Dennis P. McCann, "A Postcommunist Manifesto: Public Theology after the Collapse of Socialism," in *On Moral Business: Classical and Contemporary Resources for Ethics in Economic Life,* ed. Max L. Stackhouse, Dennis P. McCann, and Shirley Roels (Grand Rapids: Eerdmans, 1995), pp. 949-54.

In this chapter, I begin my own attempt at doing so. We begin by considering some very new things about capitalism that have not really figured as heavily as they should in most recent moral theologies. In the next section, we shall consider the extraordinary achievement of capitalism: to have liberated entire populations in twenty-five nations from poverty (about one billion human beings). At very least, we need to have this picture of what capitalism has done (and is doing) in view, for it is the essential context for our discussion of its moral and spiritual implications.

THE SUDDEN ACHIEVEMENT OF CAPITALISM

In the year 1941 there were but two capitalist powers left on Earth, and at the time things did not look at all good for either of them. The economy of the United States was in what seemed an endless downward spiral of depression and Great Britain was in visible decline. The emerging powers then were the military dictatorships of Europe and Japan and the communist dictatorship of the Soviet Union. Economist Lester Thurow gives a sobering description of how it was and, worse, what might have been had things not changed:

> The final crisis of the 1920's and the Great Depression of the 1930's had brought capitalism to the edge of extinction. The capitalism that now seems irresistible could, with just a few missteps, have vanished.[15]

Today, however, that all seems ironic to an extent that makes our very recent past seem dreamlike, if not nightmarish. But it is no dream. The "greatest generation" (to use Tom Brokaw's fine phrase) almost simultaneously defeated Hitler and put an end to the Great Depression. Then, having barely caught their breath, they waged and finally won a cold war in the hard and bitter peace that followed.[16] The events that came so "suddenly" in 1989 (to use George Will's term) were in fact the outcome of a long and sometimes seemingly hopeless struggle.[17]

---

15. Lester Thurow cited in Hernando de Soto, *The Mystery of Capital: Why Capitalism Triumphs in the West and Fails Everywhere Else* (New York: Basic, 2000), p. 208.

16. Tom Brokaw, *The Greatest Generation* (New York: Random House, 1998).

17. George F. Will, *Suddenly: The American Idea Abroad and at Home 1986-1990* (New York: Free Press, 1990).

So in that large sense our situation is about as dramatically new as it could possibly be. And this only makes the achievement seem more remarkable. For in the dizzyingly brief span of fifty years, since America's march into the theater of world war, twenty-five nations have successfully re-ordered their economies on the lines of modern capitalism. And what these nations have done would have been unthinkable to any sane person in any previous time. For they have done nothing less than eliminate real material poverty as a significant problem in their societies.

To have even suggested this might be possible during antiquity or in the Middle Ages would have landed one in a room with certain other biblically suspect people — like Galileo — who envisioned worlds that both Scripture and experience declared (or so it seemed) not possible. For if anything in the Bible was more certain than the fixed position of the earth, sun, and stars, it was surely Jesus' famous saying that "the poor you will always have with you" (Matt. 26:11). And no wonder people thought that way. In his pioneering book *The Spirit of Democratic Capitalism*, Michael Novak gives this graphic description of conditions worldwide prior to the 18th century:

> Consider the world at the beginning of the democratic capitalist era. The watershed year was 1776. Almost simultaneously, Adam Smith published *An Inquiry into the Nature and Causes of the Wealth of Nations* and the first democratic capitalist republic came into existence in the United States. Until that time, the classical pattern of political economy was mercantilist. Famines ravaged the civilized world on the average once a generation. Plagues seized scores of thousands. In the 1780's, four-fifths of French families devoted 90% of their incomes simply to buying bread — only bread — to stay alive. Life expectancy in 1795 in France was 27.3 years for women and 23.4 for men. In the year 1800, in the whole of Germany fewer than a thousand people had incomes as high as $1,000.[18]

Far worse conditions existed in Africa, Asia, and elsewhere:

> In Africa, the wheel had never been invented. Medical practice was incantatory. Illiteracy was virtually universal. Most of the planet was unmapped. Hardly any of the world's cities had plumbing systems. Potable water was mostly unavailable. Ignorance was so extreme that most hu-

18. Novak, *Democratic Capitalism*, p. 16.

mans did not know that unclean water spreads disease. Except in Adam Smith's book *the concept of development did not exist.*[19]

In our modern times, it is common to hear people speak with nostalgia about the old world that we have lost as the price of high-tech capitalism. And they have a point. But I think if they could go back in time even a few decades, they would not wish to stay very long.[20] At any rate, the reason all this began to change was — simply — capitalism. "In Great Britain real wages doubled between 1800 and 1850, and then doubled again between 1850 and 1900."[21] And that was just the beginning.

The fact itself is plain enough. But it will be instructive to put the accomplishment in a more contemporary context. (This will also help illustrate the claim I make later in the chapter that ours is not merely a culture that *contains* affluence, but is a culture *of* affluence.) In his recent book *The Virtue of Prosperity,* American Enterprise Institute scholar Dinesh D'Souza offers a trove of facts about economic existence in America. And I believe it is fair to say that very few Christian writers have really considered them as part of the context for their theologies and ethics. Among them are these notable few: In the last twenty years the percentage of Americans owning stock has risen from ten to fifty percent.[22] Between the years 1982 and 2000, the number of billionaires rose from thirteen to two hundred sixty-seven and counting. (If Bill Gates were a country he would, by himself, be number thirty-five in the world rankings on net worth.)[23] As of 1997, 144,000 American households (half a million people) were earning seven figures each year, more than 250,000 households had a net worth of more than ten million dollars, and since 1989 the number of plain old millionaire families had rocketed from 1,260,000 to more than five million — in other words, more than fifteen million people. D'Souza writes of the things that Marx failed to see coming:

> In the past two hundred years the great achievement of the modern West was to create a middle class, allowing the common man to escape

19. Novak, *Democratic Capitalism,* p. 17 (italics mine).

20. For a good discussion of the "lost world" in the context of Wendell Berry's life and writings, see Dinesh D'Souza, *The Virtue of Prosperity: Finding Values in an Age of Techno-Affluence* (New York: Free Press, 2000), pp. 135-60.

21. Novak, *Democratic Capitalism,* p. 17.

22. D'Souza, *Virtue of Prosperity,* p. 5.

23. D'Souza, *Virtue of Prosperity,* p. 12.

from poverty and live in relative comfort. Now the United States is ready to perform an even greater feat: it is well on its way to creating the first mass affluent class in world history. A mass affluent class is just starting to emerge in other European countries as well. Call it the overclass. These are the new equivalents of the lords and barons of the Middle Ages. Only today's overclass is already large and growing so fast that perhaps one day it will outnumber the peasants.[24]

And what of the "peasants"? D'Souza writes, "Americans haven't figured out that wealth in our time has been completely redefined."[25] Along current lines, the "poor" are households with incomes of $15,000 on down.[26] But the households in this grouping spend but one half of their incomes on necessities.

> Some people may be surprised to learn that 50% of Americans defined by the government as "poor" have air conditioning, 60% have microwave ovens and VCR's, 70% have one or more cars, 72% have washing machines, 77% have telephones, 93% have at least one color television, and 98% have a refrigerator. Not only are poor Americans today better housed, better clothed, and better fed than average Americans were half a century ago, in many respects they live better than the average western European does today.[27]

He explains that this happens with so little income because government figures do not include benefits "such as welfare, food stamps, unemployment provision, and rent subsidies, all of which supplement the earned income of the poor."[28] D'Souza cites a friend of his from Bombay (he is himself Asian Indian) who is said to have remarked, "I am going to move to America. I want to live in a country where the poor people are fat."[29] Certainly it will not do to downplay the real problems caused by poverty in America today. But perspectives such as this one bring a much-needed sense of balance to the issue.

24. D'Souza, *Virtue of Prosperity,* p. 16.
25. D'Souza, *Virtue of Prosperity,* p. 17.
26. D'Souza, *Virtue of Prosperity,* p. 17.
27. D'Souza, *Virtue of Prosperity,* p. 75.
28. D'Souza, *Virtue of Prosperity,* p. 75. It is also because "poor people often grossly under report their incomes."
29. D'Souza, *Virtue of Prosperity,* p. 75.

In response, the American Census Bureau is now seeking to raise the poverty level to $19,500 (which of course would immediately plunge another ten million people into "poverty"). However, remarkably, the new standard would not be purely material, but also cultural. The poor would be those persons lacking "a socially acceptable standard of living."[30] The serious implications of that non-literal definition of poverty aside, the astonishing new truth remains, as D'Souza believes it does: "If poverty is understood in its normal sense — as the absence of food, clothing and shelter — it is no longer a significant problem in America. What remains is relative inequality and the question becomes, does that continue to matter?"[31]

This question suggests an avenue of response to the most common moral objection to cultures of capitalism — that is, that they are cultures of injustice.

THE HUMAN WORKINGS OF CAPITALISM

Moral theologian Stanley Hauerwas (citing influential moral philosopher Alasdair MacIntyre) bluntly writes that "capitalism's ability [to produce · great wealth] is irrelevant as rebuttal to the essential injustice of capitalism."[32] Hauerwas's assumption here is that capitalism is successful only by means that are immoral (unjust). Given this, economist Joan Robinson would be right in comparing the successes of capitalism as she does with the activities of organized crime. She cites none less than Al Capone in support of her judgment that the difference between the two is minimal.[33] And it is certainly worth remembering that the ends do not always justify the means. The results of the actions of members of the Mob are often good — their children go to college, churches meet their budgets for ministry,

30. D'Souza, *Virtue of Prosperity*, p. 76, quoting Rebecca Blank on the Census Bureau's proposal.

31. D'Souza, *Virtue of Prosperity*, p. 76.

32. Stanley Hauerwas, "Christian Schooling or Making Students Dysfunctional?" In *Sanctify Them in the Truth: Holiness Exemplified* (Nashville: Abingdon, 1998), pp. 219-26.

33. Famous Cambridge economist Joan Robinson, to suggest this unfavorable comparison of market capitalism, cited Al Capone's sardonic remark in an interview: "This American system of ours, call it Americanism, call it capitalism, call it what you like, gives to each and every one of us a great opportunity if we only seize it with both hands and make the most of it." In *Freedom and Necessity* (New York: Pantheon, 1970).

neighborhood family businesses thrive — but the motives and actions themselves, by which these ends are achieved, are anything but good. Economists like Robinson and moral thinkers like Hauerwas feel the same is true of capitalism — that while it may bring about enormous good in the form of prosperity, its inner human workings are not good, but quite immoral.

It is very important that we have good reasons to doubt that this complaint holds true. For otherwise, no matter how strong our theological argument in affirming affluence of the right kind, that affirmation could never apply to the affluence existing in capitalism. In the rest of this chapter, then, I wish to provide those reasons before going forward into Scripture to work out the theology of affluence.

My job will not be to give a defense of capitalism. To do so would be beyond both my competence in economics and (thus) the scope of this book. And there are other works of that kind available anyway.[34] What I will do is take the lead from a comment by Michael Novak that struck me some time ago with illuminating force. "Democratic capitalism," he wrote, "is not just a system but a way of life."[35] In this chapter, my focus is on two cultural habits that go a long way toward describing the kind of "way of life" that it is. For the culture of capitalism is if nothing else one of *acquisition* and *enjoyment* of material affluence. I will use the work of social theorist Max Weber to help explain what this means for Christian teaching. Following that I will give a brief survey of classical tradition on affluence and its inadequacy for meeting this new challenge. Finally I will relate well-grounded works of others that prove that modern habits of acquisition, unlike premodern ones, do not seem to meet the tests for moral injustice. In fact, they seem unexpectedly to meet requisite tests for moral virtues. So to the extent that this is true, to the degree that these habits define the culture of modern capitalism, there is no injustice inherent in capitalism. On the contrary, there is unexpected virtue in it. At the end I argue that a similar pattern holds for common spiritual objections about materialism. I conclude that, in the light of these new kinds of acquisition and enjoyment, we have good reasons to doubt both the serious objections and, thus, we may hope to find a theology that enables Christians to integrate the experience of affluence un-

34. See the very fine discussion of this larger debate over the character of capitalism in Craig M. Gay, *With Liberty and Justice for Whom? The Recent Evangelical Debate Over Capitalism* (Grand Rapids: Eerdmans, 1991).

35. Novak, *Democratic Capitalism*, p. 29.

der capitalism into the Christian life. (I do not, incidentally, ignore the serious ecological questions modern capitalism raises, but will instead treat them in a more convenient context in tthe next chapter.)

THE SPIRIT OF CAPITALISM: WEBER'S "IRON CAGE"

Between 1904 and 1906, German sociologist Max Weber published two monumental articles on the rise of capitalism.[36] He intentionally took off from the earlier work of the great economic historian Werner Sombart, who was the first to develop the thesis that modern capitalism, more than mere economics, embodied a cultural, or more nearly religious spirit.[37] Weber tried to prove that this spirit had its roots in Protestant Christianity, especially among the Calvinistic Puritans in Britain and the United States. This "Weber Thesis" ignited a storm of controversy and debate that continues to rage today. We obviously do not have space here to delve into the controversy concerning the origins of capitalism. But Weber's theory provides a useful framework for the points I do wish to make about Christian perspectives on life under capitalism.

First, Weber made everyone understand more vividly than before that capitalism gives shape to human cultures wherever it thrives. But more deeply, he judged that the role of Protestantism in giving rise to capitalism was among the saddest ironies in human history. For capitalism by its very nature had to grow into a culture of worldliness and of the worldly acquisition of things, the pursuit and enjoyment of non-necessities (luxuries). Weber strongly assumed that the teachings and entire essence of authentic Christianity were in direct conflict with both these sorts of habitual economic actions that are requirements of capitalism. He argued that Protestantism had thus manufactured (literally) an "iron cage" from which there was no escape — except of course through becoming separate from capitalism. Many theologians agree with Weber's implication: that the relationship between true Christianity and a culture of acquisition and enjoyment of material wealth is dangerously and sadly incoherent.

36. Max Weber, *The Protestant Ethic and the Spirit of Capitalism*, trans. Talcott Parsons (New York: Scribners, 1958).

37. Robert Green, ed., *Protestantism and Capitalism: The Weber Thesis and Its Critics* (Boston: Heath, 1959), p. vii.

Whatever we think of Weber's thesis, he was surely right about one thing, and it is worth stressing. I believe that no economist or social theorist denies that capitalism *requires* that its members engage in cultural habits of acquisition and the enjoyment of quite non-essential material things (luxuries by any other name). That is what the liberation provided by capitalism is about. When capitalism really works, every member of society eventually becomes affluent to some comparative degree and (as D'Souza's numbers show) that is exactly what has happened in some nations. The cultures that capitalism helps to create do not merely contain great wealth; they *are* cultures of wealth — cultures that are animated by universal habits of acquisition and enjoyment of material wealth. This is perhaps the most startling new thing about them.

But is Weber also correct in judging that this kind of culture is thereby, for authentic Christians, an iron cage? If so, the consequences are very grave. For to live in the culture shaped by capitalism then requires that we adopt moral and spiritual habits of acquisition and enjoyment that are in opposition to the truth of Jesus Christ. No serious Christian would ever deliberately put herself in that position. But even if we are in it non-deliberately, we are in it just the same. Some Christian writers understand this implication quite clearly, and they have the integrity to bear its full consequence: to become separate from capitalism, insofar as that is really possible.[38]

Others, however, seem not to understand it very well. They are thus in the awkward (and, I believe, incoherent) position of affirming the prosperity that capitalism offers to them and to others as moral justification for their involvement, but at the same time they condemn the very cultural spirit and habits of acquisition and enjoyment that make capitalism work (and which they are engaging in themselves in their own unwitting fashion).[39]

In this light, John Wesley's thundering judgment, quoted approvingly by influential writers today, is little more than implied desperation (and self-incrimination) for people who make the claim to affirm (or at least morally tolerate) capitalism. In his widely influential book *Rich Christians*

38. See Gay, *Liberty and Justice*, pp. 22-63 (especially p. 28), for a penetrating discussion of evangelicals on the left who, as of 1990, decried capitalism on a variety of grounds, including cultural ones.

39. Notice Gay's judgment that the impression that the evangelical left gives is "somewhat paradoxical" (I would just say paradoxical). For on the one hand they denounce accumulation, and on the other they affirm enjoyment and the essential place of material things in human life. *Liberty and Justice*, p. 44.

in an Age of Hunger, for instance, Ronald Sider offers Wesley's words on Matthew 6:19-23 ("Do not store up for yourselves treasures on earth . . .") as a healthy challenge to modern Christians. Wesley was nothing if not clear: "Any man who takes for himself more than the plain necessaries of life lives in open, habitual denial of the Lord." That man, contrary to what he might think, "has gained riches and hell fire."[40] It should be pretty obvious that if we are to plant ourselves in this culture of acquisition and enjoyment (as Sider and others wish to do), we thereby perform the actions that Wesley decries as mortal sins.

This position seems intolerable as a Christian view. Without a coherent Christian way of affirming it as a human culture, we have no business engaging in capitalism. In sum, we must have a distinctly Christian way to affirm the economic habits of acquisition and enjoyment of affluence as they necessarily exist within the culture of modern capitalism. Is this possible? I do believe it is. But the contrary opinion is very widespread, in part because the entire weight of historic Christian tradition seems to be against the integration of faith with the habits of acquisition and enjoyment. For the sake of my argument, then, we must devote some space to a survey of that tradition, and to seeing that it is to an extent antiquated — old wineskins, to borrow Jesus' simile again. For in my view (with others) modern capitalism has given birth to new economic forms of acquisition and enjoyment that are unlike any that existed under ancient social economies. They are new things, and they require moral and spiritual thinking on our part that is commensurate with their newness.

ACQUISITION AND ENJOYMENT IN CHRISTIAN TRADITION

Of course we have the New Testament to deal with, and we shall do so in later chapters. But from the first centuries of Christian history, Christian theologians struggled mightily to maintain integrity in relating faith to economic life. And most of what they had to say about the acquisition and enjoyment of material wealth was decidedly negative.[41] The great St. Augustine (354-430

40. Ronald J. Sider, *Rich Christians in an Age of Hunger: Moving from Affluence to Generosity,* 20th Anniversary Revision (Dallas: Word, 1997), p. 190.

41. Two very good, if quite differing, books on the history of the question are Justo Gonzalez, *Faith and Wealth* (San Francisco: Harper & Row, 1990), and Barry Gordon, *The Economic Problem in Biblical and Patristic Thought* (Leiden: Brill, 1989).

c.e.), bishop of Hippo and the best theologian in an age of great theology, typifies the classical view of faith and wealth. His view consisted of these major points. (1) Personal property is good in the sense that God's material creation is good. (2) The acquisition of property is permitted by honest and just means — heredity, for instance, or simple work. But many, perhaps most, forms of acquisition are not — theft, conquest, oppression, demanding interest, and base mercantilism, for instance. (3) The distinction between "use" *(usus)* and "enjoyment" *(fruitio)* is basic to Christian spirituality and ethics. For Augustine, it was good to use material wealth but not to enjoy it. Proper use, he argued, was to apply one's wealth to meeting one's basic physical needs, and then to make everything left over available to the church and to the poor. To enjoy wealth beyond this was thus to violate these basic Christian norms. Augustine put it as strongly as anyone:

> From those things that God gave you, take what you need, but the rest, which to you are superfluous, are necessary to others. The superfluous goods of the rich are necessary to the poor, and when you possess the superfluous you possess what is not yours.[42]

Augustine's view on faith and wealth endured all the way through the Middle Ages and, to an extent, the Protestant Reformation.

While Luther and Calvin were less technical in their arguments on acquisition, use, and enjoyment, permitted the practice of charging interest on loans, and rejected the theology of monasticism, I do not find much support in their writings for anything like the spirit and habits of contemporary capitalism. On the contrary, my sense is that famed historian of the Reformation Albert Hyma (in his rigorous critique of Weber on this point) was right. In his estimation, Luther and Calvin were not significantly more "progressive" on economic matters than their medieval predecessors, or Augustine.[43] They were on the whole guarded against acquisition, stressing instead the principle of necessity in their teachings on charity and discouraging enjoyment in anything like the forms that create our culture of capitalism today.[44] It seems that the approach of American

42. Augustine, *In Psalmos* 147.12, ed. J.-P. Migne, Patrologiae Cursus Completus, Series Latina (Paris: Garnier, 1834).

43. Albert Hyma, "The Economic Views of the Protestant Reformers," in *Protestantism and Capitalism,* ed. Green, pp. 94-106.

44. See, for instance, Luther's essay "An Appeal to the Ruling Class," in *Martin Luther,*

Puritans like Jonathan Edwards remained an experiment in theology that largely did not catch on in academic societies. Edwards and other American Puritans indeed did seek to integrate their affluence into their Christian theology. They began to rediscover the importance of the Old Testament and its thematic doctrine of creation, especially as evident in the stories of Eden and a Promised Land flowing with milk and honey. And they began linking the experience of prosperity with notions of faithfulness and divine blessing.[45] I believe that this instinctive association of America with Eden and ancient Israel was a promising move, as will be clear in the next chapters. But it seems that the second connection — between righteousness and prosperity — was the only part of the Puritans' world-affirmative theology that stuck, becoming popularized as the Prosperity Gospel, as noted earlier.

For both Roman Catholic and Protestant intellectuals of all varieties to this day, the response to the spirituality and morality of consumption in affluent societies is most often instinctively suspicious and world-negative rather than world-affirmative. This is particularly true among American evangelicals, recent studies show. Among Protestants in the last one hundred fifty years, the most affirmative voices have been those of modernists (who of course got that name from their larger affirmation of the Enlightenment and its radical critique of orthodox tradition) and of certain popular writers whose practical orthodoxy was — shall we say — incomplete.[46] And, obviously, the true heirs of modernism in theology have shifted their

ed. and trans. John Dillenberger (Garden City: Doubleday/Anchor, 1961), especially p. 483 on luxuries. And see Calvin, *Institutes of the Christian Religion*, ed. John T. McNeill and trans. Ford Lewis Battles, Library of Christian Classics (Philadelphia: Westminster, 1960), p. 841, on the validity of acquiring through heredity but the questionable nature of that by any other means.

45. See Edwards's sermon on Deuteronomy 15:7-12, "Charity and Its Fruits," cited in John T. McNeill, *The History and Character of Calvinism* (New York: Oxford University Press, 1954), p. 342.

46. On the attitudes of Modernists in contrast to Fundamentalists in the 19th century, see Peter Dobkin Hall, "Moving Targets: Evangelicalism and the Transformation of American Economic Life," in *More Money, More Ministry: Money and Evangelicals in Recent North American History*, ed. Larry Eskridge and Mark A. Noll (Grand Rapids: Eerdmans, 2000), pp. 141-79, especially p. 177. On popular American defenders of the Prosperity Gospel, see Marsha G. Witten, "'Where Your Treasure Is': Popular Evangelical Views of Work, Money, and Materialism," in *Rethinking Materialism: Perspectives on the Spiritual Dimension of Economic Behavior*, ed. Robert Wuthnow (Grand Rapids: Eerdmans, 1995), pp. 117-41.

affirmation of capitalistic habits into reverse gear. None less than theological giant Paul Tillich could write, without fear of criticism from his peers, that "the effect of the capitalist system upon society and upon every individual in it takes the typical form of 'possession,' that is, of being 'possessed'; *its character is demonic.*[47]

Anabaptist scholars and evangelicals on the counter-cultural left have long had that intuition about capitalism, but now even mainstream evangelicals are beginning to push the apocalyptic panic button. Evangelical financial guru Larry Burkett is so troubled by the culture of consumer credit that has evolved (and is apparently so vexed by its incompatibility with the Bible) that he is now certain that we are living in the end times. That thought cannot but occur to people who wake up one day to discover that someone has locked them in an iron cage while they slept. For who but the Anti-Christ himself could offer such pleasures on plastic?[48]

But if the world does not end, who will offer guidance to Christians living under the regime of these new things? Unlike Catholic theologians, who can at least look as far back as *Rerum Novarum*, Protestants (and especially evangelicals) have very little in the way of theological and moral tradition to work with. As Princeton social scientist Robert Wuthnow has written, the broad legacy of Protestants on the materialism of capitalism is one of deep ambivalence.[49] Recent research proves that ambivalence is beginning to advance toward its natural (anti-intellectual) existential condition — despair.[50] With so much tradition and contemporary opinion against the twin habits of capitalism — acquisition and enjoyment, how may we hope to provide convincing arguments to support even a discriminating affirmation of them?

47. Cited in Neuhaus, *Doing Well*, p. 48 (italics mine).

48. See Larry Eskridge, "The Phenomenon of Financial Counselor Larry Burkett and Christian Financial Concepts," in *More Money*, ed. Eskridge and Noll, pp. 311-50.

49. See Robert Wuthnow, "A Good Life and a Good Society: The Debate Over Materialism," in *Rethinking Materialism*, ed. Wuthnow, pp. 8-15. Of course there are exceptions to this rule; for a particularly striking example, see the work of Protestant ethicist Max Stackhouse, especially his *Public Theology and Political Economy: Christian Stewardship in Modern Society* (Lanham, Md.: University Press of America, 1991).

50. Eskridge and Noll, *More Money*. If a thesis emerges from this book of very diverse essays, it is that the revivalism and biblicism of evangelicals cannot equip them for engagement of the culture. What they lack is "consistent Christian perspective tools," and "architectonic thinking." See Joel A. Carpenter's piece "Contemporary Evangelicalism and Mammon: Some Thoughts," pp. 399-405.

RETHINKING THE MORAL OBJECTION: INJUSTICE

In *The Virtue of Prosperity,* D'Souza relates an interview he conducted with T. J. Rodgers, C.E.O. of Cypress Semiconductor, on the morality of capitalism and affluence. Rodgers responded bluntly to the author's questions.

> I keep hearing feed the poor, clothe the hungry, give shelter to those who don't have it. The bozos that say this don't recognize that capitalism and technology have done more to feed and clothe and shelter and heal people than all the charity and church programs in history. So they preach about it, and we are the ones doing it. They want to rob Peter to pay Paul, but they always forget that Peter is the one that is creating the wealth in the first place.[51]

Rodgers continued in that agitated tone about one Sister Gormley, who was known for her continuous lobbying of corporations to consider more women and minorities for jobs — "a very ignorant and arrogant woman," in his view. In fact, Rodgers was so irritated by a letter from her that he took the time to write a lengthy letter of his own. In his response, he advised Sister Gormley to "get off her moral high horse," and to think about what she was saying. If he took her "politically correct" suggestions, he would put the investments of all his stockholders at grave risk, imperil the jobs and livelihood (with health insurance) of thousands of his employees, and almost certainly go under.[52] From Rodgers's quite unsophisticated moral perspective, Sister Gormley could not have been more confused than she was. For in the interest of the moral good, she had unwittingly become an advocate for the very moral evil she was crusading against: the impoverishment of thousands.

Rodgers's words sharpen the problem theologians must face. For, as D'Souza observes, "whatever their motives, entrepreneurs are doing more than anyone else to fulfill the Bible's practical mandate to improve the living standards, and the dignity, of the disadvantaged."[53] He poses this provocative but revealing question: "Who has done more to eradicate poverty and suffering in the Third World, Bill Gates or Mother Teresa?"[54] We have already considered the evidence that supports his implied answer.

---

51. D'Souza, *Virtue of Prosperity,* p. 124.
52. D'Souza, *Virtue of Prosperity,* p. 125.
53. D'Souza, *Virtue of Prosperity,* pp. 126-27.
54. D'Souza, *Virtue of Prosperity,* p. 127.

But just how significant is this answer? I have already indicated that the mere achievement of capitalism — extraordinary as it is — does not by itself give warrant to Christian affirmation of it, much less our deep involvement in its culture. Nevertheless, it does seem fairly unappreciative not to respect that achievement for what it is. Perhaps our initial reaction should be something like the response that Jesus gave to the scribes and Pharisees, who believed his power to cast out demons was from Beelzebub. With their ideological assumptions, what other explanation could there be? We, too, may be inclined to wonder, "How can Satan cast out Satan?" (Mark 3:23). Given the enormity of the exorcism that capitalism, under the auspices of unlikely liberators like T. J. Rodgers, has performed, that is at least a fair question.

Furthermore, close attention to what Rodgers was saying in the interview suggests that entrepreneurs typically acquire wealth by a most extraordinary means — one that does not look at all immoral. As background, it is very helpful to keep in mind (as many moral theologians seem not to do) that ancient Christian teaching on acquisition and enjoyment emerged in economic conditions very unlike the ones we are trying to get clear on (new things, again). For instance, in ancient and medieval economies the primary form of wealth was land — a fixed commodity — and that is one reason why these economies were nearly stagnant and almost everyone was poor. Rarely did they enjoy cycles of growth on any national scale.[55] On the contrary, in such systems the only way to acquire non-hereditary wealth was to get it (usually by force) from someone else. So in these economies, the acquisition of wealth typically (almost necessarily) happened by means of war, taxation, or (presuming a difference) outright theft. The old habits of acquisition were thus mostly immoral, to say the least. It would have been true to say that an essential injustice existed in these actions.

For the same reasons, it also was true in an almost necessary way that when someone consumed a non-essential item (that is, enjoyed it) she or he was depriving someone else of the only means available for assistance (charity). Under such conditions, who would dare to disagree with Augustine's judgment that keeping portions of wealth for personal enjoyment most often was a grave injustice? In those economic circumstances, it

55. Brian Griffiths, *The Creation of Wealth* (Downers Grove, Ill.: InterVarsity, 1985), pp. 23-31.

would be strange indeed — bizarre, even — to have moral theologians strongly affirming enjoyment as a good thing. John Wesley's words to the typical rich would indeed be on the mark. And Hauerwas's widely shared complaint about the essential injustice of acquisition would be, too. But is the achievement of affluence in modern economics colored by the immorality of what amounts to theft, or even murder? Rather clearly not.

The truth is that in modern market economies the main way that people acquire wealth is not by taking it away from someone else, but by taking part in its *creation*. This is fundamentally different from the way wealth was acquired in the ancient world — and for the most part, it is what businesses and corporations do. That is what the habit of acquisition is essentially all about under working capitalism. Walter Lippmann understood the moral implication of this uniquely modern phenomenon better than most in the first half of the twentieth century. "For the first time in human history," he wrote in his extraordinary book, *The Great Society*, people had brought about "a way of producing wealth in which the good fortune of others multiplied their own," and "the golden rule was economically sound."[56] This almost magical process at work in an entire nation is what Lippmann meant by the Good Society in his essay of that name.[57]

This is the same point that T. J. Rodgers made in his own irritable way by reminding Sister Gormley of what his corporation did for thousands of people. By running his enterprise properly, he insured the enduring liberation of people from the evils of poverty, and he established them in conditions of enduring prosperity. What this means, as Lippmann understood, is quite remarkable. Acquisition and enjoyment in an economy such as this are not just ends for oneself alone; they are also the means to similar ends for others. This example is replicated hundreds of thousands of times under democratic capitalism. So it seems that if the acquisition and enjoyment of wealth under capitalism is typically immoral, it is not immoral in the way it was under ancient economies. Indeed (like it or not), its creative liberating dynamics seem to qualify it as a candidate for virtue.

Of course, the modern form of acquisition in view might be immoral for other reasons. It might be that the entire system works only because people ignore the inefficiencies of ethics. That is the picture of capitalism

---

56. Cited in the Lay Commission on Catholic Social Teaching and the U.S. Economy's letter *Toward the Future*, p. 23.

57. Lay Commission, *Toward the Future*, p. 23.

conveyed by the old television series *Dallas*, with its main character J. R. Ewing. The Big Oil man J. R. never missed a moral shortcut in his life, and when asked the secret of his success he quickly replied, "Once you forget integrity, the rest is easy." Several years ago I bought a used car from a local dealer only to discover that they had cleverly disguised several annoying and expensive defects that I had to repair. This example, too, may be multiplied thousands of times in a free economy. People in business are free to cheat other people. But one of the lessons that D'Souza took away from his interviews with dozens of successful people in business is that, contrary to what we might expect, "capitalism makes people behave better than they otherwise would."[58]

As Adam Smith argued centuries before, D'Souza judges that "capitalism civilizes greed, just as marriage civilizes lust."[59] For instance, Rodgers explained to him that he did not write himself a huge salary because then his vice presidents would be envious, would want more money, and would have bad morale. All that would hurt his business. In this light, D'Souza contends that, in general, "The point isn't just that capitalism makes society better off; it is that capitalism makes us better people by limiting the scope of our vices."[60] Rodgers liked to think of himself as a bit of a scoundrel — he ignored speed bumps as he drove. But in running his corporation he was anything but a scoundrel — he could not ignore the "speed bumps" and be successful, too. The system not only does not prevent good behavior, it rewards it. For my part, I never went back to that car dealer, and I told everyone I knew how its managers had cheated me. (I would like to say that my actions made them repent, or drove them out of business, but, alas, they did not.) But at any rate, in any association or community, virtuous behavior towards one's fellow members improves one's standing among them. Conversely, vicious behavior does quite the opposite. To the extent that capitalism is a network of free human communities and associations, the same can be said for economic standing within it.

But perhaps the acquisition and enjoyment we have in view are immoral for quite different reasons. Maybe the modern forms of these economic actions, on the whole, do bring about good for many others, even as they dispose the agents to be morally better people. But perhaps the net ef-

---

58. D'Souza, *Virtue of Prosperity*, p. 126.
59. D'Souza, *Virtue of Prosperity*, p. 126.
60. D'Souza, *Virtue of Prosperity*, p. 126.

fect is the growth of extremes between the haves and the have-nots that are morally intolerable. One of the most common mantras of modern ethics and moral theology is that the rich are getting richer and the poor are getting poorer, and that the one happens at the cost of the other. But perhaps like real mantras, the more we repeat them, the more obvious it seems that they are true, even if they are not. Once more, I will let D'Souza speak on the subject, for it seems to me that his answer is exactly right:

> But what if these premises turn out to be false? What if the rich are getting richer *because they have created new wealth that didn't exist before?* What if we live in a society where the rich are getting richer and the poor are also getting richer, but not at the same pace? If you drive a Mercedes and I have to walk, that's a radical difference of lifestyle that might warrant speculation. But is it a big deal if you drive a Mercedes and I drive a Hyundai?[61]

In an economy based on the creation of wealth, the rich indeed get richer. But so do the poor. D'Souza makes the same judgment I am defending. "It turns out that our old categories for examining the issue are largely obsolete. We need a new way of thinking about inequality."[62] For the inequality that exists under successful modern capitalism is not at all clearly immoral in the way inequality was under ancient social economies. In D'Souza's example I see nothing clearly immoral at all in the extreme wealth and enjoyment of the one person over and against the relative affluence of the other.

It is right, nonetheless, to point out, as Ron Sider and others do, that in the U.S. some thirty million people still lack health insurance — but not as a moral criticism of modern habits of acquisition and enjoyment under capitalism.[63] For without consumer capitalism it seems obvious that there would be no health insurance at all (much less an advanced medical system with costs to insure people against). Because of modern capitalism 230 million Americans enjoy the previously unimagined benefit of medical care under the guarantees of health insurance. Because of capitalism we can actually *contemplate* extending this luxury (and it is a luxury) further to include everyone in a system of the very best medical care in history.

---

61. D'Souza, *Virtue of Prosperity,* pp. 71-72 (italics mine).

62. D'Souza, *Virtue of Prosperity,* p. 72.

63. "The Ethical Challenges of Global Capitalism" (transcript of a debate between Ron Sider and Michael Novak), *Discernment* 8, no. 1 (winter 2001): 2.

But perhaps our modern habits of production and consumption are immoral when placed in the light of another, very different and new thing that the selective success of capitalism has brought into existence. That is the enormous gap between the wealth of the fortunate nations and the poverty of people almost everywhere else. By some estimates there are around one billion people in the world who live in literal material poverty, and another two or three billion who live on the edge of it.[64] These numbers refer to suffering that is, in both its intensity and scope, hideously evil and unacceptable to the Christian. But are they grounds for believing that our habits of acquisition and enjoyment are also evil? For this to be so, at least one of two things must be true, or, as some believe, both. One is that our economic habits are the direct (or indirect) cause of poverty in these other societies. The other is that we have the moral obligation to change our habits dramatically enough so that we can redirect our wealth to elimination of poverty and suffering elsewhere.

These questions require expanded answers that go beyond the reasonable scope of the book. Nevertheless, I have included an addendum on globalism and the ethics of global poverty as an epilogue, and in it I have suggested the direction that Christian thinking might take. To the first consideration, I will simply point out that pioneering new work in world economics strongly encourages us not to think of our economic habits as a primary or even secondary cause of worldwide poverty. If anything, they are a primary cause of whatever prosperity these poor nations have, and a dramatic reduction of our consumption and production would thus have the unintended outcome, in the long run, of creating more poverty. Moreover, if this research holds, the primary causes of poverty in these societies are legal and political, and thus internal to those societies, not external to them. Regarding the second issue of our obligations, I will argue that globalism (our technical connectedness with people everywhere in the world) does not by itself generate the strong moral obligations for affluent Western Christians that moral writers commonly claim that it does. In the light of certain key biblical narratives on social ethics, I do not believe that the obligations we have to the "global poor" are in conflict with rightly formed habits of acquisition and enjoyment. For the time being, however, I believe it is best to put these arguments on hold and to put them to the test at the end of our investigation, rather than at the beginning.

64. Sider, *Rich Christians*, pp. 1-20.

Now, what all this means in part is, as the writers of the Lay Commission Document (cited just above) indicate, that one effect of capitalism has been that the "ancient dichotomy between self-interest and the common good has at the very least been greatly diminished."[65] In other words, Adam Smith was right in believing that capitalism would make something possible that had never been widely possible in economic life before — the pursuit of socially "enlightened" self-interest. The strong way to put this implication is to say that it makes possible — encourages rather — the pursuit of material gain for individuals without doing any harm to society, or to other nations. On this view, the properly formed pursuit of self-interest is generally good for everyone and everything concerned.

RETHINKING THE SPIRITUAL OBJECTION: *PLEONEXIA* AND MATERIALISM

Christian writers do not just claim that the habits of capitalism are socially unjust. Moral theologians like Hauerwas also typically assert that the habits of modern economic culture are very like what the ancients called *pleonexia*.[66] This is the spiritually corrupting vice of insatiable desire to have more and more material things. Now, there is no doubt that our modern habits include a desire for more; to consume is simply to acquire and to enjoy one more thing or other. And there is no doubt that this desire sometimes is insatiable and spiritually corruptive. But is this desire in every instance a vice along the lines of the one described by the ancients? Is the desire for more in every instance an indication of the modern evil of materialism?

This is a very difficult question for Christians, in large part because whatever answer we give grows from interpretations of difficult biblical texts. Indeed, just as there is a strong negative disposition toward affluence in moral theology, there is a time-honored tradition of asceticism in the spiritual teachings of the church. The ancient monastic vow presumes that life with a minimum of possessions (poverty), and certainly without luxuries, is spiritually better than life with abundance. Even among Protestants, certain elements of this tradition are making a strong comeback in our

65. Lay Commission, *Toward the Future*, p. 23.
66. Stanley Hauerwas, "Christian Schooling," pp. 219-26.

day. Their main form is not rigorous asceticism, but a gospel of simpler living, which extols the virtue of radically reducing one's consumption for spiritual as well as moral reasons. This is in response to a growing awareness that something is badly wrong — spiritually wrong — with the way the economic culture is affecting the spiritual character of the church.[67] The trouble with these approaches is that they cannot very well integrate the strong biblical theme — and it is a very strong theme from beginning to end — of physical delight as God's ultimate vision for human beings (as I argue in later chapters). The only way to make this point, however, is to go through the texts in detail, and then to offer an alternative to these more ascetic approaches as we go along.

But are there broader cultural and psychological reasons for thinking that our economic habits are self-destructive in a spiritual way? Quite a few philosophically diverse thinkers believe so. Conservative Christians like Don Eberly and William Bennett, among others, like to extol the inner virtues of previous generations in contrast to those of today.[68] On the more liberally expansive side, writers like Wendell Berry, Joseph Schumpeter, and Daniel Bell all predict that among the fruits of modern capitalism will be the ruin of the human spirit. In 1976, Bell wrote the highly regarded book *The Cultural Contradictions of Capitalism*, in which he brilliantly sharpened Weber's picture of capitalism's evolution from a culture of frugality, hard work, and delayed gratification into one of rank hedonism and debauchery.[69]

But if we consider my earlier argument that capitalism rewards virtue more than it does vice, the spiritual situation does not seem nearly that grim. There is a spiritual connection, after all, between dignified work — the creation and realization of one's vision — and reaping the fruits of that work in relative security and freedom. Perhaps too few scholars and Christian theologians have had this experience to appreciate it; I do not know. But I gather that what entrepreneurs do is not entirely different from what scholars do when they envision and write (and even market) their courses,

67. See Wuthnow, *Rethinking Materialism*. All the authors in this collection focus on the negative spiritual and moral effects of acquisition in American society. They also, however, reveal the awkward ambivalence I remarked on earlier. See pp. 8-15, in which Wuthnow treats ambivalence as a "legacy" of Christians on this subject.

68. For a very good survey of conservative Christian worries about affluence, see D'Souza, *Virtue of Prosperity*, pp. 48-49.

69. See D'Souza, *Virtue of Prosperity*, p. 49.

articles, and books. The sense of spiritual goodness and completion that comes when these efforts are successful is unmistakable to anyone who has had the great good fortune to have and to enjoy them.

For instance, I imagine that the makers of Mercedes-Benz automobiles take immense pride in the engineering and craftsmanship of these superb cars. I imagine that the production of these vehicles brings with it feelings of fulfillment and aesthetic pleasure that are not unlike what the great masters of visual art experience when they produce great art. I think we would have to have very powerful reasons for judging that these feelings are unhealthy. Furthermore, I know many people who can afford luxury cars like the Lexus or Mercedes, and (aside from the investment advantage that gives them — these cars keep their value), I also know how much pleasure they get from the nearly perfect performance of those vehicles. I think it is very like what other friends of mine get from the pieces of fine art that they own, or from the great books that they read. I see no reason not to make this comparison. Outside of base resentment, I see no reason at all to think that either form of affection is unhealthy materialism. Why not instead wish that everyone could enjoy life at those levels?

There is a growing body of writing that is devoted entirely to showing that gaining wealth does not bring gains in happiness. Clearly this is sometimes the case; there are lots of people whose habits as consumers look very much like what Walter Benjamin called "the fetishism of merchandise." Buying stuff does not always make people at all happy. Often it leaves them empty, especially if their lives are empty to begin with. D'Souza addresses this issue in the context of high technology; his comments seem to me as sensible as they are honest and amusing:

> This *condescension,* however, fails to take into account the genuine fascination, charm and delight that new acquisitions and toys give us. Wouldn't you like to have a Jacuzzi with a built-in music system in your bathroom? How about a St. John outfit that makes you the very definition of elegance? Or a TV screen that drops out of your ceiling? Or a computer system for your car that talks to you and gives you street directions? These are fairly cool items.[70]

In response to those who complain that the accumulation of wealth brings

---

70. D'Souza, *Virtue of Prosperity,* p. 243 (my italics).

nothing but unhappiness, D'Souza recalls a friend's use of the familiar quip that "people who say that money doesn't buy happiness simply don't know where to shop."[71] That, or they have never seen the looks I used to see every year on Christmas morning when my kids woke up to shiny new bicycles, or to some brand new computer game station. Only a pure curmudgeon could look into their delighted faces and see the spiritual corruption of *pleonexia*. As will be argued later, we human beings are designed by God to enjoy material things — in the right way, of course. The point, though, is that there is a right way.

But not all people do enjoy things in a way that is right. People who lack spiritual resources and are miserable to begin with often become even more miserable amid their possessions. Increased wealth merely gives them more ways to be unhappy. Even people who are not miserable to begin with may become spoiled and lost in mindless, obsessive consumption. That is what mindless and thoughtless people do when they become rich. They become mindless, thoughtless rich people. I have known quite a few people in that condition. But I also know people — many of them Christians — who have a deep spiritual sense of things about them, and who are also very affluent. These people are not miserable; on the contrary, they know that wealth is not the foundation of their existence. But they love being rich both for the freedom it gives them to enjoy life and for the immense power it enables them to offer on behalf of others. In the lives of these people affluence is itself a very great good.

In my introduction I cited the statement that Michael Novak made to D'Souza in an interview, and it pertains to this point. A good number of rich people are learning, through wealth, that there is more to life than bread, and it is affluence that thus "leads people to God."[72] Among other things, Novak's comment implies that, just as there is a true spirituality for being poor, there is a genuine spirituality for being rich. It remains to see from our scriptures what that unusual kind of spirituality might be.

When D'Souza contacted Daniel Bell, whose 1976 social critique of capitalism was among the fiercest of its generation, Bell strangely refused to talk about his earlier dire view of its failings. He had apparently withdrawn his influential thesis without notice. And in their telephone conversation Bell seemed annoyed by his own previous perspective, noting that

71. D'Souza, *Virtue of Prosperity*, p. 243.
72. D'Souza, *Virtue of Prosperity*, pp. 143-44.

"the truth is that the world is a much better place today than at any time during the twentieth century."[73]

At the end of his discussion D'Souza — himself an immigrant from a poor nation — offers one last bit of wisdom to intellectuals in the West. He counsels that their alarm over affluence seems to many people on the outside almost comical, like strangely thankless whining:

> At a time when people in poor countries are trying desperately to better their condition, you cannot lecture them about the moral and social perils of affluence; they would surely think that you were joking. It's not that they would disagree with you; they simply wouldn't know what you were talking about.[74]

Do Western thinkers truly mean to imply that the poor are really better off in conditions of non-affluence? For those seeking liberation from poverty for themselves and for their people, that indeed seems a strange and self-defeating premise to adopt.

At the end of this chapter, then, I come to the provisional conclusion that modern economic habits of acquisition and enjoyment as they flourish under capitalism are not necessarily immoral. Nor is it obvious that they are always destructive to the human psyche and thus to the inner spiritual strength of society. They can be shaped into habits that are immoral and destructive, to be sure. In a society like ours, excessive hedonism is an option. But it seems that it is not a necessity, and the evidence is the affluent people in whom it is not present. It remains to see whether sacred Scripture supports this judgment. If it does (and I shall argue that it does), it remains to see how and to what extent it does so. In the rest of this book, then, on this assumption, I shall seek to forge a theology of affluence for Christians seeking to live with integrity within this culture of capitalism.

73. D'Souza, *Virtue of Prosperity*, p. 141. When asked about his previous understanding of capitalism as the cause of spiritual and social decay, Bell responded, "Don't talk to me about that. It's all bullshit." P. 142.

74. D'Souza, *Virtue of Prosperity*, p. 232.

CHAPTER TWO

Genesis: The Cosmic Vision of Delight

Our end is in our beginning.

T. S. ELIOT

As in most matters of Christian theology, we must begin our quest for answers at the beginning — with the story of creation in Genesis. The other great biblical narratives all speak in the language given by Genesis. The Law, the Prophets and Wisdom, and even the Gospels and Epistles of the New Testament are so thoroughly immersed in the vision that is introduced in Genesis that they cannot really be comprehended in any depth apart from it.[1] That is because the book's authors crafted the story of our beginning to serve also as an image of what the purpose and inevitable end of the world will be like. The story thus also reveals in picturesque literary terms what the world should be like, and so is a guide to moral and spiritual living here and now.

Unfortunately, few Christian writers on faith and wealth apply this common theological principle when they engage our particular subject. And by not putting the topic of faith and affluence in these very basic terms of creation, they routinely invite very serious, almost predictable de-

---

1. This point is made very forcefully in the scholarly but readable essay by George Landes, "Creation and Liberation," in *Creation in the Old Testament,* ed. B. Anderson (Philadelphia: Fortress, 1984), pp. 135-51.

fects into their theological analysis and judgment. This problem is typical of the most influential books we have on faith and economic life.[2]

Christian writers today seem more concerned about warning us against making an idol of wealth, which is at heart what materialism is. And they are right to be concerned. There is widespread agreement among scholars in our culture that obsession with material wealth is rampant — inside and outside of churches.[3] And no doubt it is true that a great many people respond to their affluence in that unfortunate manner. Perhaps we have dulled ourselves too often to the constant warnings of our scriptures, from beginning to the very end, that the power mammon has over people is extraordinary. It is godlike, almost, even for people who sincerely profess faith in the true God. I suppose it is something like alcoholism in that respect. The scope of its devastation to souls, to lives, and to entire societies

---

2. This criticism applies most clearly to Ron Sider's *Rich Christians in an Age of Hunger: Moving from Affluence to Generosity,* 20th Anniversary Revision (Dallas: Word, 1997). In spite of constant urging by critics for years, this newest edition of the book still offers no treatment of the creation story and its themes, much less an account of how they become integrated in the Hebrew and Christian narratives of wealth and poverty. While Sider affirms the goodness of creation (and rightly resists the charge that he promotes asceticism), he nevertheless offers nothing like a *theology,* or integrated Christian view of creation and culture as a framework for his ethics. To the extent that he has such a theology, however, it seems more in keeping with his own Mennonite heritage than with traditions that have historically affirmed the institutions of society as part of the good order of God. It is also fair to say that another important work, Gordon's very rigorous *The Economic Problem in Biblical and Patristic Thought* (Leiden: Brill, 1989), also fails generally to integrate the themes of creation (particularly those of Gen. 1, as his focus is mainly on "Yahwistic" source, or "J" — roughly Gen. 2-3) with those of fall and redemption. In a different way the very recent book by Craig L. Blomberg, *Neither Poverty Nor Riches: A Biblical Theology of Material Possessions* (Grand Rapids: Eerdmans, 1999), does the same thing. The section on Genesis 1-12, pp. 33-39, under the subheading "From Eden to Sinai," makes no thematic connection between the strong vision of material delight in Eden and the promises made to Abraham, the patriarchs, and Moses. Amazingly, Blomberg comes away with the "manna model" of the wilderness and its norm of "enough" for "daily bread" as the frame of reference for Christian ethics. His reasoning and my criticisms of it occur in relevant discussions of Old and New Testament texts below.

3. See, for example, the widely influential book by Robert Bellah et al., *Habits of the Heart* (New York: Harper, 1985). This is a most provocative, if not very cheerful, essay on the present state of the American character. Also the more recent collection of essays by evangelical Christian authors, *Rethinking Materialism: Perspectives on the Spiritual Dimension of Economic Behavior,* ed. Robert Wuthnow (Grand Rapids: Eerdmans, 1995).

cannot easily be overstated, but those who are caught in its grip are the last to know.

But while we dare not be complacent about the dangers, as prevalent as they are in our new cultures of affluence, we must also take care in forming our judgments. For like alcoholism, materialism is invisible. It is first and foremost a spiritual condition. Of course it also has external symptoms — troubled behaviors, many of them immoral — that grow from within. And very often these behaviors are so exaggerated that diagnosing the nature of the illness is quite straightforward. When someone is falling down drunk, violent, abusive, and dysfunctional every day, anyone can see that this person is a true alcoholic. Likewise, when someone like Imelda Marcos uses her riches as First Lady of the Philippines to accumulate 100,000 pairs of shoes (while her very own people suffer in abject poverty), few would dispute the public's judgment that she was sick with greed. Instances like these are perfectly clear. But warrant for judging someone to be an alcoholic is not always so unambiguous. If we encounter someone at a gathering who we think is imbibing a bit too enthusiastically in spirits, it would be unwise (and quite unfair) immediately to suspect — much less to form the strong belief — that he must need treatment for his drinking. It may turn out that his daughter has just had a baby, or that he has gotten an unexpected raise, or is seeing an old buddy for the first time in years. In short, he may just be celebrating, having a good time, enjoying a moment in life that is to be enjoyed.

I believe that something like this ambiguity exists in our efforts to spot out materialism. Genesis helps us to see that it does, and to appreciate the danger of the Pharisee that lurks within the moralist. For it introduces the biblical truth, in the clearest possible terms, that God has in fact designed human beings to enjoy life in the material world. It urges us to understand that there is a godly condition of delight (as I shall call it), which is not just good but paradigmatic. That is to say, it reveals the vision that God has for all human beings. It is God's intent from the beginning, and is thus the end that he has in view for humanity forever. It is therefore the frame of reference for the sort of vision that Christians ought to have for humanity in the here and now. There is much to qualify and explain, to be sure, and I do not wish to get out too far in front of my own arguments. But Genesis is in my view absolutely essential both to seeing that this claim about delight really is true, and then to seeing what it entails for our understanding of modern affluence and the constellation of questions that it poses for faith.

CREATION: NOT DIVINE BUT SACRED

Most scholars agree that the ancient Hebrews were the first people to develop a religion of true "transcendence." In other words, they were the first to picture God as altogether above and beyond nature. Their God was not to be confused at all with the creation. Images of God were fiercely forbidden. Thus they were also the first people whose religion demoted the material world from the status of divine being to that of clear non-divinity.[4] In contrast, the myths of the other ancient nations show that they venerated the sun, moon, and stars, and believed that all of what we call nature was a world of living, personal, divine self-consciousness, a realm of movement, will, and activity. If not literally divine, the world of nature was for nearly all ancient peoples a place of myriad natural powers through which human beings encountered the divine.

Even though we shall speak later of the sacredness and preciousness of nature in biblical terms, it is true to a great extent that the Bible removes this living soul of divinity from the world. The theme of God's "otherness," or transcendence, thus brings with it a commanding "No!" to idolatry, to use Karl Barth's terminology. And this transcendent "No!" has immense importance to our search for economic identity. One side of this is obvious and has received considerable attention lately. In its broad terms, the warning is indisputable and real. This fundamental distinction of status and value between the creator and his creation is basic to every spiritual teaching in the Bible on how we are to relate to wealth (and not relate to it). It may be true that (most) affluent Westerners are in no danger of fashioning a literal golden calf, or going back to the worship of astral bodies (at least not where I live). But it is the nature of our culture of affluence that we are very vulnerable to giving mammon the throne of our lives, where God alone belongs. The truth is as simple as it is familiar, but let's state it anyway: We do not belong to things, but to God. That is to clarify true worship and all of life in the most basic way. If we really live in the light of this truth, we cannot go very far wrong.

Furthermore, though, even as the narrative demotes and diminishes the status and value of the world, in the context of mythology, it also does something else that is very remarkable. For it does not (as many seem to

---

4. See the standard work by Henri Frankfort, *The Intellectual Adventure of Ancient Man* (Chicago: University of Chicago Press, 1977).

think it does) reduce nature to the level of a mere object with which we humans can do as we please. For among the deepest themes of the narrative is that this creation that God majestically calls forth into being is *good*. It is good in its individual parts, and it is good as a cosmic whole, as an integrated system. In fact, in this integrative, cosmic sense, the text informs us that God declared it to be *very good* (Gen. 1:31).

All commentators on Genesis agree that this language is not just functional, as in "that hammer is good for driving nails." It is moral and religious; it is the language of divine blessing. The idea is not that the creation is good merely for human utility, although (properly understood) this is part of what makes it good. It is good rather in the sense of being a pure and holy thing, as something that God respects, loves, and takes delight in for the perfect, purposeful whole that it is.[5] While nature has no share in God's divinity, it does have a share in God's goodness and good pleasure. While our theologies have mostly missed it in their explanations of why God created in the first place, the narrative almost overflows with the love and joy that God feels as he brings forth this world. We must keep this idea in the background as we go now to our crucial discussion of the story's teaching on human identity: that we are made in the image and likeness of God.

THE IMAGE OF GOD: HUMAN DOMINION OVER NATURE

It is widely agreed by both defenders and critics of Christianity that this demystification of nature helped to give the green light to the aggressive movement and progress in science, technology, and economic life that we associate with Western civilization.[6] And it is true that the Western mentality is to some extent rooted in a biblical worldview. The concept of human superiority in value and dignity over nature is enormously strengthened in the creation story by its claim that God made humankind in his very image and likeness. This teaching about human identity has been very controversial throughout Christian history, and it remains so today. From earliest times theologians debated its meaning, and nowadays people dis-

---

5. Gerhard von Rad, *Genesis*, trans. John Marks (Philadelphia: Westminster, 1972), p. 52.
6. See, for example, the classic essay by Lynn White Jr., "The Historical Roots of Our Ecological Crisis," in *Science* 155 (March 1967): 12-26. His idea popularized the theory of the great historian Arnold Toynbee; see James Nash, *Loving Nature* (Nashville: Abingdon, 1991).

pute not only its meaning but also its proper application to ethics, especially in the field of ecology. But certain recent biblical scholarship, not as familiar to theologians or laypeople as it should be, can help us to anchor this basic doctrine in its original setting and to sharpen our sense of its first meaning. It also turns out that this scholarship leads (in my view) to unexpected and fresh applications for our investigation of faith and affluence. In making this application, we will also have to consider this doctrine in the context of modern environmental concerns about the relationship between Christian doctrine and the ecological problems of the West. For the argument I wish to make in defense of a godly approach to affluence depends to an extent upon points that emerge from engagement of criticisms that environmentally concerned people commonly make against the biblical doctrine in view. I will thus offer a brief defense of my own against these criticisms and then make the application to the questions we have about human affluence.

To begin, all ancient peoples searched desperately for a clear sense of identity. Like us, they asked the basic questions, "Who are we?" "What is it to be human?" "Why are we here?" "What is life all about?" Their answers were often pretty grim. The Babylonian creation story, *Enuma Elish*, taught that human beings were made to bear the burdens of the gods.[7] Experience had taught them that being human, for the vast majority, was hard. If there was real hope, it was in an afterlife (and even that became doubtful for some). The inference is understandable: since we would never will such hardship on ourselves, it must be the gods who willed it so. Many of us today can identify with the world-weariness of the ancients.

But Genesis offers a contrast to the ancient pattern and to our modern disillusionment and fatigue. It certainly agrees that life is hard. There is no shallow optimism anywhere in the story — or in the Bible at all, for that matter. But Scripture does not attribute life's troubles to God's will. The context for evil and suffering is not the doctrine of creation, but rather that of the fall. And it is remarkable that the creation story does not begin with a primal explanation of the burdensomeness of life as the consequence of our sin against God. The very first picture that Genesis gives of our identity and God's vision for us and for the world is instead "good

7. See Alexander Heidel, trans. and ed., *The Babylonian Genesis*, 2nd ed. (Chicago: University of Chicago Press, 1963), esp. pp. 118-26; and Frankfort, *Intellectual Adventure*, esp. p. 182.

news." In an otherwise cold and dark world the words are warm and bright: "Then God said, 'Let us make humankind in our image, after our likeness'" (1:26).

There have been many theories and debates about just what this language means.[8] As Old Testament scholar J. Richard Middleton points out, this diversity of interpretation stems from perennial failure throughout the history of Christian theology to interpret this text exegetically in its historical and textual context rather than in the abstract.[9] Moreover, Middleton shows convincingly that, while systematic theologians even today continue to speculate on what the image of God means (is it reason? morality? capacity for relationships?), "there is at present a virtual consensus among Old Testament scholars concerning the meaning of the *imago Dei* in Genesis."[10] These scholars have carefully noted the "predominantly 'royal' flavour of the text," in rhetorical combination with the blessing-mandate of dominion and rule that the text explicitly gives to human beings — typically royal functions. In brief, many literary clues make it clear that the God who speaks and acts in Genesis 1 is a divine monarch — a "King presiding over 'heaven and earth.'"[11]

By describing humankind as created in the image of this God, the text confers royal status upon them (remarkably, upon both men and women in equal measure). Other external research into idiomatic conventions of the Ancient Near East shows beyond controversy that the expression "image of God" was a commonplace reference to the monarch — the king or queen. The idiom makes perfect sense when we realize that these societies were theocratic: the monarch quite literally served as the earthly representative, presence, will, and authority of whatever deity the people worshiped. As the image of God, the monarch was an incarnation of divine rule, with all the

---

8. See the survey of this doctrine in Carl Braaten and Robert Jenson, *Christian Dogmatics* (Philadelphia: Fortress, 1984). Also Karl Barth, *Church Dogmatics*, III/1, trans. and ed. Geoffrey W. Bromiley (Edinburgh: T&T Clark, 1958), pp. 192-206. Some traditions have focused on the intellect, others on morality, others on spirituality, others on relationality and personhood, still others on creativity and freedom. Barth judges that the dominant theory in a given time usually says more about the time and culture than about the meaning of the language of Genesis.

9. J. Richard Middleton, "The Liberating Image? Interpreting the Imago Dei in Context," *The Christian Scholars Review* 24, no. 1 (Sept. 1994): 8-25.

10. Middleton, "Liberating Image?" p. 11.

11. Middleton, "Liberating Image?" p. 12.

dignity, value, and freedom to make binding judgments that we would associate with that role.[12] With all of that material in the background, then, the familiar passage in Genesis gains fresh meaning: "Then God said, 'Let us make humankind in our image, after our likeness; and let them have dominion over the fish of the sea, and over the birds of the air and over the cattle, and over all the earth, and over every creeping thing that creeps upon the earth'" (Gen. 1:26). As the great Old Testament theologian Gerhard von Rad put it, "Just as powerful earthly kings, to indicate their claim and dominion, erect an image of themselves in the provinces of their empire, so man is placed upon earth in God's image as God's sovereign emblem."[13]

The most extraordinary thing is not the idiom itself, but its revolutionary application to the human race. By stating that God made humans in his image, Genesis thereby gives *all* human beings a royal identity comparable to that of a king or queen, as well as royal obligations commensurate with the role. That is to say, on this interpretation, not just some, but *all* human beings have this authoritative status before God, and *all* human beings are thus called upon to represent on earth God's rule over heaven. To be made in God's image most basically means to have been given dominion over the earth, under God. Much is promised here — not just the supremacy of humankind, but the rudiments of what would become our modern ideas concerning the dignity and "inalienable rights" of every human person. The universality of this teaching is so revolutionary for its time (or any time) as to be breathtaking.

In Genesis, then, human identity is expressed first in the language of royal dominion and calling. Unlike ancient myth, this language does not deify any human beings — we are not to act as gods in the absolute — but it does dignify and bless the whole race with the highest creaturely status possible. This role inherently demands conformity with the will of the One who created us and placed us on earth. Our realm of rule is ultimately not our kingdom, but God's. But as God's, it is ours, too. The peculiar theme of dominion is thus the dominant one in this part of the story. God blesses the first humans and then commands them to go forth to "fill the earth and subdue it" (Gen. 1:28).[14] The image is one of a God-derived value, free-

---

12. See especially David J. A. Clines on parallel usages in non-Israelite nations such as Syria and Egypt, "The Image of God in Man," *Tyndale Bulletin* 19 (1968): 53-103.

13. Gerhard von Rad, *Genesis,* p. 60.

14. The Hebrew word for "subdue" is a very strong one. Writes von Rad: "The expres-

dom, dignity, power, and royal effect over the whole earth and its inhabitants. There is therefore a fundamental repudiation of any religion or theory which puts human beings on the same plane as God. But also, on the other hand, this doctrine rejects the notion that humans are on a level equal with — or even beneath — the various elements of nature.

This (in my view) indispensable doctrine of human dominion is objectionable to a growing population of thinkers in our day — and not only outside of our churches. It seems that Christian writers, too, especially ones with strong environmental concerns, are very reticent to stress anything that promotes the supremacy of human beings over non-human beings. (As a professor in a Christian liberal arts college I could relate many an anecdote to support this sense of things.) Because of this state of affairs, I think it will be helpful to give some space to consider the major objections, and then to offer a brief defense of the doctrine against them. It turns out, also, that parts of this defense are very instructive as context for understanding how the doctrine of human dominion is linked with the desired condition of material affluence and delight.

HUMAN DOMINION AND THE ENVIRONMENT

It will be difficult to make the application of this doctrine of human royalty and dominion that I wish to make to the topic of affluence unless we first anticipate certain indirectly related objections. The language of Genesis in affirming human dominion is so strong that, as we have mentioned, critics like Lynn White, Jr., commonly blame it for the ecological crisis that has come with the rise of industrial and high-tech capitalism. And it will do no good whatsoever for Christians to downplay this language, as Christians with environmental interests so very often do. For it seems logically clear that we cannot downplay the notion of human supremacy in value relative to non-human beings without also downplaying assertions of human rights and dignity as we have understood these notions in the Judeo-Christian traditions of the West. It is in fact strangely incoherent for Christians to proclaim themselves advocates of human rights and at the same time deny (usually on environmental grounds) the assertion that human

---

sions for the exercise of dominion are remarkably strong: *rada*, 'tread,' 'trample' (e.g. the wine press); similarly *kabas*, 'stamp.'" *Genesis*, p. 60.

beings have transcendent value and dignity among the other good creations of God. Nor will it do to set a model of "stewardship" over and against the image of dominion as an alternative to it. For the text makes unmistakably clear that the kind of stewardship in question (and there are many different kinds) is that of royal dominion under God. The two analogies are complementary, not antagonistic to one another. And I trust that the larger biblical force of this statement will be clear enough by the end of our next subsection, or at least by the end of the book.

But if there are compelling reasons to affirm human supremacy, there is also much to weigh against doing so. Critics of the doctrine explain the global ecological crisis as a failure of our Western worldview, with its anthropocentric, detached, and brutal lack of reverence for nature. On the surface the argument seems valid. For a people will hardly destroy a redwood forest if they believe that the great trees are a people with a divine nature and purpose. Native Americans, so long as they were true to their spiritual traditions, could not imagine deliberately wiping out the buffalo by strangling its range with barbed wire and shooting the remnant for hides (or just for mean sport). We can accuse primitive cultures of many evils, but not of calculated, wanton savagery against nature. That seems destined to be a sad part of our legacy as "civilized," "Christian" Western Europeans. But if not our biblical view of nature, what made some of us capable of doing these things? Does the concept of the Royal Man and Woman necessarily engender arrogance and indifference to the welfare of nature? Is there a direct line from the ideology of human dominion in Genesis to the desire certain people have to wipe out whole species of plants and animals for gain?

First we must step back and do some serious theological reflection on the narrative of Genesis 1 and its picture of God. The six days of creation give us a picture of God using his great power — his dominion. In the ancient world, light was widely understood to be the purest form of divinity. Hence the worship of the heavenly bodies — the sun, moon, and stars. In Genesis, the God of Israel speaks — and light comes into being at his royal command. The sun, moon, and stars do not appear in the story until three "days" later. This is a narrative way of presenting what theologians have classically termed God's omnipotence. Simply in terms of its mammoth *quantity*, as we have seen, the effects of this power are staggering. It is power in its maximal form, beyond anything we can well imagine. But certain modern theologians have also pointed out — I believe rightly — that the deeper truth about God's mighty power is not its scope, as great and glorious as that is. The deeper truth is about the personal *quality*, the personal character and direction of God's power as he puts it to use. For again, when he creates, the God of Genesis does not act from mere selfish interest, as the gods so often do in ancient myths. On the contrary, he first creates out of sheer delight in the goodness of his creation.

The classical doctrine that says that God created to glorify himself is thus true, but very misleading as commonly stated, and it has led to many unfortunate sermons and catechism lessons about "God everything, human beings nothing." Of course it is to God's glory that he creates, but when he creates he both enriches himself and glorifies everyone and everything else. That is the glory of God. By his power God frees, orders, and empowers other beings to be themselves, to be what is closest to their essences as individual beings, as parts of a cosmic whole. In his royal greatness, God uses power to liberate other beings from nothingness to an existence that is good. Unlike the power we may see around us, God's power expresses itself in sovereign, royal love.

If some communities today fail to appreciate God's power, others have often not appreciated the servant-form that is its true glory.[15] The delight of God is other-centered rather than self-centered. His joy is comparable to that of an artist in the sheer rightness and integrity of an artwork, or a parent in the birth of a strong and vigorously healthy child. His joy is in a world completely in harmony with itself, everything in its proper place, *shalom*. For the sun, moon, and stars, God made the heavens and light. For the fish and birds, he designed the seas and the sky. For plants, animals, and humans, God made the dry land. Everything was in its place, and that placing was *good* for every being described. And the whole creation was very good. In this sense, the God of power in Genesis 1 is also a servant of his creatures. He rules. But he also serves with great passion and compassion. His rule empowers and magnifies his subjects. It does not oppress or diminish them. The spirit that moved Jesus to wash his disciples' feet did not originate there and then. It goes all the way back to the first moments of creation.

15. Classical Christian theology such as Herman Bavinck's *The Doctrine of God,* trans. William Hendriksen (Grand Rapids: Baker, 1977), presents God's power mainly in the context of God's abstract omnipotence. A modern exception is the work by Emil Brunner, *The Christian Doctrine of God,* trans. Olive Wyon (Philadelphia: Westminster, 1949). Also Karl Barth, *Church Dogmatics,* vol. 2/1. These works bring together the omnipotence and love of God with focus on the work of Jesus Christ as the supreme expression of God's power.

Such is the model of dominion that is presupposed in the language of Genesis about human rule and dominion over the earth. God's lordly passion for his world makes us royal and supreme, but in such a way that it also makes our earth sacred. God's "Yes!" to human beings as rulers includes within it a carefully ordered "Yes!" to the whole cosmos and everything in it created by God. In the simple language of the text, it is very good. Whatever human dominion is in Genesis, then, it ennobles us for the purpose of ennobling everything else. Like our God, we too are servants in royal form.

Furthermore, the text soundly refutes another, related kind of objection to the doctrine of human dominion. This objection normally comes from certain feminist writers, who understandably look upon any language of power and authority with suspicion. Influential writers of theology like Sally McFague and Catherine Keller discern in these ancient notions a powerful agenda — to give divine legitimacy to hierarchy, including that of patriarchy.[16] I have already indicated that the text does indeed enforce a hierarchy between God and human beings, and between human beings and nature. In my view that sort of hierarchy is of maximum benefit to all parties, for reasons already stated. But I do not think there is any clear ground in this text for building anything like that kind of hierarchy between any human beings. In Genesis 1 God declares both the man and the woman together as being made in his very own image and likeness. So even if there is any other kind of hierarchy between men and women (which I do not believe there is or should be), it would have to prove its legitimacy on quite different grounds, not on this doctrine of human dominion.[17]

It is very important to stress, especially as context for understanding godly forms of being affluent, that the value, dignity, and rights that follow from this precious doctrine belong to *all* human beings. With that being so, the framework is in place for building a spiritual and moral view of af-

---

16. See Middleton's summary of their arguments, "Liberating Image?" pp. 13-14.

17. A careful reading of Genesis 1 reminds us the man and woman were both made in God's image and to both he gave dominion. In the second creation narrative of Genesis 2-3, in spite of traditional readings, the text makes clear that the man and the woman are coequal partners in life, each to be committed to the well-being of the other. For an extended discussion of male and female in Genesis 2-3, see Phyllis Trible, *God and the Rhetoric of Sexuality* (Philadelphia: Fortress, 1978).

fluence as it should be. This pre-democratic idea follows from reverence for the royal dignity of every individual.[18]

But to return to the environmental challenge, we must take note that God not only made human beings from the earth, but also placed them in the garden "to till and keep it" (Gen. 2:15). As the later history of Israel and the land will show, there is much more in common between Genesis and Native American thought on the sacredness of the land and its inhabitants than has typically been acknowledged in either tradition. For somewhat disparate reasons, pollution of the land and the wanton destruction of animal and plant life ought nevertheless to be just as great a sacrilege and desecration to Christians as it is to Native American people. While insisting on the supremacy of human beings, the dominion-theology of Christians must at once also be a rich source of energy for a fierce, but theologically well-formed environmentalism.

So the biblical notion of human dominion over nature in no conceptual way leads to the anti-ecological view that environmentalists rightly oppose. In fact, with a little more space, we could easily draw out the point that the particular notion of dominion in this text actually entails the contrary. Since it is dominion that represents God's view of nature, and since God's view of nature is that it is sacred, it follows that humans must rule over nature with a respect that is commensurate with that truth.[19] Our role is to set the creation free from harm, to bring out its potential — not to inflict evil upon it.

So it seems that whatever the sources of anti-environmental attitudes are in the West, they are not in the Judeo-Christian doctrine of human dominion, but in the metaphysics of some other, utilitarian sort of worldview. But the rigorous reader will not yet be satisfied. For even if the basic doctrine of human dominion does strongly entail a creative and redemptive approach to the ecology, on the premise that nature is sacred, it by no means follows that these intuitions are compatible with the larger affirmation of capitalism that I am making in the larger context of this book. Is there a way to affirm capitalism (as it seems we must, for reasons already noted) and at the same time affirm the ecological principles of true human

18. The issue of "rule over" comes to a head in the biblical narratives on the establishment of monarchy in Israel. God warns against this system as unnatural and open to abuse. See John Bright, *The Kingdom of God* (Nashville: Abingdon, 1953), pp. 32-33.

19. On this argument, see my article "Can Protestants Let the Trees Do the Talking?" in *Religion and Liberty* 10, no. 2 (March and April 2000): 5-7.

dominion? I believe there is. However, to work out a complete explanation would really require another book for anything like a complete treatment. And so I will not even try to give one in this book. Nevertheless, it seems that I should at least offer something, even if it is but an outline of what that treatment might include.

One way to integrate the ecological doctrines of Scripture with capitalism is to propose the existence of a kind of capitalism that is entirely different from what we have now. This is the strategy of a good many "greens" (including Christian ones) who have come to terms with the reality that is capitalism but do not think that the planet can sustain modern *consumer* capitalism for a very long time without breaking down. A good example is the book *Natural Capitalism* by ecologists Paul Hawken, Amory Lovins, and Hunter Lovins.[20] These authors propose societies in which everyone drives "green cars," and where the entire energy system is retooled from top to bottom.

Among explicitly Christian greens are Mark Walden and Frank Cougar. Walden is on the editorial staff of *The Green Cross,* a publication they bill as "a Christian environmental quarterly," published under the auspices of Ron Sider. Cougar is a frequent contributor. Walden and Cougar are aware of the modern economic dogma that societies must consume at high rates in order for economies to sustain growth and create wealth. One might have thought that this was among the safest assumptions anyone could make about the economic essentials of successful capitalism — for (as noted in the first chapter) it is the emergence of the consumer economy that has unleashed the wealth-creating powers of capitalism since the 1950s. There has never been a non-consumer form of capitalism that has managed to work.

Nevertheless, Walden and Cougar believe it is a myth that we must consume as we do or else decline.[21] Furthermore they are convinced (and this is the green dogma) that to continue present forms of consumption (in this they seem to include, questionably, all forms of production) will inevitably cause the depletion of enough resources to bring the world consumer economy to collapse. We can avoid this disaster, they believe, by taking what they call a "middle path of downsized levels of consump-

---

20. Paul Hawkin, Amory Lovins, and Hunter Lovins, *Natural Capitalism* (Little, Brown, 2000).

21. Mark Walden and Frank Cougar, "The Human Consequences of a Consumer Society," *Green Cross* 2, no. 2 (summer 1996): 13-15.

tion."[22] With that they envision a world in which energy sources are re-
newable, farming is all organic, recycling is the norm, manufacturers produce mainly durable products, the economy is decentralized to scale, and
society adopts non-material definitions of success (this may be a good
thing, because I would think in this set-up there won't be much of any).
In addition they pile on high tax rates for "resource depletion" and tax reforms "to aid the restructuring process." We will also have to have
"shorter work hours" for "community purposes," a scientific understanding that society "cannot continue on its present course," and a social ethic
that finds fulfillment in "living together" rather than in separate units.[23]

Not being a professional economist I will not develop my suspicion
that this proposed social economy is but a utopian fantasy. But even if the
economics, such as they are, were feasible, I am inclined to agree with
Dinesh D'Souza's conclusion about these alternative capitalisms. Redesigning entire societies is fairly difficult under the best of circumstances.
The likelihood of completely redesigning our own (as well as implement-
ing the "new order" elsewhere in the world) is practically zero. Why would
anyone seriously believe that anything like this could happen in the real
world? I do not know. I only know I find this sort of thinking unrealistic,
and, in its Christian form, messianic. At any rate, D'Souza helps bring this
discussion back to earth: "The deliberate halting of growth rates, either in
the West or in the Third World, is incomprehensible."[24]

D'Souza also joins a growing community of other Christian theorists
on the subject who believe that our best hope for the environment lies in
the advance of both wealth creation and high technology. The one enables
us to liberate people from poverty. The other offers our best chance at
knowing how to do so with minimum damage to the ecosystem.[25]

Moreover, D'Souza points out something else that environmentalists

---

22. Walden and Cougar, p. 14.

23. Walden and Cougar, pp. 14-15.

24. Dinesh D'Souza, *The Virtue of Prosperity: Finding Values in an Age of Techno-
Affluence* (New York: Free Press, 2000), p. 150.

25. D'Souza, *Virtue of Prosperity*, p. 150. On this school of thought see also Robert
Royal, *The Virgin and the Dynamo: Use and Abuse of Religion in Environmental Debates*
(Grand Rapids: Eerdmans, 1999); and "The Cornwall Declaration on Environmental Stewardship," *Religion and Liberty* 10, no. 2 (March and April 2000): 9-11. This declaration calls
for the integration of environmental stewardship with property rights. More than one hundred Christian leaders from a variety of backgrounds have signed it.

generally overlook. He cites Peter Huber's provocative but true statement that "the rich, not the poor, are the ones actively committed to conserving wildlife, forest, seashore and ocean."[26] It is not the loggers and fishermen in the American Northwest, or the small farmers of the Brazilian rain forest who are preserving the environment. They have neither the luxury nor the vision to do so; they are too busy trying to make a living. In fact, they normally view the environmental movement as the "enemy." Like it or not, it is people like Ted Turner who buy up millions of acres of land, keep it from destructive development, place vast herds of bison upon its grasslands, and leave them untouched for posterity. And there is truth in the notion that landowners care a great deal more about their property than any government agency or lobby ever will. So there is some real sense in thinking that the more people that rise from poverty to prosperity, the better things will be for the environment.

This point, however, allows that strong regulatory agencies exist for constraining owners who act to the (fallen) contrary. And it also allows that the eschatology of the green community is to an extent alarmist, failing to take into account that our technology may well solve at least many of our most serious problems, such as the extermination of species in the rain forest, or the effects of carbon emissions on the global climate. Meanwhile, again, there is not space to develop anything like an environmental view or ethics in this book. And so we must come back to its main focus, which is the relationship in Christian theology between faith and affluence. We simply suppose for now that the cultivation of affluence is not unambiguously incompatible with the environmental intuitions that we have affirmed.

HUMAN DOMINION AND DELIGHT

To return to our main theme, then, human dominion in Genesis expresses itself not just in these powerfully creative and redemptive terms, but also in the language of productive work, abundance, flourishing, and unashamedly physical delight. There is a sorrow about ancient civilization. Much of this sorrow stems from the profound awareness that we hu-

---

26. D'Souza, *Virtue of Prosperity*, p. 148. Quoting Peter Huber, *Hard Green* (New York: Basic, 1999), pp. 149-53.

mans are finite in our mortal flesh. There is something in our human longing for eternity, expressed in our greatest cultural achievements, that finds our existence in time and space, inside these mortal bodies of ours, troublesome and prison-like. We feel like birds with our wings clipped. Perhaps this is the reason why religions so often tend toward otherworldliness and spiritualism. To an extent, this ancient problem is at the root of our current search for economic integrity. It is widely known that both Thomas Jefferson and Karl Marx rejected a fully biblical Christianity because they believed it was too otherworldly. They echoed the sentiments of Nietzsche, who declared that, in essence, Christians were "haters of the body," and "the great despisers of the earth." And in truth a good many Christians have presented their faith as if it were concerned exclusively with the afterlife.

But these thinkers did not hear very well the "Yes!" that God speaks in Genesis and elsewhere to the creation. Throughout Genesis 1, the text affirms the material world as both real and "good" (an affirmation that is repeated throughout the story) — as something that truly ought to be. To the world of light, land, sky and seas, the heavenly cosmos, and the earthly collection of plants and animals, God gives a joyous blessing. Like an artist, he gazes admiringly upon the whole creation and is pleased to say that it — all of it — is very good (Gen. 1:31).

In this light, I suggest that the goodness of the world is not just the ground concept for rules about respecting the earth; it is also about its capacities to bring royal delight to human beings — to be delightful, and about our human capacity (like God's) to be delighted by it. It is about the cosmic harmony, or *shalom*, which is pleasing to God and thus ought to be received in delight by human beings. Moreover, if we think about it, the goodness of the creation that is described by Genesis 1 is unthinkable apart from its materiality. Materiality is as essential to the goodness of the created order as the physical body is to a fully human identity.[27] The common idiom that says that we humans *have* bodies is not quite consistent with the imagery of Genesis 2. It is more appropriate to say that, as completely human beings, we *are* bodies.[28]

---

27. For a thoroughly rigorous and challenging study of the body in the Old Testament, see the recent work by John Cooper, *Body, Soul, and Life Everlasting* (Grand Rapids: Eerdmans, 1989).

28. See Barth, *Church Dogmatics*, III/2, esp. pp. 325-436.

In Genesis 2:7-9, this last point about the body is suggested by the imagery of God forming the man from the ground and placing him and the woman like a small king and queen in a pleasure garden with all its delights. The idea is earthy and wonderfully extravagant — that we are of, by, and for the earth. We are fashioned from the earth to live upon the earth, not merely to dominate in the abstract, but to execute our dominion by cultivating, caring, bringing forth the created potential of the earth and other beings. The story makes it very clear, too, that the end of this sort of working, cultivating rule over nature is enjoyment of the fruits of the earth. The Garden of Eden is nothing if not a vision of this truth about God's will for human beings. The concept of dominion thus includes something like the regality and majesty of delight that we naturally associate with royal status. Such a person is indeed a steward of creation, and a servant, but such terms are inadequate quite to identify one who is royal, "every inch a king," as Shakespeare said of Lear.

It is true that we are more than mere bodies; we are also spiritual beings. God breathed his breath into the first human, and thus brought him to spiritual life. And we are rational, moral beings, and much else besides. But our fullest spiritual, rational, and moral capacities are not easily imagined apart from the body. The experience of physical majesty is the experience of human freedom in the real world. That is why, for the ancient Hebrews, life apart from the body was not life at all, but mere existence. The quintessential vision of life in its full expression is the physical man or woman in his or her garden of delight. It seems to me that the enjoyment of pleasure in this larger existential setting is quite distinct from and opposed to what we normally think of as hedonism, covetousness, or the greed of *pleonexia*. It is the expression of deep godliness and humanness. It is a natural state of good pleasure in the good things of God and God's world. In this condition, human beings were apparently best placed to encounter, to know, and to respond to their creator and to other beings.

Genesis 2 thus makes clear that bodily life is essentially good. The story pictures this goodness in the setting of an oriental pleasure garden, lush with fruit and vegetation, teeming with life of all sorts, its beauties enriched by the flowing of four great rivers out of its heart. The man and the woman lived with royal effect, and that was good. There are indeed images of creative, productive, fruitful work (we will get to the issue of warnings and obligations in due course). But on the whole they are pictures of enjoyment and pure delight in the world. They are pictures of blessing for self-actualizing freedom to enjoy life as a gift. We must ponder the original divine permission, "You may eat of every tree of the garden," which expresses much more than mere concern for their nutrition. The first vision of material human existence we get from Scripture is not a narrative of just "getting by" on a diet of "daily bread," a counsel of "just enough." Rather, it opens to us the vast, superfluous horizon of freedom for delight that God gave to human beings in the beginning.

The whole view is one of almost embarrassingly extravagant excess. Of course the term "affluence" is a modern economic one, and so we ought not use it without qualification to describe this original state of affairs and vision of human existence at its ontological best. But with qualification, the term applies quite well, I think. For while they had no money, no equities, no real estate, no jobs, no technology — no capital in our modern sense of the word, their condition of flourishing had the same sort of effects as those things can have upon us. Eden set the man and woman free from servitude to want, it unleashed them to dream, to use their creativity, to work in productive and rewarding ways, to reap the fruits of their labor, and to take human pleasure in the whole of life, in the image of God, and in his good pleasure. Capitalism has brought us closer to recreating that condition than has any other economic system in the history of the world. We might say that Eden enabled them, in their work, also to be at rest. It was a good place for them to be.

This helps us to picture the kind of bodily life that is good. In academic circles, we often think of this narrative as making an implied attack on the pagan notions of God that surrounded Israel — this is one of the established commonplaces of biblical scholarship.[29] But as Middleton perceptively observes, "Genesis may also be read as polemical against Near Eastern notions of *being human*."[30] His point is not exactly the one I am making, for it is about the implied attack that Genesis is making on inequality as justification for oppression. We shall come back to that point very shortly, for it is at the core of biblical ethics for the rich. But before attending to that widely affirmed idea, we need to see that the story is even more basically an assault on barrenness. The entire material existence of the man and the woman is one of unabashed splendor. That they were na-

---

29. See Gerhard Hasel, "The Polemical Nature of the Genesis Cosmology," *Evangelical Quarterly* 46 (1974): 81-102.

30. Middleton, *Liberating Image?* p. 18.

ked and not ashamed confirms the pure, direct, and unspoiled relationship that they had with the world of physical delight. The story impresses upon us the truth that abundance, fruitfulness, and excess are the proper conditions for a full life of delight. And it forces us to make a distinction that is too seldom made between the carnal lust of hedonism and the dignity that is delight.

In our fallen world, there is a false enjoyment of things that is dark, demonic, and evil. The creation story does not ignore this reality. (And the prophets will later help us to identify this kind of gratification for what it is.) But to understand it properly, we must first know what the true and good kind of delight is, of which the other is a cruel mockery.

The vision that comes through in the story of Genesis, then, helps to explain why it was that God's promises have always been material in nature. It is not accidental or gratuitous that in the following narratives of Abraham and the patriarchs God promises them worldly wealth, power, and flourishing — both for them and for their descendants. No matter of chance that the promises to Moses were of a land flowing with milk and honey, or that Job is the epitome of a man whose circumstances embody his rightness with God and so forth.[31] What God promises is nothing less than the condition he intended for people in the beginning. The theme underlying these promises is no less than the nature of creation itself — for human beings redemption just is being restored in new circumstances to the old order — God's order — of the world. And it is not by chance that Jesus himself, for all the many ambiguities that attend his economic life and teaching, never ceased to proclaim the kingdom of God as a great messianic feast, and to live in a manner that (among other things) expressed the reality of that future kingdom in the present. As we shall see in later chapters, the banquet begins with his bodily Incarnation and is secured forever by his bodily resurrection after real bodily death on a cross. The narrative of Genesis demands that we take very great care in heeding the warning near the end of the Gospel narrative of Christ, when a woman of doubtful reputation breaks the seal on a jar of pure nard and pours it

---

31. It seems that Craig Blomberg, in his often very informative book *Neither Poverty Nor Riches,* did not make this essential connection between the ontology of creation and the later material promises of God to Israel. Perhaps that is why he so readily dismisses the paradigm of Eden as relevant to Christians, and supports the notion that Proverbs 30:8-9 and its counsel of moderation ("give me neither poverty nor wealth") is a summary of the paradigm biblical ethics, as his title suggests. As I will argue, I think this view is quite mistaken.

over Jesus' head (John 12:3). Judas could not get past the extravagance of the act, and even less so Jesus' tacit approval of it. When the time comes, we will return to that enigmatic text.

At any rate, the narrative of Genesis strongly supports the sentiment of Lear, as he replies to his daughter's complaints about his excesses. "O, reason not the need: our basest beggars are in the poorest things superfluous: Allow not nature more than nature needs, man's life is cheap as beast's."[32] Old Lear knows that he is waging war for the human soul. There is a difference between his love of royal effect or majesty and his daughter's lust for money and things. As the great psychologist William James wrote:

> Man's chief difference from the brutes lies in the exuberant excess of his subjective propensities. His preeminence over them lies simply and solely in the fantastic and unnecessary character of his wants, physical, moral, aesthetic, and intellectual. Had his whole life not been a quest for the superfluous, he would never have established himself so inexpungeably in the necessary. Prune down his extravagances, sober him, and you undo him.[33]

The creation story suggests that physical and material delightfulness (superfluity) is needful for healthy human well-being everywhere.

It is no doubt why delightful physical actions like getting in good shape, buying a fine new dress or suit, having one's hair done well, shaving and putting on a good aftershave, or getting behind the wheel of a finely tuned car elevate us from various states of depression and discouragement. The same is true of curling up in a pleasurable sitting room in front of a fire in winter, and of grilling steaks on a cedar deck on a warm spring evening. The story of Genesis makes clear that not all excess and extravagance is wantonness. Not all "who come eating and drinking," as Jesus did, are "drunkards and gluttons." Human delight is a precious expression of God's glory, of human dignity, and of the goodness of life in this world. In its proper form it is a sacrament to God's dominion over chaos and darkness. And it is the condition of affluence alone that makes full delight possible.

---

32. *King Lear,* 2.4.

33. William James, *The Will to Believe,* cited in Robert Bly, *Iron John* (New York: Vintage, 1990), pp. 224-25.

HUMAN DOMINION AND THE FALL

Of course affluence, being necessarily a state of considerable freedom, makes other things possible, too. The words, "You may eat of every tree of the garden," are about God's blessing and our freedom. Nevertheless, consistent with the notion of image bearing as being a representative (that is, not absolute) kind of dominion, the freedom of the man and the woman was limited. "But of the tree of knowledge of good and evil you shall not eat, for in the day that you eat of it you shall die" (Gen. 3:17). As we know, though, the serpent persuades the woman and the man that this limit is but a cloak for God's envious fears. "You will not die. For the Lord knows that if you eat of it your eyes will be opened, and you will be like God, knowing good and evil" (3:4). At this point the woman discovers an altogether new form of enjoyment, one that is anything but delightful. The power of attraction is great and she and her husband both eat. The judgment of God over this disaster confirms the serpent's horrible half-truth: "Behold, the man has become like one of us, knowing good and evil" (3:22).

According to biblical scholar Malcolm Clark, the idiom of "knowing good and evil" was judicial — that is, about having rightful authority to make judgments.[34] His careful research confirms the traditional view of the fall as a quest for equality with God. The first humans wished to be their own gods, little miniature Yahwehs, autonomous rulers of their own universe. The story is thus a warning to the whole human race, but especially to those who are given the freedom that comes with affluence. Perhaps we may think of sin in this context as false dominion. Whatever the ancient doctrine of original sin means (and we cannot go into its mysteries in this book) it carries the idea that all human beings have this disposition to try to rule on their own, in the absolute. We all have this desire somewhere within ourselves to be ridiculously tiny versions of God, answerable to none but ourselves. Our text makes clear that this disposition is at the root of alienation between humanity and God, between human beings and each other, and also the earth. Because of it thorns and thistles emerge from cracked soil. Drops of sweat break from the brow. Work becomes hard and tiresome. The world falls under a curse. In this world there is land, but no Eden.

34. Malcolm Clark, "The Legal Background to the Yahwist's Use of 'Good and Evil' in Genesis 2–3," *Journal of Biblical Theology* 88 (Sept. 1969): 266-78.

It is very difficult to give a brief summary of what follows between Genesis 4, in which Cain slays his brother Abel, and Genesis 12, wherein God calls Abram and a new narrative of Israel begins. But the importance of this material in connecting creation with Israel is too great to leave out completely. So I offer just these few closing comments:

First, these narratives convey the bleak truth that the world has become full of the sort of dominion that came with the mind of the serpent. If servant-dominion describes the human condition that God made in the beginning, we might well call the sort of quality that now generally gives shape and direction to human power "serpent-dominion." Outside Eden, Cain slays his brother Abel and God drives him into exile. In response, he and his sons build a city and name it after themselves — a kind of self-centered anti-creation. The line of Cain grows in its evil to such an extent that God regrets having made human beings in the first place. He decides to destroy the culture of Cain by means of a purifying flood, and does so. But even amid such evil, destruction is never the ruling theme of the narrative. Redemption and hope are.

For example, good things come forth amid and almost in spite of the growing evil of Cain's family line. The city he founds is a context for all kinds of spiritual and moral chaos, but it is also a birthplace for the arts, technology, and animal husbandry — all good things. The message is that our scriptures, even at this grim point in the story of sin, do not advocate separatism. While they do stress the power and pervasiveness of serpent-dominion in the world that human beings fashion, they nevertheless also proclaim that the forces of cosmos, the integrity of God's good creation, are greater still. Sin cannot overcome or contain them, not even in the evil city of Cain. Greater is he who is in us, we may paraphrase, than he who is in the world.

And furthermore, at the same time, with the birth of Seth, who replaces Abel, God begins a new line of human beings. In this family line, what grows is not sin and evil but righteousness, crowned with the birth and life of Noah, the one who is to "redeem us from the curse which is on the ground" (Gen. 5:29). The narrative works very hard to remind readers that we — all of us — are the descendants of Noah, not Cain. Our legacy is thus in the promise, in grace and righteousness, and not in unredeemable evil. This important truth comes through most clearly in the covenant that God makes with Noah, his sons, all their descendants and with all created things. In this fallen world it is true, on the one hand, that "the imagination of man's heart is evil from his youth" (8:21). But on the other, it is also true that God still affirms humanity and the world. For God reaffirms the truth that human beings retain the value and dignity of creatures made in his image and likeness (9:6), and that human authority over the earth is a good thing, even in a world now filled with dominion of the contrary sort (9:1-2).

In a world like this, affluence, like any form of power, is bound to be rare, the condition of a privileged few. And it is bound to be dangerous, the fruits of a struggle for power and the lust to keep it. Nevertheless, even in this world, the narratives of Abraham and Israel that follow prove beyond doubt that God is undeterred. They reveal that he is unmoved by difficulty and danger, as great as these are. They reveal a God who is as resolved as he can be to have a world in which human beings do not merely survive, but flourish in true *shalom* and, therefore, in material delight. They are not merely narratives of divine rescue, but of cosmic redemption, and material affluence is part of redemption. I believe this is the best explanation we have for the central place the narratives ever after give to wealth as the incarnation of God's promise and blessing. The challenge for Christians is to figure out what this truth means in the context of the narratives of Jesus as the Christ, and what affluence thus means for the Christian faith. But we have miles to go before we get to the Gospels. First we must follow our theme into the narratives of Israel in the exodus and exile, and we must consider the economic themes that arise in the Law, the Prophets, and in the books of Wisdom.

CHAPTER THREE

The Exodus: Land of Liberation and Delight

*Possession of the land is the earliest eschatological motif in
Israelite religion. It is the ultimate goal of the people. But it
is more; the land is the sanctuary of YHWH, his dwelling
place on earth.*

YEHEZKEL KAUFMANN[1]

THE GOD WHO LIBERATES

Many of us learned the story of the exodus in Sunday school; others of us
got our first images of this great event in sacred history from those spectacular scenes in the film *The Ten Commandments,* with Charlton Heston
as Moses. But we very well may not have learned that the biblical story of
Israel's exodus from Egypt contains deeply serious theology. To the ancient
Hebrews, and to historic Judaism, the exodus was (after the creation of the
world) the most important event of all time. It was the event in which the
true God of the universe came forth at long last to fulfill the promises he
had made so long ago to Abraham, Isaac, and Jacob. In doing so, this God
revealed his nature and his vision for the world more completely and more
widely than ever before in human history. So it is believed by Jews and

1. Yehezkel Kaufmann, *The Religion of Israel* (Chicago: University of Chicago Press,
1960), p. 241.

Christians alike. The narrative of the exodus is as basic to Old Testament theology as the narratives of Christ's Incarnation are to New Testament theology. And in Christian theology the exodus is second only to the life of Christ in its contribution to our doctrine of God.

In recent decades we have begun to learn that the narratives and collections of laws connected with the exodus also provide very important frames of reference for modern political and social theology. Whatever criticisms we may have of the contemporary movement known as liberation theology, it is incontestably true that these (mainly Latin American Catholic) theologians are absolutely right in their larger sense of what the exodus means in social terms. Gustavo Gutiérrez, perhaps the premier liberation theologian, states well the core intuition of its theology. He writes, "The Liberation of Israel is a political action."[2] It is the story of a God whose very nature it is to liberate the poor from the oppressions of poverty.[3] In this view, God identifies intensely and especially with the poor. So it follows that the people of this God must (if they are faithful to his nature and will) be disposed to be and to do likewise. North American theologian Ron Sider has been stressing for years to fellow evangelicals (who have not always been attentive to the idea) that "the God of the Bible wants to be known as the liberator of the oppressed."[4] His assertion only gains strength from the obvious interest in justice for the powerless in the corpus of exodus laws.

There is little controversy among Christian scholars over the points we have considered so far. I certainly do agree with liberation theologians, and with Ron Sider and others, who stress that the God of Scripture has a peculiar interest in setting the poor free from poverty. There is no doubt that in the exodus God liberates a poor and oppressed people, and this is an essential part of what the exodus narratives reveal about the nature and will of God generally. My disagreement with liberation theologians is not about the centrality of this liberation, but about the form that this liberation takes, and also about its implications for moral and spiritual theology.

2. Gustavo Gutiérrez, *A Theology of Liberation,* trans. and ed. Sister Caridad Inda and John Eagleson (Maryknoll, N.Y.: Orbis, 1989), p. 155.

3. For a useful critical treatment of liberation theology, see Norman K. Gottwald, "The Exodus as Event and Process: A Test Case in the Biblical Grounding of Liberation Theology," in *The Future of Liberation Theology,* ed. M. Ellis and O. Maduro (Maryknoll, N.Y.: Orbis, 1989), pp. 250-60.

4. Ronald J. Sider, *Rich Christians in an Age of Hunger: Moving from Affluence to Generosity,* 20th Anniversary Revision (Dallas: Word, 1997), p. 43.

In this chapter I will stress the prominent biblical theme (down-played by liberation theologians) that divine liberation in the exodus takes the form of material delight. Moreover, I will argue that material delight (affluence properly achieved and enjoyed) emerges in this narrative as a paradigm for our spirituality and ethics. In my view, the pronounced theme of affluence in the literature that is linked with the exodus is thus vastly more important than Christian interpreters commonly suppose it is.[5] On the contrary, the inclination of almost all Christian scholarship on the subject is to downplay the significance of this theme for Christians. Nevertheless, I am convinced that it is the very theme, going back through Jacob, Isaac, Abraham, and Noah, that connects these stories with the narratives of creation, and thus with God's original vision for human existence. It remains to be seen just how this vision of material flourishing and delight is manifested and enshrined in the distinctly Christian texts and in Christian theory.

But as they are, these texts of the exodus are as near as anything we have in sacred Scripture (except perhaps for Luke's Gospel) to a theology that is uniquely aimed at the concerns of wealthy people seeking God. And my interpretation encourages us to think of material affluence in a considerably more favorable light than is typical in Christian scholarship on wealth.[6] Unfortunately, it has mainly been defenders of the so-called Prosperity Gospel who have stressed these narratives of wealth as models for believers in our day. Their readings lack proper nuance, and their applications thus seriously distort the sense of Scripture on how faith relates to affluence.

This chapter consists of two main parts. The first focuses upon what I will call narratives of the land. These texts simply relate the entry of Israel into the land of Canaan, and they convey the purpose of God's agency in

---

5. For example, the most complete recent attempt to offer a biblical theology of wealth is by Craig L. Blomberg, *Neither Poverty Nor Riches: A Biblical Theology of Material Possessions* (Grand Rapids: Eerdmans, 1999). A major thesis of the book is that the patriarchal blessing of wealth was exceptional, linked as it was to God's special promise to them of a land. Blomberg does not inquire into the more primary question of why God would liberate the Hebrews by just that means.

6. In *Wealth as Peril and Obligation: The New Testament on Possessions* (Grand Rapids: Eerdmans, 1995), as the title suggests, Sondra Ely Wheeler offers an entire account of New Testament teaching on wealth without even discussing the predominant Old Testament theme of wealth as a divine *blessing*. It would seem that "peril" and "obligation" are at last the only terms left for Christians in understanding conditions of material affluence.

bringing that about. Following conventional Old Testament scholarship, I understand this material as providing the larger context in which we are to interpret the key legal texts that follow from the events in view. The second part of the chapter thus considers ancient Hebrew laws and spiritual and ethical teachings that pertain to the material condition of affluence. In this discussion I shall seek to show what the essential principles are in these texts, and how they might apply to affluent Christians today.

As I write on these texts, I am well aware of the intricacies that exist in the academic disciplines of tradition-historical criticism and textual hermeneutics. I will enter into these issues only to the extent that I think is helpful to my explanations and argument. But my decision not to go into them in depth seems to me reasonable. For one thing, there is no agreement among scholars on most of the form-critical and redactional problems in the compositional history of the writings in view. It would require almost an entire book to review and to sort through this material, and even then it would still be unclear what its implications are. But for another, as indicated in the introduction, I firmly believe in the divine inspiration of the biblical canon. So (for me) whatever the merits of these speculative historical and philosophical studies (and they do have them) are, I do not think they are *essential* to writing Christian theology. As I explained earlier, I do not see how, on inspiration, they can be. I shall proceed on the assumption, then, that we can get the essential meaning of these texts by reading them in the light of narratives, and in the context that the framers of the Bible deliberately gave them in the canon.

THE PROMISED LAND OF DELIGHT

As we follow the biblical narratives from Noah to the events of the exodus and Moses, we cannot fail to notice the unifying theme of promise. In the light of God's promises to Noah and all his descendants (that is, all of us) and to the entire creation, the story narrows its focus to God's dealings with Abram. God promises to Abram that he will make of him a great nation, that he will make his name great and that his blessing will extend to all the nations of the earth (Gen. 12:2-3). Genesis 13 describes the great wealth that Abram thus began to acquire, and the theme of prosperity rises in the narratives of Isaac, Jacob, and Joseph (20:14-16; 24:35; 26:13; 30:43; and 47:27). These men all have lives marked by hardship of one sort or another — the crowning example being the irony of Joseph's captivity and triumph in Egypt — but the literal force of God's promise remains. The four hundred years of slavery and poverty that follow thus seem worse even than they otherwise would, for the contrast they strike in the story with what the reader knows to be real. The narrative does not directly answer the natural question of why this God of delight would permit his people to suffer such intensely non-delightful things. The problem of God and evil that vexes many a modern believer is, alas, not new.

But at any rate, in his good time, God delivers on his promise. God finally takes action. The first chapters of the book of Exodus are about God's mighty acts of redemption as performed through the (again) ironic figure of Moses, who like Joseph arises through the political ranks of Egypt to become the hero of Israel. By the end of these dramatic events enacted between Moses and Pharaoh, who represents the greatest power known on earth, the incomparably greater power of this God proves too much even for him.

And to add insult to the injury just inflicted, as the Hebrews prepare their exit from captivity, God tells them first to go ahead and "plunder the Egyptians" before going (Exod. 11:2-3). This part of the narrative has been something of an embarrassment to scholarly commentators on the text. And they have spent no little effort seeking to gloss over the apparent immorality of the action.[7] It seems that the strain of embarrassment still exists, judging from Craig Blomberg's most recent way of understating the matter: "Plundering the Egyptians shows that God wants his people to go into their new land with a measure of wealth."[8] Blomberg hastens to add, however, that the Hebrews did spend much of the spoils on the tabernacle (so we suppose that diminishes its questionable ethics). Furthermore, he stresses that that their new-gotten affluence "quickly lured them into idolatry" (so we see the perils), and that very soon they were on their daily diet of manna, anyway. The episode of the manna, he observes, was "the dominant method of providing physical sustenance for God's people in the desert." This method, he explains further, was designed by God to prevent them "from becoming too well off."[9] In Blomberg's view, the perennial

---

7. See the summary of literature and the various pained attempts at explanation in Brevard S. Childs, *The Book of Exodus* (Philadelphia: Westminster, 1974), pp. 175-77.

8. Blomberg, *Neither Poverty Nor Riches*, p. 38.

9. Blomberg, *Neither Poverty Nor Riches*, p. 38.

truth for Christians in this part of the story, then, is thus quite contrary to the one I am about to make. In the light of his interpretation of Paul, in 2 Corinthians 8:15 (a reading that we shall also have to challenge in a later chapter), the primary point of the narrative (and all of Scripture on wealth, in his view throughout his book) is "about avoiding extremes of riches or poverty."[10]

Without going into a detailed critique of this interpretation, I must simply state my objection that it, like most other attempts to bring the episode of the plundering (that extends to the brutal conquest of the Canaanites) into line with a presumed-to-be-better Christian morality, does not square very well with the conspicuous theme of the narrative. That theme of course continues the one that began in Eden, endured to Noah, and grew strong again in the narratives of the patriarchs. It is the promise of God to bring his people quite deliberately into conditions of material prosperity and power *in the extreme*. Despoiling the Egyptians is simply the resumption of that theme in the context of a new one — that is, the theme of God and justice. In the end both the Hebrews and the Egyptians "get theirs." (And by the way, under the circumstances, I see nothing immoral about either outcome.)

Moreover, constraining the rebellious Hebrews to daily portions of manna in the desert is indeed temporary, as Blomberg does note, but (so I judge) precisely because it is *not* the model or normative paradigm in the story (contrary to his interpretation). As the text will make explicit, it was but a preparatory testing, a step toward the long-envisioned goal of what life would be in the new land. And as I will argue in a later chapter, Paul's use of the manna episode comports entirely with this understanding of it as exceptional, provisional, and not at all the epitome of faith and virtue in the ordinary course of economic life for Christians.

The long-awaited entry into the Promised Land, flowing with milk and honey as it was, secures this link between the story of redemption in the exodus and the vision of creation we have considered in Genesis. In doing so, it helps to sharpen our understanding of just what form the liberation of God's people takes. It takes the form of creation. And, of course, the creation is all about extremes. It seems more than strange that a God who purportedly disapproves of extremes of wealth (not just extremes of poverty) would have created the world he did in the first place (we remember

---

10. Blomberg, *Neither Poverty Nor Riches*, pp. 38-39.

Eden), called Noah and the patriarchs into the light of affluence as he did, and now leads a whole people into a rich land to become an extremely wealthy nation.

The biblical language describing the land and its conditions of affluence and possibilities for delight is nothing if not extreme. For all the form-critical and redactional problems that exist in scientific studies of the book, there is little controversy over the widely held judgment that Deuteronomy (in its final form) is late in comparison with other writings of the Pentateuch, and that its character is deeply interpretive and theological.[11] In this view, Deuteronomy "constitutes the center of Old Testament theology."[12] Moreover, its canonical function, in giving the series of speeches to Israel by none less than the towering figure of Moses, is clearly to interpret the Torah in an authoritative theological sense to the nation — it is in that light a theology of Israel's history, and of the law.[13] And in its reflections on Israel's experience in the exodus, the frame of reference for spiritual and moral life in the land is not at all focused on the virtues of moderation, in the context of daily manna and the like. The wilderness is not the spiritual and moral context for the spiritual and moral opportunities and challenges that await Israel on the other side of Jordan. That context, rather, is the Promised Land. So if this canonical understanding of the book is at all on track, then the land and its qualities ought to come into our focus, too.

Scholars of Deuteronomy have for a long time now believed that its framers were also deeply involved in the shaping of the prophetic writings of the Old Testament.[14] And if that is true, it helps contemporary Christians to understand what the theological assumptions of the prophets' writings were on the subject of affluence. It means that the prophets understood Israel's sins in the context of these powerful, creational Deuteronomic terms. (More on the prophets in the next chapter, however.)

The propriety of this focus on the challenges of affluence becomes unmistakably clear in the text. The figure of Moses explains the nature of Israel's situation in almost Eden-like terms:

11. See Brevard S. Childs, *Introduction to the Old Testament as Scripture* (Philadelphia: Fortress, 1979), pp. 204-6.

12. Childs, *Introduction to the Old Testament*, p. 204.

13. Childs, *Introduction to the Old Testament*, p. 213.

14. Childs, *Introduction to the Old Testament*, p. 204.

> For the Lord your God is bringing you into a good land, a land of brooks of water, of fountains and springs, flowing forth in valleys and hills, a land of wheat and barley, of vines and fig trees and pomegranates, a land of olive trees and honey, a land in which you will eat bread without scarcity, in which you will lack nothing, a land whose stones are iron, and out of whose hills you can dig copper. And you shall eat and be full, and you shall bless the Lord your God for the good land he has given you. (Deut. 8:7-10)

Out of the waters of chaos and destruction, God had once again created a cosmos, a good world, in which his beloved creatures might have life as he envisions it for them — in material delight. It is very important to see that the form of liberation is creation in this sense, and what that means.

But as it was in Eden, so in this new land the great affluence that God had given them made possible something other than the delight he had in view. As in the garden, there was more than one tree from which to eat. The words of delight in prosperity are barely out of the speaker's mouth when these words of warning follow:

> Take care that you do not forget the Lord your God, by failing to keep his commandments, his ordinances, and his statutes, which I am commanding you today. When you have eaten your fill and have built fine houses and live in them, and when your herds and flocks have multiplied, and is multiplied, then do not exalt yourself, forgetting the Lord your God, who brought you up from the land of Egypt, out of the house of slavery, who led you through the great and terrible wilderness. (Deut. 8:11-15)

The warning then gets still more specific about the spiritual danger that comes with this great, new affluence, which exceeds anything they had ever imagined for themselves. After explaining that the manna and other trials in the wilderness were "to humble you and to test you, and in the end to do you good" (not, again, it seems, to establish a norm for their expectations, vision, and ethics), the real danger becomes clear:

> Do not say to yourself, "My power and the might of my own hand have gotten me this wealth." But remember the Lord your God, for it is he that gives you the power to get wealth, *so that he may confirm his covenant that he swore to your ancestors, as he is doing today.* (Deut. 8:17-18, italics mine)

As in Eden, violation of the moral order meant death. The consequences cannot but remind readers of that original choice:

> If you do forget the Lord your God and follow other gods to serve and worship them, I solemnly warn you today that you shall surely perish. Like the nations that the Lord is destroying before you, so shall you perish, because you would not obey the voice of the Lord your God. (Deut. 8:19-20)

It seems that material abundance is as dangerous for the freedom that it creates as it is good in its potential for bringing about cosmic good in and through delight. Creation of this kind necessarily makes possible a fall.

At this point in our discussion of the exodus, several things seem clear enough. First, God's purpose in setting his people free from slavery and poverty was, at bottom, linked with his larger purpose for human beings in the beginning. It was to place them in conditions where they might be free to cultivate a spirituality and materiality of true dominion and delight. The form that liberation took in the exodus was indeed that of the creation in a new context and setting. And if it is true that this purpose grew from God's very will for human beings, and was not merely a means to some higher, spiritual end, then we would not expect it to change in the unfolding of redemptive history. As we shall see, it does not change, not even in the Prophets and Wisdom books or in the Christ-narratives of the New Testament, with their stress on the evils of the rich and on the sufferings and poverty of the righteous. In this light, we must view affluence not merely as a circumstantial or relative good, but as a cosmic good. Once again, the condition of material affluence, in this light, is good in the same way that we have learned to think of the creation as good.

Second, the text of Deuteronomy makes it very clear that the good of affluence has certain very serious challenges built into it. The most basic challenge for making the good of affluence actual — for bringing about from it true delight — is most essentially spiritual in nature. It is to have the right spirituality of affluence at the core of one's material life. As the text expresses it, amid their great wealth God's people are to instinctively bless God, even as they themselves are blessed. Perhaps it sounds like a platitude to jaded moderns, but the truth is that this spirituality of blessing and the awareness that one just is blessed in affluence is the wellspring of all the other goods that can follow. It is not the end of the matter by any means, for a spirit of blessing toward God (which is very close to the notion of being grateful) and being blessed has to grow into dispositions and actions of a moral kind toward fellow human beings. And we are about to enter into the important matters of morality that arise in the corpus of Old Testament law. But the root of the ethics clearly is in a proper spirituality in response to the cosmic good of affluence. But as we shall see more clearly yet, the prophetic ethics of Scripture follow from this affirmation of affluence, not from its denial. That of course means that their challenge to God's people is to be affluent in the right way, not to cease being affluent altogether.

But third, likewise, the root of evil in responding to material affluence is also primarily spiritual. The text expresses it in those fall-like terms of autonomy, the attitude that "by my own hand" I have got this wealth. This is not the spirit of blessing, dominion, and delight. It is the spirit of self-serving arrogance and pride of the worst sort. In Moses' speech we thus begin to get a sense of the difference between these attitudes toward affluence. We shall continue to explore this difference in our discussion of the Law, and then the Prophets. For these very different spiritual responses to affluence bring about very different kinds of morality in economic life. And as I shall indicate at the end of the book, we may apply this intuition quite directly to our response to global poverty — which is as much a spiritual challenge to wealthy Christians as it is an ethical one (in my view).

THE HERMENEUTICS OF AFFLUENCE

Before going on to the exodus law and its challenges for the affluent in Israel, I want to devote a little space to anticipating an objection that I have encountered from time to time. I have never seen the objection in print — perhaps because it is not in the end a very convincing one. But I have encountered it in discussions, especially with people who are determined to resist the main point I am making in this part of the book — that the condition of affluence in the text is a cosmic good, at the core of God's eternal vision for human beings.

The objection simply is that what we moderns mean by affluence is so very different from what the biblical text means that we may not make the application of the one to the other. In other words, the affluence that Deuteronomy blesses as a divinely grounded good is nothing like the affluence that contemporary people enjoy under the regime of our high-tech economies. The difference is not only in degree but also in the kind of wealth that is commonly available now. As one person put it to me, Abraham was rich by ancient standards, but he would be poor by the measures we use now. On this person's view, then, God indeed affirms being affluent in the way that Abraham was, but not in the way that someone like a Bill Gates or a Warren Buffett is. The principle is that these men are just too rich for God to approve.

But is that so? Is it true that the very different kind of techno-wealth, together with the extraordinary amounts of it they (and we) typically have, render the words of Deuteronomy, just cited, useless as a framework of theology for modern Christians? The principle that would make it so seems to me constrictive to an extent that most believers (including me) would normally judge improper and even destructive to the claim of biblical authority in matters of modern life as a whole. For what if we applied the same logic to other topics, such as technology? It is clearly true, we should admit, that the text of Scripture does give a guarded but strong affirmation to the development of artificial technology (Gen. 4:22). But it is also true that the writers of this text (which affirms crude metallurgy) never imagined anything like modern industry, the computer chip, the passenger jet, or the human genome project. But surely it does not follow (on common Christian assumptions about the truth and inspiration of Scripture) from this obvious truth about the ancient horizon of the text that its *theological* affirmation of technology has no important bearing on our modern debates about its development and use. Of course the Amish, for example, have based their choices about technology on issues of degree and kind, but it seems rather arbitrary, does it not, to affirm the technology of the axle and wheel, but not the drive shaft, or the computer? It is kind of quaint and winsome that someone like Wendell Berry refuses to use a word processor — he writes on an old Royal manual — but (assuming he affirms at least the older technology) surely there is nothing philosophically or morally binding in his decision. We might develop the same sort of rebuttal by using subjects like knowledge, or political systems of freedom in contexts of race and gender. If the concepts involved are so unstable that they cannot cross time, it is hard to see how we could affirm the inspired meaning and authority of the Bible at all.

I do not wish to press further into the matter of hermeneutics, for soon we would reach the point of no return, I think. But furthermore (and finally) it is not exactly true that our concepts of affluence and poverty are as unstable as my acquaintance suggested they are. It seems that we define them conceptually in pretty much the same way as people did in ancient times. For poverty, in essence, is simply not having enough material means to afford the food, clothing, and shelter required to sustain physical life over time. On the other hand, affluence is essentially having more than enough for this purpose. On this conceptual understanding, in spite of cultural differences, we know poverty and affluence when we see them. I think it is true that when we read descriptions of Abraham, Isaac, Jacob, Joseph, Job, David, Solomon, Zacchaeus, and others we do not instinctively think that we are reading about people who just thought they were rich, but were in reality poor. We know that we are reading about people who really were rich, even though they were not affluent in the same way that we are. I believe it is very safe to say that the teachings on wealth and poverty in the Bible, while they arise in pre-modern economic settings, do find their conceptual — and thus spiritual and moral — way into our own time and its vastly different circumstances.

THE LAW: WHERE DELIGHT AND COMPASSION EMBRACE

Scholars agree that the many laws of Israel express an "exodus vision" of society. The laws are repeatedly grounded in words which Israel recited in worship: "For I am the Lord your God, who brought you out of Egypt."[15] The implication is clear: Israel's national life was to reflect the character of the God who redeemed them from bondage. The God who liberated had molded a people of liberation. The logic is the same as in the story of creation, where God used his great power to liberate other beings by creating them, and to make them flourish as the beings they truly were. Human beings were created for the purpose of representing God's servant-dominion, or kingdom, on earth.

The laws (many of them baffling, harsh, even senseless to the modern person) always come back to that gentle, constant refrain of God's compassion for powerless people. Over and again, the law makes special provision for the widow, the orphan, the poor, the alien, and the one who so-

15. On the connection, see the very readable book by James Limburg, *The Prophets and the Powerless* (Atlanta: John Knox, 1977).

journs without a home. Through this spirit of compassion, the seemingly countless laws of the Old Testament breathe the spirit of God's one true law, which requires that if we love God we will also love our neighbor as ourselves (Lev. 19:18).

One of the most important and compelling sections of Scripture for understanding the exodus vision is the Holiness Code of Leviticus 17–26.[16] It is particularly remarkable in its association between holiness and the marketplace. There is indeed guidance on ceremonial and devotional worship, on personal moral habits, and on much else besides. But its religious concerns extend with special force to Israel's economic life.

Many laws created a liberating force in the lives of the poor and powerless in Israel. For instance, fields were not supposed to be harvested to the margins. Landowners were to leave grain and fruit around the edges so that the "poor and the sojourner" might glean from the remains (Lev. 19:9-10; 23:22). Israelites were not to abuse the "stranger" or "sojourner," but instead to "love him [or her] as yourself" (Lev. 19:33-34). In doing business "just weights" and measures were to be used (Lev. 19:35-37). Elsewhere, laws protected the poor from unfair lending practices. No collateral was to be required of a poor borrower, and wealthy persons were not to take advantage of the needy by charging interest on loans (Exod. 22:25-27).[17]

Furthermore, Leviticus 25 proclaims a "sabbath" for the land every seventh year. Its intent is not just to give the land rest, although this is sound ecology. It also aims at enhancing economic humaneness in Israel for both animals and working people. It is to provide food for "yourself, and for your male and female slaves and for your hired servant and the sojourner who lives with you; for your cattle also and for the beasts that are in your land all its yield shall be for food" (Lev. 25:1-7), thus extending the "gleaning law" established in Leviticus 19:9ff. This concern for the poor and powerless (including the earth and animals) is indeed in the very soul of the law. It is essential to the whole biblical vision of delight, and shalom.

---

16. Its name is derived from its repeated words: "You shall be holy, for I the Lord your God am holy." The teachings of the "Holiness Code" gave Israel a summary and "definition" of holiness. They are thus of utmost importance to a biblical vision of life. For detailed discussion of the Holiness Code and questions about its literary history, see Childs, *Introduction to the Old Testament*, pp. 182-84.

17. This is the basis for the historic Christian condemnation of charging interest as immoral (usury). More recent Christians (siding with Jewish tradition) have pointed out that the text forbids charging interest to a poor brother. It is not a blanket prohibition.

Laws of tithing (Lev. 27; Num. 18; Deut. 14) were also, in part, to help the poor — especially the Levites and priests, but the origins and history of this practice are as murky as its place in the ethics of giving in certain congregations is overstated.[18]

Deuteronomy 15 also proclaims a "year of release" every seventh year.[19] In this year all loans to Israelites were simply to be cancelled (Deut. 15:1-6)! Furthermore, lenders were not to refuse loans to the poor just because the seventh year was soon approaching. The logic in both laws is similar: "there will be no poor among you" (Deut. 15:4). But (note the realism) since poverty will never be completely eradicated, "you shall open wide your hand to your brother [or sister], to the needy and to the poor, in the land" (Deut. 15:9, 11). Hebrew slaves were also to be liberated every seventh year (Deut. 15:12). Again the logic is grounded in God's actions and character: "you were a slave in the land of Egypt, and the Lord your God redeemed you; therefore I command you this day" (Deut. 15:15).

These texts confirm that God wished his nation to be a decent society. In keeping with the narratives of blessing, the legal and moral texts breathe a spirit of mercy, giving the poor special upward movement. Israel, given its history as a slave nation, was never — never — to forget the poor. As the prophets later remind them, in doing so they would forget who they were in the deepest sense of their identity, that they too were once slaves, and in forgetting their identities they would (despite their pious rhetoric) forget the God who redeemed them from bondage.

In our modern super-economies we cannot realistically consider a slavish imitation of practices such as canceling debts every seven years. No one seriously considers this an option because it would obviously destroy

---

18. On the problems of its history in tradition, see Kaufmann, *The Religion of Israel*, pp. 189-93. Ron Sider seriously misleads readers by representing the tithe of Deuteronomy 14 as being primarily a form of charity for the poor (*Rich Christians*, pp. 74-75). It is true that this tithe went to the Levites every third year, but its normal purpose was to fund a massive feast of delight and blessing (Deut. 14:22-27).

19. For a discussion of the relationship between Leviticus and Deuteronomy in Israel's history, see Barry Gordon, *The Economic Problem in Biblical and Patristic Thought* (Leiden: Brill, 1989), pp. 11-12. Their approaches to economic life are essentially alike in principle, but in Leviticus, later than Deuteronomy, some scholars detect what Gordon describes as "new vistas." These are "fresh insights concerning the possibilities of economic growth; a new universalism (concern for life beyond the culture) and a renewed probing of the meaning of work" (p. 15). These observations, especially the first one, are pertinent to some of our later points about the sympathy of Leviticus to productivity, growth, and delight for all people.

our banking system and its ability to empower people through the creation of jobs and so forth. The poor would suffer most from such economic devastation. Scripture calls us rather to contemplate its deeper values in new settings, to "sing unto the Lord a new song" in new situations. Rather, through careful analysis of our own situations we must think creatively about how to infuse our economic environments with the sort of compassion that causes an upward lift for those who are weakest. We must think this through on all levels of economic life, from the political to the deeply personal. The text allows no compartmentalization between the Christian life and the economic identities we seek as societies and as people. That the principles of compassion must be enshrined in social systems is unmistakably clear in the laws of Israel, but most especially in the much-discussed provision of a year of release or "jubilee." Moreover, the Holiness Code, among other legal texts, strongly validates the modern insight that a free economy must be framed by a legal and political system that encourages the right choices and protects the weak from the wrong ones.

THE JUBILEE AND ECONOMIC LIFE

Perhaps the most remarkable and controversial section of the Holiness Code is Leviticus 25, which (along with its counterpart in Deuteronomy 15) spells out the requirements of the jubilee. It is not as fashionable as it once was to argue that the jubilee supports modern socialism (or something very like it), and thus that it exposes the great godlessness of Western capitalism.[20] But if commentators widely agree nowadays that the jubilee gives no warrant for state socialism, many writers judge that it does give strong support for programs of charity and for social policies that have the

20. John Gladwin of the Church of England's Board for Social Responsibility, writes of the jubilee: "God saw a need for a redistributive principle whose aim was to restore justice and peace. The operations of the free market in land sales and its impact on people are not trusted in Scripture." Cited in his essay, "Centralist Economics," in the volume of essays edited by Robert Clouse, *Wealth and Poverty: Four Christian Views* (Downers Grove, Ill.: InterVarsity, 1984), pp. 185-86. An entire community of Christian scholarship, mainly of European descent, once blossomed on this understanding of Leviticus 25 as a biblical manifesto of socialism. See the monumental work of Robert North, S.J., *Sociology of the Jubilee* (Rome: Pontifico Istituto Biblico, 1954), esp. pp. 175-89.

goal of a more just society than would otherwise exist. This application seems right.

But these writers also understand the jubilee to enshrine principles that greatly weaken Western notions of property rights. And in response, Christian defenders of Western legal traditions often come off as evasive in facing the values that seem to emerge from the jubilee. They commonly claim, for instance, that the jubilee was never actually put into practice, or that it is simply not relevant at all to modern economic systems.[21] But as an account of the texts, this response to the claim simply will not do, no more so than spiritualizing the texts of affluence will do on the other side of the issue. For as Jesus made clear, specific laws may pass away, but the universal truths embodied in the laws will not pass away, not a single "jot or tittle." A credible biblical theology of economic life must include a convincing account of the jubilee.

As stated above, the entire context of the laws is a pervasive concern for the poor as an expression of true godliness, and the jubilee (regardless of whether it was put into practice) functions throughout Scripture to make this point emphatically to God's people.[22] Thus it is that Isaiah used the jubilee to help us imagine the coming kingdom of God in its full material manifestation (Isa. 61:1-2). The "jubilee kingdom" was a realm of freedom from oppression of every kind, including material poverty. The coming of the kingdom would be the day of release for the captives of the earth, a day of liberation and joy to the whole world in the most comprehensive manner imaginable. In Luke's Gospel we find that Jesus used the jubilee in precisely this way as the typological framework in which to understand his entire mission on earth as the Messiah of God, the Holy One of Israel whose mission was to "proclaim liberty to the captives" (Luke 4:18). As we shall see in our discussion of the Gospels, this was indeed a spiritual jubilee, but it was not only that. The liberation of Jesus Christ also contained a powerful, prophetic social message that was indeed Good News to the economically and physically poor (Luke 4:18-19). The physical liberation of the captives thus

21. For instance, defender of reconstructionism David Chilton writes that "The Jubilee was *typological*: that is, it was a symbolic prefiguring of the work of Jesus Christ." By this he means that its application today is symbolic only and contains no significance for real economic life. See his *Productive Christians in an Age of Guilt Manipulators* (Tyler, Tex.: Institute for Christian Economics, 1981), pp. 156-57, and the whole chapter on the jubilee.

22. On the complex matter of its practice see Blomberg, *Neither Poverty Nor Riches*, pp. 44-45.

becomes a glass through which we begin darkly to see the fullness of God's plan in Jesus Christ to bring about a kingdom of justice and peace. Here we see both the metamorphosis of the jubilee as a law and its constancy as a principle. And (as I will try to show) this point entirely supports the view I have proposed on affluence and delight. For what does the jubilee accomplish but the very quintessence of delight?

But to return to the text and its meaning with respect to property, every fiftieth year was to be a year of "jubilee," when all land outside walled cities returned to the family who originally owned it.[23] On the Day of Atonement (note the context of worship), in the fiftieth year, a horn was to be blown in the land to "proclaim liberty to all its inhabitants." The picture is powerful. Israel's great celebration of freedom from spiritual oppression was also a day of real-world economic restoration. When the horn blew, all Israel knew again that the realms of spirit and earth belonged together.

The explanation for this restoration of land is particularly important because it gives the principles behind the jubilee, and these remain the subject of intense debate. The text puts the explanation in the voice of God: "The land shall not be sold in perpetuity, for the land is mine; for you are strangers and sojourners with me" (Lev. 25:23). A good many — indeed most all — writers on the subject infer from this explanation of the jubilee that its logic was that of "an ultimate relativization of private property," as Craig Blomberg judges it was.[24] Likewise, Ron Sider (unlike the more radical liberationists) grants that Leviticus does not exactly *abolish* private property, but he believes that it teaches a doctrine of "stewardship" that seriously weakens our modern, Western tradition of property rights, which are vintage Adam Smith. The basic premise of this kind of stewardship is that, strictly speaking, we do not own property. Instead, we must realize that we are, in Sider's words, "only stewards" of what *God* owns.[25] He thus

---

23. Gordon observes that the law seems to favor non-agrarian forms of economic life. See examples in *The Economic Problem*, p. 19. He speculates that the reason for this was that rural people were more vulnerable to abuses in the credit system than were businesspeople in the towns and cities. This may have been true, but his explanation ignores the religious vision of the land as sacred and as a trust from God to his people that cannot be violated.

24. Blomberg, *Neither Poverty Nor Riches*, p. 45.

25. Sider, *Rich Christians*, p. 70. In Sider's view generally, while he is aware that the text does not support communism, the jubilee is on the whole inconsistent with notions of property in the works of Adam Smith, and in the ideological heritage of the United States. See pp. 92-93.

believes that the jubilee (and all Scripture, for that matter) radically weakens our personal right to use and to enjoy wealth. This weakened claim to ownership (and its implied critique of affluence) increases the force of obligation that affluent people have to share their possessions, and it strengthens the rights of the community (church or nation) to establish systems that distribute wealth more evenly across the board to meet the basic "needs" of people.[26] As is well known, liberation theologians, too, judge that the jubilee warrants radical intervention into economic life by churches and governments to insure the fair redistribution of property.

On the surface, this seems to be a reasonable point of view. For the text does introduce a peculiar notion of property rights, and on that basis it does aim to liberate and restore people — at least some of them — to the desired conditions of life through the compulsory re-allotment of land. And Sider is no doubt correct (as well as in line with all mainline Christian moral teaching) in thinking that the jubilee provisions are a model of some kind for the institution of social mechanisms in law and policy that protect people from losing everything they have. However, it is also important to be as precise as possible in understanding the principles involved. For they are not exactly consistent with those of contemporary models of stewardship.

For one thing, to the extent that the jubilee involved the legal distribution of property, the shares were unequal to begin with. The Levites got no land; first-born sons received twice the land given to the other sons (Deut. 21:17); daughters neither owned nor inherited anything. And non-Israelites had no share in the land. They could perhaps lease land and use it for a while, but they could not really buy and own it. For the jubilee would actually take it back from them and return it to the native owners.[27]

And then there were the slaves. It is an intriguing irony that the same exodus which Gutiérrez and other liberation theologians herald as a repudiation of slavery and all social hierarchy also affirms the limited buying and selling of slaves (Lev. 25:39-40).[28] Israelite slaves were released on the

---

26. In the newest edition of *Rich Christians,* Sider stresses the validity of property ownership more unequivocally than he did in earlier ones.

27. For an extended discussion of the economics of this, see the commentary by Baruch A. Levine, *The JPS Torah Commentary: Leviticus* (Philadelphia: Jewish Publication Society, 1989), beginning on p. 474. See also the somewhat more accessible (to laypersons) commentary by John Hartley, *Word Bible Commentary: Leviticus* (Dallas: Word, 1992), beginning on p. 415.

28. Gutiérrez, *Theology of Liberation,* p. 295.

seventh year, and they (provided they were male or married to a male Israelite who lived on the land) would have benefited from the jubilee. But non-Israelite slaves were neither released nor given a share in the restoration of land. So the principle of redistribution, whatever it was, was certainly nothing like an egalitarian one. Hebrew males certainly had primary advantages; Gentile slaves came in a distant last.

But to continue, it is mistaken to picture the jubilee as first and foremost a policy for the execution of just stewardship of the sort that Sider and others have in mind. Writers on the subject almost universally miss the point that its provisions applied only to members of the original Israelite tribes. The poorest people in society were unaffected by it. For aliens, sojourners, non-Israelite debtors and slaves possessed no land in the first place and thus had no share in its repossession on the day of jubilee. Their economic need, however dire, played no role in the redistribution. Strange as it may seem, given the function of these texts in modern theologians' discourse, the people whom the jubilee helped were not the poor, but the families of original affluence. The jubilee (if practiced) guaranteed that they endured in their landed affluence regardless of whether they wanted (or deserved) it.

Of course (as just noted) there are provisions elsewhere in the law that prove beyond question that the affluent Israelites had obligations of justice to the poor within Israel. But the jubilee itself gave none. It created no obligation for the rich to sacrifice their surplus land and its benefits in order to serve the real needs of these poor. On the contrary, in the event that a poor non-Israelite had managed to acquire land through what would have amounted to a lease, the jubilee provided that he (for women would almost certainly have not been able to buy or sell land) would lose possession rights the moment the horn blew because the deed of ownership returned to the native owners. In that instance, the land was released, and the industrious non-Israelite was disinherited (creating another inequality). The jubilee did nothing directly to restore such people to their estates.

What the jubilee did was restore property and all its power to the old landed families, the true Israelites, and there is no condition relating to whether they needed it or not. Of course, if they had for some reason become poverty-stricken, the year of release would have released them from poverty. (Again, assuming that the jubilee was ever practiced.) No doubt many would have sold their land knowing they would get it back again, precisely because they had come up short in their finances and needed to lease their capital to meet expenses. No doubt some had become impoverished in the most literal sense, and such people would have experienced the jubilee as the most basic kind of liberation. But the mere liberation of such people from poverty simply was not the explicit and driving logic of the jubilee. It seems that the main purpose of the jubilee was rather to preserve the original integrity of the land as God had apportioned it in the beginning. And in that way its aim was to preserve the substance of the promise of delight to the people of Israel, too. In sum, the jubilee made it harder for the people to ruin the basic structures that God had created to secure their prosperity.

In his classic 1954 study of Leviticus 25, Robert North pointed out that the jubilee, properly understood, actually "stresses and safeguards the function of private property as an *incentive* to industrious energy."[29] The strength of North's monumental argument lies in his careful reading of the text itself. In fact, Leviticus 25 not only affirms and safeguards the property rights of each tribe, it declares such rights to be unalienable, as unalterable and absolute as the God who gave the property to them. In contrast to the way in which Blomberg, Sider, liberation theologians, and others interpret the concept of ownership, the logic is that *because* God owns the land, and they are thus sojourners *with* God, the land cannot be sold in perpetuity. For if they are with God in the way God envisions it, the land must be with them — it was the essential context for them to be with God. Sider, Blomberg, and others are entirely right to think that the jubilee takes away Israel's absolute control over property. But they seem not to recognize that this limitation thereby also prohibits the sort of need-based actions that they advocate in the name of good stewardship. For by limiting the property rights of non-Israelites or other buyers to a form of leasing, rental, or temporary investment, it literally prohibits the liquidation or sharing of assets for ethical purposes. And on the other hand, it not only limits the property claims (to land, anyway) of non-Hebrews, it simply prohibits them from having any landed property at all.

This suggests a theocratic notion of "stewardship" for the Hebrews that more resembles what we find today in the Middle East — where Israelis and Arabs engage in a great struggle for possession of the Holy Land —

---

29. North, *Sociology of the Jubilee*, p. 163. North observes that the law was very carefully and ingeniously designed so that its constraints on abuses also "helped structure the economy so that certain types of growth were more likely to occur than others." P. 19.

than in the modern West. Each side strengthens its claim to the land by asserting that God gave them the land in the first place, and so their propriety over it is irrevocable. So in this light, it is not a weakened notion of ownership that guarantees the liberation of Israelites. It is stronger one even than they themselves might have preferred. For Hebrews, the doctrine of property is thus much stronger — not weaker — than anything in our philosophical traditions in the West. And this has to mean that the moral implications of the jubilee are very different from the ones commonly supposed. If anything, the jubilee is a warning against a cavalier or careless attitude toward property rights and a key to the liberation and delight of societies.

The parallel account in Exodus 19 helps to clarify things, at least somewhat.[30] As Old Testament scholar Robert Hubbard has argued, we should imagine the jubilee as a repetition of the exodus itself, as a re-entry of Israel into the land.[31] In the book of Exodus these two ideas are connected: the earth belongs to God, and Israel (if faithful and obedient) shall live on that earth a royal life of delight and dominion. In chapter 19 the logic of ownership comes out in just these terms of dominion and delight. It says, "for all the earth is mine" (note the claim of absolute ownership) and "you shall be to me a kingdom of priests and a holy nation" (Exod. 19:5-6). The idea of God's absolute ownership generates the idea of Israel's royalty, proximity to God, and special (holy) dominion upon the earth. As the book of Revelation would later phrase it, God is shaping a "race of kings." Likewise, in further support of this interpretation, we must note that in Leviticus 25 the movement of the text is from sojourning with God in the land toward a life of abundance, not one of scarcity. "You will keep my decrees and observe my laws and do them in order that you may dwell in the land securely. The land will yield its fruit, and you will eat your fill" (Lev. 25:18-19).

To put this vision in the context of economic systems, we note from the text that the morality of the jubilee must not be abstracted from the affirmations of banking, lending, and general productivity at one's work which come through everywhere in these laws. The provisions for loans

30. This connection was brought to my attention by Old Testament scholar Dr. Raymond Van Leeuwen, who was then professor at Calvin College and is now on the faculty at Eastern Baptist College.

31. On the jubilee as an institutional exodus, see Robert Hubbard, "The Go'el in Ancient Israel: Theological Reflections on an Israelite Institution," *Bulletin for Biblical Research* 1 (1991): 3-19.

make little sense without an affirmative view of a moneyed financial system. The provisions for fairness in business, "you shall not wrong one another" (25:14), make little sense apart from an affirmation of business and commercial enterprise. And the restoration of property was simply essential to the flourishing of the people.

As we just stated, the whole point was a secure and abundant life. The purpose of the release was to protect the Israelite families structurally from poverty and to empower them for both lives of redemptive action and delight in the abundance of the land. Having satisfied the moral conditions laid down by God, Israel would be satisfied in the physical realm. The words, "the land shall yield its fruit and you shall eat your fill" (Lev. 25:19), summarize the entire jubilee vision. And as we noted earlier, eventually they broaden in diverse ways, throughout Scripture, to become the messianic vision for all human beings; such a vision, I believe, ought to be at the core of our Christian vision today. We should not sell off this vision in perpetuity any more than Israel should have done so with the land. For the one cannot exist for very long without the other.

I believe it is very difficult to go beyond this broad interpretation of the jubilee to give a detailed account of its moral and social applications to economic life today. Nevertheless, several authors do suggest that its implications are not at all as negative toward modern democratic capitalism as is widely supposed. In a summary of his own thorough study, North concludes that "[Leviticus] 25 implies that the independent small property-owner is the backbone of a representative government."[32] Regardless of whether North's implication is the only legitimate one, the exodus vision of Israel was indeed about economic liberation. And the basic unit of this liberation was fundamental, landed liberty for Israelites, including (as in the Garden of Eden) an invitation to dominate, cultivate and enjoy the fruits of the land. Moreover, Old Testament scholar John Hartley writes that placing the jubilee inscription, "to proclaim liberty throughout the land" (Lev. 25:10), on the Liberty Bell in Philadelphia was in fact not an improper use of that text (again contra Blomberg).[33] At the end of his very lengthy commentary on Leviticus, Hartley writes:

32. North, *Sociology of the Jubilee*, p. 218.
33. Blomberg, *Neither Poverty Nor Riches*, p. 45. He writes, "Ironically, some of the most stalwart contemporary defenders of American freedom miss entirely the larger context in which this proclamation is embedded and the distinct significance of the Jubilee. Here, if ever, is the ultimate relativization of private property."

The Jubilee manifesto has not been lost on the pages of a forgotten Old Testament book. It has had a leavening effect on social thought in the West, as the inscription of the words of v. 10, "proclaim liberty throughout the land," on the Liberty Bell attests. This legislation has contributed to the Western idea that every family has a right to own property. The view of land ownership herein, however, is revolutionary. It promotes responsible work that attends ownership of property, and at the same time it promotes responsible brotherhood of all Yahweh's people arising from their faith in Yahweh. This wonderful manifesto will continue to feed both the eschatalogical vision and utopian thinking until the kingdom of the Lord Jesus Christ is fully established.[34]

If we add the important qualification that this liberty and right to property belonged to the Hebrews, and strengthened their claims even more so than anything that Locke, Jefferson, or Adam Smith advocated, then Hartley's judgment seems right. Furthermore, if the interpretation just considered is at all valid, the jubilee is an uncompromising manifesto of delight as the vision of life in the world that God fairly demands. I judge, then, that any idea of social justice that does compromise the integrity of that vision, as we seek to expand it to include all human beings, is thus, no matter how strident its appeals to the contrary, in violation of the jubilee.

MORAL OBLIGATIONS AND MORAL PROXIMITY

This is a good place to introduce an idea that we will look at in more detail later in the book. It is what I call the principle of "moral proximity." I believe that the social ethics of the Bible enshrines this principle, and that it is very important to modern Christian ethics. It is especially important now, because of the recent occurrence of globalism — that is, the figurative shrinking of the world by means of high technology. The shrinking effects of globalism have created a great deal of confusion and distress among sensitive Western Christians about their moral obligations in economic life.

Among the new things of globalism is the technological interconnection of almost all people in the world with each other. In the context of

---

34. Hartley, *Leviticus*, pp. 447-48.

modern capitalism and its achievement, this means that any wealthy person in any economically advanced society is within technical reach of almost any poor person in any other undeveloped society. As we go about life under modern capitalism, then, we naturally wonder what our obligations are to poor people living in these other, economically poor nations. A very prevalent and influential answer in the moral literature is that the technical features of globalism make our obligations to those people very strong, perhaps just as strong as they are to the people who are near to us in location and significant relation. We will consider the arguments in support of this view as we go, but let me indicate now that I believe this reasoning greatly oversimplifies and distorts the entire matter of Christian moral obligation. And I believe it does great personal damage in some people by creating in them a kind of messianic despair and desperation that does not comport with the vision and spirit of the Gospel.

The principle of moral proximity helps prevent this damaging oversimplification and distortion. In brief, this principle states simply that our moral obligations in economic life are greater or lesser in proportion to their moral proximity to us. I will have occasion to elaborate the terms of this definition later. But the texts of the exodus are instructive in beginning to understand what it is about. The idea is not entirely different from that of the traditional Roman Catholic principle of subsidiarity, which means that social problems ought to be handled first by the people and agencies nearest in location to them rather than by remote ones.[35] Careful analysis might well prove that this principle entails what I am calling the principle of moral proximity, for it requires that our moral focus normally be on the problems and issues that are nearest, that we know best and care about most. At bottom, what this principle teaches is that what we naturally believe by intuition — that our obligations to some people (our own children, for instance) are much greater than they are to certain others — is really true. I will delay making my proposals on what this implies for moral theology on global poverty, but obviously the implications are fairly important. For at very least, this intuition builds a moral perspective into our thinking that has primary focus on our immediate human networks

---

35. On the principle of subsidiarity, see *Toward the Future: Catholic Social Thought and the U.S. Economy,* by the Lay Commission on Catholic Social Teaching and the U.S. Economy (North Tarrytown, N.Y., 1984), pp. 5-7.

and communities, and it inherently weakens the claim that our focus ought rather to be on the most remote ones.

It seems that something like this moral principle operated in the ethics of ancient Israel. For one thing, the people within Israel had no developed system of obligations in their ethics toward people living outside their national boundaries. That does not mean that they had no obligations to people on the outside, but only that whatever obligations they may have had, say, to the Assyrians, were negligible in the context of Israel's ordinary national life. The moral focus was intensely on moral life within the significant community, and thus being a "light unto the nations." For another, as noted several times, the obligations that Israelites had were clearly strongest within their own families and tribes, then within their religious community as Jews, and only then within the broader fabric of society. The principle existed that some people are morally closer to us than others. I believe it existed in order to make the demands of morality in economic life reasonable, bearable, and humane. For without this moral perspective and its graduated limitation of moral duty, for the seriously dutiful person, the vision and blessing of material delight would be impossible to accept. Thus, without this limiting principle, Israelites could not have affirmed the vision that God had for them, nor could they have allowed themselves to cultivate a spirit of delight in the Promised Land. The weight of unlimited obligations to the poor would have crushed and impoverished them. Perhaps the principle was also to prevent the sort of desperate, joyless, messianic zealotry that so often takes over in movements of social reform — the spirit for which Jesus rebuked Judas with the famous words, "You always have the poor with you, but you do not always have me" (John 12:8). Or perhaps, as suggested with the jubilee, it was to prevent the destruction of the very sources from which wealth might come to bring relief to at least some of the poor. Or perhaps the wisdom of the notion includes all these purposes.

In coming chapters we shall consider this principle of moral proximity again, in the life and teaching of Jesus, in the context of economic life in the church following Pentecost, according to Luke in the book of Acts, and in an addendum to the book, in the light of recent pioneering work in the economics of development, I will apply this principle to the ethics of global poverty in the circumstances of globalism. I will argue that the new realities of globalism do create moral obligations for wealthy Western Christians, but not obligations of the ultimate sort that influential Christian writers judge that they do.

CHAPTER FOUR

The Prophets and Wisdom:
Economic Life and Eternal Life

We are what we eat.

LUDWIG FEUERBACH

THE DARK SIDE OF DELIGHT

In the preceding chapters we have seen that affluence is a cosmic good, a creation of God for the purpose of the free human cultivation of delight. Prosperous people are supposed to understand this condition as a sacred blessing and the Law challenges them to adopt attitudes, thoughts, and habits that are in keeping with this view. But we have also seen that from its very beginnings in Eden this condition of real freedom necessarily brings about the possibility of both spiritual and moral evil. And the freedom of affluence creates the possibility for uniquely destructive kinds of evil. The stories of creation and of the exodus teach that evil exists and has gained a foothold within the world and within us. The traditional language about this reality is that we are "fallen," and the systems of the world are fallen, too.[1] And the chaos that the freedom of affluence can

1. For a very good treatment of demonic evil and the social order in Scripture, see Stephen Mott, *Biblical Ethics and Social Change* (Oxford: Oxford University Press, 1981), p. 6.

bring about is commensurate in greatness with the goodness of the cosmos that it embodies.

The writings of the prophets are largely about the unique evils that people can bring about by means of affluence. All the prophets describe behaviors that realize the worst fears of the speaker in Deuteronomy. The nobility of Israel under the monarchies did everything he warned could happen once the people became rich. With rare exceptions they became arrogant, shallow, oblivious to the suffering of the poor, hard of heart, greedy, shamelessly oppressive, and self-indulgent. And just as the speaker had warned, because of these sins the nation was doomed to perish from the earth.

The story of the exile is mainly about Israel and its wealth. It is a biblical fact that a main reason for the exile was economic immorality. Israel's spiritual life had gone bad, to be sure, but some prophets (Amos, for example) barely mention their heresies in doctrine and worship. Bad doctrine and false worship are not to be underestimated. But all the prophetic writings prove that Israel's spiritual downfall was most clearly evident in the breakdown of virtue in the economic realm. Their evil was less obvious in their theology and worship than it was in their ethics of business, in their political policies, and in their manner of eating and drinking.

More intensely than any group of writings in the Old Testament, the Prophets teach that, just as economic life is on balance the measure of God's blessing, so is it a measure and mirror of the soul. When we come to the Gospels we shall see that Jesus' entire mission embodied this principle of prophetic tradition. And it is entirely consistent with — in fact it follows from — the claims I have made about the place of material delight in God's vision and purpose for his people. It is the sense of cosmic good in affluence that makes the behavior of Israel's monarchy and upper class not just wrong, but evil in a nearly ultimate sense.

In this chapter we are going to first examine the teachings on affluence in selected prophetic texts. For simplicity and brevity, we will single out the book of Amos as representative of prophetic tradition on economic life. In the second part of the chapter, we shall look at the Wisdom books. In this part, we will pay special attention to the book of Proverbs and at its developed theology of wealth and poverty.

AMOS AND THE EVILS OF THE AFFLUENT

It seems that the message of Amos came when economic times were reasonably good in Israel.[2] Modern archaeology supports the general picture given by the book of Amos that it was a time of financial prosperity for the nation.[3] The tradition is that Amos was a herdsman and "dresser of sycamore trees" in Tekoa near Bethlehem (Amos 1:1; 7:14), and that the Lord called him to prophesy during the reigns of Uzziah and Jeroboam in Judah and Israel respectively (Amos 1:2). Scholars agree that the message of Amos, while distinctive in several respects, is broadly representative of the Latter Prophets on the subject of economic life.[4] And so we trust that a more complete review of the other prophets would not reveal significant theological conflict between Amos and them.[5] I have chosen to ignore the fiendishly tangled debates over the form-critical, tradition-historical, and redactional problems with the setting and composition of the book. But I presume it is reasonable to accept the judgment of Brevard Childs that what counts most in using the book is "how the message of Amos was appropriated and formed to serve as authoritative scripture within the community of faith."[6] I also believe his comment on the historical grounding of the book is worth noting: "It is of great theological importance that a high degree of historical particularity has been preserved in Amos' preaching."[7] For this particularity brought home to the book's original readers that God really did destroy the Northern Kingdom of Israel for the economic sins of its rulers. And that God really did so is indication of how seriously readers in our day must take the prophet's message.

The rhetorical disposition of Amos makes his book unusual (even for the prophets) in its severity, which is nearly unqualified by mercy. Most of

2. See James Limburg, *The Prophets and the Powerless* (Atlanta: John Knox, 1977), p. 55. The preaching of Amos seems to have begun around 760 B.C. and was primarily aimed at the Northern Kingdom; see also Brevard S. Childs, *Introduction to the Old Testament as Scripture* (Philadelphia: Fortress, 1979), p. 400.

3. Limburg, *The Prophets and the Powerless*, p. 55.

4. Limburg, *The Prophets and the Powerless*, p. 62; also J. Barton Payne, *The Theology of the Older Testament* (Grand Rapids: Zondervan, 1962), pp. 247-49.

5. This assumption also finds support in the discussion of the prophets in Craig Blomberg, *Neither Poverty Nor Riches* (Grand Rapids: Eerdmans, 1999), pp. 69-81.

6. Childs, *Introduction to the Old Testament*, p. 400.

7. Childs, *Introduction to the Old Testament*, p. 409.

the Latter Prophets begin with oracles against Israel, and only then do they turn against the nations outside. In contrast, Amos begins with a bitter judgment against the nations. But he (or whoever the book's author or editor was) has not done this for traditional or ethnocentric reasons. He has cleverly used this approach as a rhetorical device to set up his audience for a great fall. After finishing the last judgment against the nations, as his Hebrew audience might have begun to feel smug, Amos turns on them with great ferocity.

> Hear this word that the Lord has spoken against you, O people of Israel, against the whole family that I brought up out of the land of Egypt: You only have I known of all the families of the earth; therefore I will punish you for all your iniquities. (Amos 3:1-2)

This is indeed the exodus vision that we considered earlier — only, once again, in reverse: God liberated Israel from Egypt and made them the only people on earth that he has "known." They are indeed his special people. (Later in the book Amos indicates that God has known the other nations, too, only in different ways.) And *therefore* will he punish them for their iniquities. Contrary to expectation, their privileged place in God's plan makes their evil even more intolerable than otherwise. It seems that Jesus' assertion that "to whom much is given, much is required," is therefore a reiteration of an old truth. (And the rhetoric of Amos indeed should prevent Christians, too, from presuming on God's grace in the wrong way.)

It seems we must distinguish between two kinds of economic evil in Amos. The first is that people directly exploit the weak in order to increase their own wealth. The text of Amos describes this evil in graphic poetry:

> They sell the righteous for silver, and the needy for a pair of sandals — they who trample the head of the poor into the dust of the earth. (Amos 2:6-7)

> They hate the one who reproves in the gate, and they abhor the one who speaks the truth. Therefore because you trample on the poor and take from them levies of grain, you have built houses of hewn stone, but you shall not live in them; you have planted pleasant vineyards, but you shall not drink their wine. (Amos 5:10-11)

This cold and deliberate treatment of poor and defenseless people in Israel is shameful, and obviously so. But lest we become smug — for most of us do not deliberately exploit or oppress anyone — we must consider the second sort of evil that Amos condemns.

One of the harshest passages in the Bible is Amos's speech to the women of Northern Israel, who apparently are occupied with building fine resort homes on Mount Samaria:

> I will tear down the winter house as well as the summer house; and the houses of ivory shall perish, and the great houses shall come to an end, says the Lord.
>
> Hear this word, you cows of Bashan, who are on Mount Samaria, who oppress the poor, who crush the needy, who say to their husbands, "Bring something to drink!" The Lord God has sworn by his holiness: the time is surely coming upon you, when they will take you away with hooks, even the last of you with fishhooks, through breaches in the wall you shall leave, each one straight ahead. (Amos 3:15–4:1-3)

These women are not the perpetrators, but Amos accuses them, too, of oppressing and crushing the poor. Their behavior implicates them in the evildoing of others.

The message of Amos is clear enough. The rulers of Israel have engaged in political, economic, and business tactics that are oppressive, and deliberately so. Therefore God is going to destroy everything that they have. Furthermore, even though they are not the agents of the evil, the wives of these men are nonetheless deeply implicated in it, and God will bring devastation upon them, too. One of the most severe and widely cited passages of Amos gives a kind of summary of how God viewed them.

> Alas for those who lie on beds of ivory, and lounge on their couches, and eat lambs from the flock, and calves from the stall; who sing idle songs to the sound of the harp, and like David improvise on instruments of music; who drink wine from bowls, and anoint themselves with the finest oils, but are not grieved over the ruin of Joseph! Therefore they shall now be the first to go into exile, and the revelry of the loungers shall pass away. (Amos 6:4-7)

Amos thus denounces their enjoyment of fine things as "revelry," and he declares that God's verdict upon them is already irreversible and final. In a stunning reversal of the exodus, he declares, God is going to send them back into captivity.

But while the broad lines of prophetic tradition on the evils of social injustice are clear enough, it is no light or uncomplicated matter to know exactly how to interpret and to apply the prophets' writings to contemporary social ethics. As noted earlier, liberation theologians seek to recover and to proclaim the prophetic word of God to the wealthy nations that exist in our day, and to do so in a manner that defines the needed ethics of global poverty. In this "prophetic" Christianity, the major premise of the moral argument is that Christians living in affluent societies are (unwittingly) guilty of sins that are very like the ones that the wealthy classes of Israel committed. On that premise, it follows that the divine condemnation of the rich in Amos and the other prophets applies to the vast majority of people living and working under capitalism in the developed societies of our day.[8]

In North American discussion, no one has advocated this prophetic argument more strenuously in public debate than Ron Sider has done. In his discussion of the prophets and the "prophetic" teachings of Jesus, for instance, he makes the remarkably bold pronouncement that "many rich 'Christians'" may have reached the point "when neglect of the poor is not forgiven. It is punished eternally."[9] His basis for this extraordinary judgment simply is the fractionally low (by his standard) amount of money that Western Christians give to the global poor:

> North Americans and Europeans earn sixty-one times as much as the people in poor countries, but we give only a tiny fraction of our affluence to the church. Most churches spend much of that pittance on themselves. Can we claim we are obeying the biblical command to have a special concern for the poor? Can we honestly say we are imitating God's concern for the poor and oppressed? *If the Bible is true, can we seriously hope to experience eternal love rather than eternal separation from the God of the poor?*[10]

8. Walter Brueggemann also makes fairly direct (and in my view facile) applications of the prophets' message to modern consumer culture. See *The Prophetic Imagination* (Philadelphia: Fortress, 1978). For a critique of Brueggemann and others on this level see Mark Daniel Carroll R., *Contexts for Amos: Prophetic Poetics in Latin American Perspective* (Sheffield: Sheffield Academic, 1992), pp. 141-43.

9. Ronald J. Sider, *Rich Christians in an Age of Hunger,* 20th Anniversary Revision (Dallas: Word, 1997), p. 62.

10. Sider, *Rich Christians,* p. 62 (italics mine).

It seems, then, that unless the fraction increases, Sider thinks it likely that God is going to condemn the vast majority of Westerners (professing Christians included) to eternal damnation for the very same reason that he destroyed Israel.

Perhaps someone will protest that we mortals never have grounds for making judgments of this ultimate kind, for doing so presumes the complete knowledge of people and circumstances that none but God can have. Nevertheless, justification of Sider's statement rests entirely on the premise that the commonplace economic behavior of ordinary Western people is strongly comparable to what the wealthy people of the prophets' day did. Sider seems to think the comparison is obvious, for he gives no explanation or defense of his assumption that this comparison is a good one. However, I believe there are very good hermeneutical reasons for thinking that the comparison is facile, that it does not hold — and that the devastating judgment that follows from it is perilously misplaced and unfair.

THE HERMENEUTICS OF MORAL EVIL IN THE PROPHETS

Perhaps the most fundamental problem with the hermeneutics of prophetic Christianity is its failure to stress the distinctive nature of the political and social economy during the time of the prophets. The political order was a monarchy gone over into tyranny, and the social economy (mainly based on marketing of commodities) was completely under the control of a ruling elite. These rulers of Israel were in the nearly omnipotent position of being able to set rates of taxation, fix prices, and generally bully their way around the economic precincts of the nation. That is, of course, the downside of monarchies (about which God had warned them). In a society of this sort power is concentrated in the monarch and it extends only to those who are favorably connected with the throne.

It is very important to notice and to understand that the prophets all aimed their diatribes first and foremost at the king and at the ruling classes that extended the arm of his rule. For they were the ones who were uniquely charged by God to protect and to promote the welfare of the nation. They were especially to take care to protect the poor and powerless members of society, who were otherwise completely defenseless. When these rulers instead used their powerful positions to exploit, to impoverish, and to oppress the very people they were responsible to defend — and did so merely for their own self-gratification — they obviously committed sins that were very evil indeed. And especially in the context of the exodus and the teachings of Torah, we can well appreciate the severity of God's judgment against them.

The notion of moral proximity has bearing on this discussion. Given the nature of the political and social economy, there was very close, direct moral proximity between the rulers of the nation and the people that God called them to rule. Being responsible for the people — especially their economic welfare — went with the job. In a word, it *was* their job. Their responsibility for the economic conditions of the poor in society thus could hardly have been greater or more direct than it was. And what about the wives of those rulers? True, they may have lacked the direct power their husbands wielded, but by marriage they wedded themselves to the entire moral situation. It became proximate to them, and them to it. They thus acquired responsibility for their actions in response to it, and unfortunately they chose to affirm the evil of their husbands in a deliberately implicit way. While the people suffered misery inflicted by their husbands, these women used the profits of that misery to indulge themselves. They deliberately exploited the oppression of the poor people they were supposed to serve, and so they were guilty of oppression, too. (In the next chapter, we shall come back to this matter of guilt by implication.)

In this light, it seems fairly obvious that what these rich people in Amos did was as deeply evil as it could be under the circumstances. But is it at all obvious that ordinary Western Christians are routinely committing evils comparable to theirs? Is it clear that the behavior Sider describes — giving too little a percentage of their income to the global poor — is anything like what Israel's ruling class did in spiritual and moral quality? If the comparison were between these rulers and a Ferdinand and Imelda Marcos, for example, then I would find the application reasonable and appropriate. For these notorious figures were in a comparable position of authority and power, they had moral obligations commensurate with that position, and they used their nearly unlimited powers, nevertheless, in similarly destructive, inhuman, and self-indulgent ways. History contains thousands of comparable examples, as does our world today. But ordinary Western Christians are not in a position that is even vaguely comparable to theirs. Ordinary people living under democratic capitalism, raising families, working one or two jobs, saving for college, for care of aging parents, and for retirement, contributing to churches and local charities — and giving but one or two percent of their income to people in remote parts of the world — just do not fit the description of the evil men and women in Amos. To suggest that they do is hermeneutically improper, and the judgment that follows from it — that God condemns them, too — is perilously unfair. (Peril accrues both to the judge and the judged, and the injustice is obvious.)

But there is yet another vexing problem with prophetic Christianity, one that we have to consider at some point in our discussion, and this seems as good a place as any to do so. It is the standard or measure by which prophetic Christians judge that Western people are indeed giving enough of their means to pass the crucial moral tests. What is most troubling, perhaps, is that writers like Sider and others make this test as important to faith and life as anything, but they do not make the standards required for passing it at all clear. In fact, the standards that they do give often seem almost arbitrary and self-serving. Worse, they seem to entail an odd and self-defeating sort of relativism and, in the end, not really to be moral standards at all. Given the extraordinary demands that representatives of this movement make upon ordinary Christians to adopt the right moral standard, this failing could not be more serious than it is. I will continue to treat Sider's presentation as emblematic of the argument in view.

"PROPHETIC" CHRISTIANITY AND
THE SEMANTICS OF MORAL STANDARDS

Sider challenges affluent Christians in developed societies to give more of their income to the world's poor. But how much more does he believe they (we) have to give in order to pass the ultimate moral test? The most obvious answer is in his use of John Wesley's comment, as noted earlier. Wesley, as we recall, argued that anyone who enjoys the goods of this world while others (any others) within our reach are in need thereby commits a very grave sin, one that merits damnation and hellfire.[11] As we have seen, Sider quotes this statement approvingly, and from his discussion of the prophets and other prophetic texts, one could reasonably infer that he, too, condemns the enjoyment of any superfluous wealth whenever we might use it instead to meet desperate human needs. In other words, one would natu-

11. Sider, *Rich Christians*, p. 190.

rally think that Sider favors something very like a "utilitarian" approach to economic ethics. As also noted earlier, the main principle of utilitarian ethics is, as the term suggests, the deliberative, proper utility of one's resources. On this principle, we are obliged to make the best use of our resources that is possible without harm to ourselves, and that normally means seeking to meet the greatest needs that are within our power to meet. On this view, because of global poverty (in modern context, where in theory it is within our power to meet the needs of anyone in any part of the world), it is very hard, if not impossible, to see how any wealthy person could ever be morally justified in just enjoying some part of his affluence. For it is always within our power to use this affluence to meet the life-and-death needs of someone else.

Sider often seems to be affirming utilitarianism of this sort for rich Christians. For instance, in a key summary he offers the conclusion that "we must decide between the kingdom of heaven and the life of affluence."[12] In this passage he states quite unequivocally that the "Christian life" (in contrast to the "life of affluence") is one that grows from distinctions between "necessities" and "luxuries," embracing the one for our own good but denying ourselves the other, so that we may provide necessities to others who do not have them.[13] Statements like these are so commonplace in Sider's works that anyone might be forgiven for concluding that his moral view is strictly utilitarian. Indeed, every year that I have used *Rich Christians in an Age of Hunger* as a classroom text I have asked my students how many of them think this is his view. And each time, almost every hand has gone up — yes, Sider thinks that we ought not to enjoy non-necessities in a world of hunger.

But a few discerning students always withhold an opinion, for they notice that Sider's view of affluence is not quite that straightforward. They notice (often with exasperation) that in another crucial passage of the book, in which he is affirming consumption of necessities only and condemning the enjoyment of luxury, he hastens to explain that he is not using the term "necessity" in its ordinary sense. We might have thought that, in the context of economic existence, this term could have but one sense: that which is minimally required for adequate food, shelter, and clothing. But in this passage, Sider puts the term in quotes, and then he strangely

12. Sider, *Rich Christians*, p. 106.
13. Sider, *Rich Christians*, pp. 106-7.

99

notifies his readers that his usage is non-literal. "'Necessities,'" he writes, "is not to be understood as the minimum necessary to keep from starving." It rather means, he explains, what is "necessary" for a standard of living that "would have been considered [in ancient Hebrew society] reasonable and acceptable, not embarrassingly minimal."[14]

Now this is among the most important passages in Sider's book, for in it he is giving his bottom line, his understanding of those crucial standards that we are to use in forming our judgments about the moral life of afflu-ence. We presume that these are in fact the sorts of standards he has used in forming the judgment that a good many of us are very likely going to be damned eternally to hell. So we might expect that this would be among the most lucid and illuminating passages in his entire discussion. But quite ob-viously, his terminology is anything but clear.

For one thing, in this new usage of the term, a "necessity" can refer to something that we do not need for survival (hence the quotation marks). But if words mean anything, something that we do not need is just not a necessity. There is no way around the fact that something that we do not need is to one extent or another superfluous, and to that extent it is a lux-ury. Of course I realize that we can use the term "necessity" in causal senses, as in "for me to get to Paris, a plane flight is a necessity." But it is aimless and self-defeating for Sider to use the term that way. For then any luxury can qualify as a necessity of one sort or another. (Bill Gates "needs" a 30,000-square-foot house in order to run experiments with new technol-ogy.) But by putting the term "necessity" in quotation marks, that is ex-actly what he does. He begins labeling literally superfluous items — com-parative luxuries — as "necessities."

At any rate, in this very crucial passage about standards (that we are to confine our habits to proper necessity) it seems that Sider takes a semanti-cally tortuous and roundabout way to affirm the enjoyment of certain lux-uries — the ones that are, in his view, "necessary." So, by inference, his view does not seem to be that of a rigorous utilitarian (such as Wesley). But what then, we wonder, is his view, and what are the standards by which he makes his strong moral judgments about lifestyle? More significantly, what is the all-important standard you and I must adopt in order to live an au-thentically Christian life?

In certain passages, Sider explicitly affirms the enjoyment of wealth,

14. Sider, *Rich Christians*, p. 69.

and we might expect that in these instances he would offer clear standards for doing so with integrity. Consider the following example: In his discussion and moral analysis of Deuteronomy 14, he first presents the tithe it describes in quite utilitarian terms, as if it were focused entirely upon the use of Israel's affluence to help the poor. But later in the book, he mentions the tithe again, and this time refers to its actual purpose, which was to fund a nationwide feast in thankful celebration for the blessings of God in the land. The people were to take ten percent of their income and spend it on meat, strong drink — "whatever you desire" (Deut. 14:26).[15] The prominence and theological implications of this feast, we might think, would prompt Sider to reconsider the apparent lack of balance in his picture of the proper lifestyle, and perhaps even offer some concrete guidelines for his readers. Unfortunately, he takes from it only this limited and somewhat vague permission: "God wants his people to celebrate the glorious goodness of creation."[16] Given Sider's very strong judgments against the enjoyment of luxuries in an age of hunger, serious readers will rightly want to know just how this glorious goodness can be celebrated in good conscience.

But we do not get anything like the clear statement we need in order to resolve this tension. The closest Sider comes to a clear statement of his standards for enjoyment is the statement cited at the beginning of this section. It is that in ancient Israel the standard for limiting and affirming affluence was what they deemed "reasonable," "acceptable," and not "embarrassingly minimal." So these terms apparently describe the standard that Sider takes from Scripture and uses to form his moral judgments about lifestyle. But is it at all clear what the norms for meeting these standards are, or that they really are true moral standards at all? It is hard to see how they are.

For one thing, what people in ancient Israel would have deemed a "reasonable," "acceptable," and not "embarrassing" level of affluence would obviously have been vastly different from what someone living in the United States in the twenty-first century would deem so. But assuming that Sider does not intend that we adopt Israel's norms for what is reasonable, acceptable, and unembarrassing, it seems that those norms must change from one time, place, and culture to the next. What is deemed rea-

---

15. Sider, *Rich Christians*, pp. 74-75.
16. Sider, *Rich Christians*, p. 100.

sonable (and all the rest) in one culture will differ greatly from what meets that standard in some other culture. So even if it does become clear what the norms are for a particular society (and the norms will inevitably vary within societies, too, as they do in ours), in what sense are these true moral norms, much less moral norms of the sort by which to make universal, ultimate moral (even prophetic) judgments? It seems that standards such as these lead instead to a form of cultural relativism about lifestyle. But this of course defeats the entire purpose of prophetic Christianity.

For instance, I fail to see why someone like Bill Gates could not appeal to this standard in defense of his own level of affluence. For all he would have to say in response to the criticism that he is too rich is that what is reasonable, acceptable, and unembarrasing as a level of affluence in his immediate culture is quite different from what people in the prophetic Christian community understand by that standard. Of course his critic could assert in return that his own norms are valid and Gates's are not, and thus that Gates is indeed too rich, and enjoys too much of what he owns, but what would the grounds be for doing so? I think Gates would be well within his intellectual rights to accuse anyone who made this argument of being arbitrary, judgmental, hypocritical, and transparently self-serving all at the same time.

And that, of course, is a problem many of us have encountered in our dealings with Christians who seek to use standards of this sort to set forth social norms for everyone. I vividly recall a former student of mine declaring with great dogmatic certainty, in defense of Sider, that he (the student) had finally decided it was "all right to have a car, but not a big or very expensive one." So he judged for all of us. But he did not like my next question, which was simply, "How big and how expensive a car will you let me have?" Of course what seemed quite acceptable to me seemed morally reprehensible to him. But on what grounds did he make this severe judgment (even as he drove around in his Ford Escort, as I believe it was, to and from activities linked with his Christian liberal arts degree at a cost of about eighty thousand dollars in the end)?

Of course Sider and agreeable others are convinced that this "standard" (we must use the quotation marks) originates in Scripture. His appeal is to the saying in Proverbs 30:8-9 — "give me neither poverty nor riches" — as the key. Sufficiency, he says, is the biblical norm for material possessions. Craig Blomberg has recently offered a similar view of biblical standards for affluence. He asserts that Scripture condemns affluence in the extreme and encourages a lifestyle of moderation, one marked by "neither wealth nor poverty."[17]

But if it is true that the Bible on the whole teaches that "sufficiency" (as with "necessity," quotation marks seem appropriate) is the norm, then what the Bible teaches unleashes exactly the same sort of relativism and arbitrariness of judgment that we just discussed. For this reason alone, I would be skeptical of the interpretation. Furthermore, it seems clear enough from our study of the creation and exodus narratives that the biblical standard for measuring the spiritual and moral integrity of affluent people does not lie in whether they exceed the arbitrary limits of "sufficiency" or "necessity." As I will argue, there is no good reason to take the wisdom saying of Proverbs 30:8-9 to enshrine the final standard for Christian lifestyle. This is hardly unexpected. For as our earlier discussions suggest, what makes affluence a cosmic good is just that it creates freedom for human beings and, in that light, that it makes possible the proper dominion, dignity, and delight which otherwise would be impossible.

It follows, then, in the abstract, that the more affluence someone has, the better off she is. For more affluence just increases her freedom and thus her possibilities for executing proper dominion, achieving a life of dignity and delight, and so forth. But of course there is no such thing as affluence in the abstract; it is always affluence in a context of problems and obligations — and those in a fallen world. And we have yet to discuss the issue of global poverty and our obligations. But our discussion of Amos, to whom we now return, will help us better to understand what the norms are that God has used in forming his judgments of the affluent people of Amos's day.

MORAL EVIL AND PROPHETIC GRIEVING

I do not think there is any support at all in Amos or in prophetic tradition generally for the model of strict utilitarianism or for its modified form of simpler living based on some standard of "necessity" or "sufficiency." In interpreting Amos's diatribes against the enjoyments of the ruling rich, Old Testament theologian Gerhard von Rad notes that "we have to remember that all asceticism and *any kind of suspicion of material good was*

---

17. Blomberg, *Neither Poverty Nor Riches*. This is the larger theological thesis of the book as a whole.

really very alien to Jahwism as such."[18] He asserts (in support of points we have considered thus far) to the contrary that "eating and drinking, taking one's enjoyment, in a word, every material blessing that enhanced the quality of life, were accepted in simple thankfulness from Yahweh's hand . . . it can only have been extreme indulgence which necessitated the raising of such complaints about the enjoyment of material things."[19] I propose that this judgment is exactly right, and that "extreme indulgence" is a very different spiritual and moral behavior than merely having and enjoying prosperity in the extreme. I propose that the important contrast is not between extreme wealth and some properly moderate level of enjoyment, but is between extreme indulgence on the one hand and true delight on the other. But the question arises: when is the enjoyment of material affluence indulgence, and when is it delight? This question is at the heart of our entire investigation. I believe that Amos is of great help in suggesting the framework for an answer.

We return to the passage in which Amos condemns the eating and drinking of the people under judgment:

> Alas for those who lie on beds of ivory, and lounge on their couches, and eat lambs from the flock, and calves from the stall; who sing idle songs to the sound of the harp, and like David improvise on instruments of music; who drink wine from bowls, and anoint themselves with the finest oils, but are not grieved over the ruin of Joseph! Therefore they shall now be the first to go into exile, and the revelry of the loungers shall pass away. (Amos 6:4-7)

In the light of von Rad's comment, which confirms the entire human vision of creation and exodus, as we have seen, the moral judgment is not against enjoyment of very fine things — even in a time of hunger. For all times are times of hunger; the prophecy therefore would also have to be against David and against the whole vision of delight that God gave Israel in the first place. Only on the shallowest of readings would someone judge that the evil of Israel's rulers was simply in having ivory beds, eating good meat, drinking wine from bowls, and being bathed in oils while others elsewhere — generally — starved. I have already given my hermeneutical

18. Gerhard von Rad, *Old Testament Theology,* vol. 2, trans. D. M. G. Stalker (New York: Harper & Row, 1965), p. 137.

19. Von Rad, *Old Testament Theology,* p. 137.

perspective on the poor who were relevant to the moral judgment of Amos.

In the key passage there are two allusions that I believe are exceedingly important to answering our larger question. One is the reference to King David. After all, King David sang, played music, danced into the night, ate the best meats, and drank fine wines. And in these things he is an archetype of delight, not evil. The rich rulers under Jeroboam were doing, on superficial inspection, the same things that David did (and perhaps they responded that way to Amos when challenged by him — hence the allusion). But the prophet hears something evil in the music. He feels evil in their manner of sleeping, eating, and drinking. He sees it in the eyes, hears it in the shrill laughter, conversation, and empty noises of the great, hollow houses. He smells it in the grilling of the meats, in the fragrances of the wines, and in the perfumes that they pour upon themselves. He senses pure evil — but why?

The root of their evil is exposed by the second allusion in the last words: "but are not grieved over the ruin of Joseph." Commentators generally take this as a reference to Northern Israel, and to the social and economic ruin that came upon its people as its rulers ate and drank.[20] Their whole spirituality expresses a lack of proper, sacred grief for the suffering around and about them. These are the leading figures of Israel. They identify themselves with the majestic power and glory of King David. But they know nothing of the passion and sacred grief for the nation and its poor, to which his songs and music attest. They have lost touch with brokenness and so they have lost their own souls. Their celebrations have become frivolous, disgusting, and pathetic displays of self-indulgence. Their music is nothing more than idle song. It is as removed from godly delight as the east is from the west.

But there is a deeper level still to this prophetic judgment and the scene that the text creates. It is the scene of a great royal banquet. We have considered the theme of material delight and the important theme of feasting — eating and drinking always in the right way before God and other human beings. Soon we will consider this theme in the context of the Gospels and their narratives of Christ, and we will discover that they frame his entire mission by this theme. The one who came "eating and drinking" was, as we shall learn, Lord of the Banquet, the messianic feast of God with

20. Carroll R., *Contexts for Amos*, pp. 262-63.

his people. If we wish to see, however, what eating and drinking look like when done in the wrong way, there is no more vivid picture than the one Amos gives. In "eating and drinking" this way, they ate and drank their own iniquity to their own destruction.

I do not wish to be misunderstood as saying that the evil in Amos is only spiritual and not a matter of lifestyle. For had they truly grieved, perhaps there would have been no summer homes or beds of ivory. There most certainly would have been less of what the narrator calls lounging (and which I take to be the evil form of rest). Proper grief at the ruin of a people would have shifted the entire focus from where it was. In Amos the entire focus of the ruling rich was upon themselves, and not at all upon the people under their watch and care.

The music no doubt, too, would have become deeper and more powerful. But Amos wisely does not fall into the trap of legalism, seeking to pinpoint some politically correct substance to use for bed making, or perhaps whether, in this world of need, beds might not be necessary at all. For the prophet, it is a matter of finding one's true humanity. It is a matter of becoming a mature person with a vision from the Lord and a heart for people, especially the poor and powerless. The rich must be liberated not from riches but from the selfish mind and heart of the serpent. We must have the mind of God, the true Lord, who is our servant. We must strive toward the light of the exodus vision and recover the spirituality of redemptive power, which turns our delight into love. As Jesus knew, there must always be a certain sacred grief in the joy of God's people: "Blessed are those who mourn." This, I think, is the starting point for affluent people in modern societies today: we cannot be righteous unless we have a proper sense of grief. What exactly this entails is a matter we shall pursue in due course.

THE MORALITY OF NATIONS

In applying the words of the prophets to contemporary teachings on affluence, there is one more thing we ought to stress. It is that they were not only interested in the morality of Israel, but also in that of surrounding nations. In the first two chapters, Amos delivers an attack upon no less than six non-Israelite groups: Syria, Gaza (home of the Philistines), Tyre, Edom, Ammon, and Moab. The crimes for which he condemned them were diverse, but a common thread ran through them. Each nation used its might to dominate other people in order to expand national power and wealth.

Syria "threshed Gilead with the threshing sledges of iron" (Amos 1:3), and its hammering of a weaker people like wheat into bits of grist, Amos predicted, would lead directly to its own destruction. Gaza "carried into exile a whole people to deliver them up to Edom" (1:6), evoking images of gratuitous abduction for mere profit in the slave trade. For having done such a thing, "the remnant of the Philistines shall perish,' says the Lord God" (1:8). The crime of Tyre was similar and the result just as bad (1:9f.).

And Edom? "He pursued his brother with the sword, and cast off all pity, and he maintained his anger perpetually, and he kept his wrath forever" (1:11). The image is of relentless, pitiless onslaught against a brother — that is, someone with whom a pact or covenant had been made. Again, destruction is the consequence of breaking one's word.

Finally, the Ammonites had "ripped up women with child in Gilead, that they might enlarge their borders" (1:13). And the Moabites "burned to lime the bones of the king of Edom" (2:1ff.), desecrating a sacred burial site. Both are instances of brute insensitivity toward another, weaker people. Justice requires nothing less than the destruction of such brutish nations.

The logic of these moral judgments is familiar by now: it is the logic of the exodus. To whom God has given liberating power, there is now the obligation to be a force of liberation — not oppression — in the world. Using power for self-interest alone is the very quintessence of national immorality. One of the most interesting passages in the Old Testament, Amos 9, shows how the exodus-logic extends to all peoples the Lord has blessed.

> "Are you not like the Ethiopians to me, O people of Israel?" says the Lord. "Did I not bring up Israel from the land of Egypt, and the Philistines from Caphtor, and the Arameans from Kir? The eyes of the Lord God are upon the sinful kingdom, and I will destroy it from the face of the earth." (9:7-8)

Not only Israel has gone through an exodus. So have these other nations, and perhaps more that the text does not mention. Whether they know it or not, they have been freed and empowered by the Lord. The Philistines and the Syrians, too, are (in a different way) God's people and have received liberating power from his hand, although they are not expected to know or express it in the same way as the Hebrews.

This means that God does not judge and punish these nations arbitrarily. Judgment occurs within an active moral universe. The prophet appeals to his audience's humanity, to their own desires and longings for liberation and delight. And he appeals to the fact that God has granted them these dreams. He implies that there is no good excuse for treating human beings in an inhuman manner. It is a living law of nature that we crave liberation and delight and, just as we crave these things for ourselves, we ought to crave them for everyone. If we are true to our own longings we will hate oppression wherever it exists, in whatever form. If we have received such power ourselves, and we nevertheless use that power not to liberate but to oppress others, then we are on the way toward death as a people. God will act through forces of history to reverse the liberating energy and he will send us back into the darkness. Israel will go back into slavery, Syria back to Kir, the Philistines into the abyss. Those in high places who abuse the weak and powerless will inevitably themselves be brought low. Amos's message to the nations is that we live in a moral universe in which justice is required, and justice will be done.

And enthusiastic national religion will not help:

> I hate, I despise your festivals, and I take no delight in your solemn assemblies. Even though you offer me your burnt offerings and grain offerings, I will not accept them; and the offerings of well-being of your fatted animals I will not look upon. Take away from me the noise of your songs; I will not listen to the melody of your harps. But let justice roll down like waters, and righteousness like an ever-flowing stream. (5:21-24)

Justice is in the essence of God, and it must be in the essence of God's people — both his special people and the peoples of the earth. Amos the prophet reminds us that righteousness is indeed closely connected with societal justice. Righteousness and justice are not the same, but they are very closely related.[21] Justice is righteousness expressed in the social order. The prophet thus reminds us that the matter of national morality is not a marginal religious concern, but right at the center of what controls our future with God. The economic life of Israel and the nations cannot be untangled from the eternal lives of people.

---

21. See Mott, *Biblical Ethics*, pp. 59-63, on the close connection between the concepts of "righteousness" and "justice."

PROVERBS AND WISDOM

The Wisdom books of the Old Testament — the Psalms, the book of Proverbs, Ecclesiastes, the Song of Solomon, and the book of Job — all in different ways probe the mysterious interaction between faith, morality, and wealth. Since space permits only a summary, our focus will be on the book of Proverbs, which presents the worldview of biblical wisdom in a most interesting way, and it gives special attention to the realm of economic life.[22] In fact, I believe it can impart wisdom in areas where our understanding of the world is too simplistic. For instance, popular preachers today teach that true faith nearly always produces wealth, and that wealth is a sure sign of God's blessing, while poverty is an indication of the contrary. They claim that "God wants his people to prosper," and that "faith will bring material wealth."[23] In spite of the Prosperity Gospel's appeals to Proverbs for support, we shall see that biblical wisdom discourages us from picturing the moral world as this straightforward and predictable. There is a note of truth in the popular preaching (and this is usually neglected by its critics), but Proverbs helps us to see and appreciate the much greater complexity and mystery of moral life in the economic realm.

On the other hand, Proverbs can also impart wisdom in areas where our understanding of the world has become too complicated and negative. For example, liberation theologians generally believe that the world system is so deeply corrupt that true righteousness normally results in poverty. Thus the poor are essentially identified with the pious as the true people of God. Thus material wealth is seen as the reward for compromise and compliance with oppressive powers. Thus it is generally assumed that the wicked prosper and the prosperous are wicked. And of course there is a grain of truth, too, in their appeal to the Wisdom books of the Old Testa-

22. For the main body of this section on Proverbs I am indebted to a paper by Raymond C. Van Leeuwen, "Wealth and Poverty: System and Contradiction in Proverbs," read at the Religion and Theology Department Colloquium at Calvin College and at the Society of Biblical Literature in 1990. See also by the same author, "Enjoying Creation — Within Limits," in *The Midas Trap*, ed. David Neff (Wheaton, Ill.: Victor, 1990), pp. 23-40. For a concise review of other Wisdom books on wealth, see Blomberg, *Neither Poverty Nor Riches*, pp. 57-62.

23. For a review of the writings of the Prosperity Gospel, see Marsha G. Witten, "'Where Your Treasure Is': Popular Evangelical Views of Work, Money and Materialism," in *Rethinking Materialism: Perspectives on the Spiritual Dimension of Economic Behavior*, ed. Robert Wuthnow (Grand Rapids: Eerdmans, 1995), pp. 117-41.

ment for support. Nevertheless, we shall see that Proverbs keeps faith in the moral order and in human beings. It warns against simpleminded optimism, but it recovers something of the simplicity of childlike faith in God and the workings of his world.

It is true (and must be stressed) that Proverbs portrays the condition of being rich as a good thing, and that of being poor as an evil: "Wealth is the ransom for a person's life, but a poor man has no means of redemption" (13:8).

And again, "The wealth of the rich is their fortress; the poverty of the poor is their ruin" (10:15). Proverbs such as these succinctly support the point just made on the goodness of affluence resting in the freedom that it creates for human beings. Overcorrecting, critics of the Prosperity Gospel often overlook the essential truth of which it is a distortion. Material wealth brings empowerment, strength, and freedom. Poverty brings powerlessness, and leaves people trapped and powerless to change their situation. These proverbs merely restate the biblical affirmation of dominion, delight, and flourishing. True human life is not just rich in spirit but also in physical and material goods. On the flipside, material poverty is an assault on the whole person — body and soul. Therefore, it is crucial to say that "God wants his people to prosper." Without this basic affirmation we weaken the whole Christian vision of dignity, worth, and rights for people. And we weaken the moral force of our conviction that poverty is as evil.

Some proverbs do teach that our economic lives are wired as they ought to be to the cosmic moral order. Righteousness will have its reward, not only in heaven but also on earth, and unrighteousness will end in material ruin. There is in fact a system of rewards and punishments, says Proverbs, and these include material gain and loss. Riches will be the direct reward for righteousness, and poverty the just consequence of irresponsible action (or inaction):

The reward for humility and fear of the Lord is riches and honor and life. (22:4)

Whoever trusts in the Lord will be enriched. (28:25)

The appetite of the lazy craves, and gets nothing, while the appetite of the diligent is richly supplied. (13:4)

One who is slack in work is close kin to a vandal. (18:9)

A slack hand causes poverty. (10:4)

These proverbs picture a moral universe that is working the way it should. The righteous people prosper, and the unrighteous are impoverished. However, we must be very cautious in drawing conclusions from these proverbs. Does this ideal situation always exist, so that the claims of these proverbs are always true?

We must understand something about the nature of the proverbs. Old Testament scholar Raymond Van Leeuwen points out perceptively that different proverbs often make contrasting points.[24] For example, Proverbs 26:4 says, "Do not answer fools according to their folly, or you will be a fool yourself." But the next verse directs the wise person to do the contrary: "Answer fools according to their folly, or they will be wise in their own eyes." So what does Proverbs teach? Are we to answer fools or not? Van Leeuwen points out that our answer depends on the situation. Proverbs is telling us that sometimes it is wise to answer a fool, but sometimes it is not. And the wise person knows both this truth and which proverb to apply to each situation in which he encounters a fool. Van Leeuwen writes, "We need to realize that proverbs are true with regard to the particular situation they fit. What the German poet Goethe said of languages is better said of proverbs: 'He who knows one, knows none.'"[25]

Applied to faith and prosperity, the truth of Proverbs is that sometimes the world works according to clear justice. In those situations, the proverbs just cited ring true, and thus declare those situations good. In these situations the righteous are the rich, God identifies with them, and they with him. The wicked are the poor, and God does not identify with them. But ancient Israel learned the hard way that the world does not always operate justly. Anyone who thinks that it does is in danger of severe disillusionment and disappointment with God. I have known many students and colleagues who have lost faith in God altogether because their simplistic understanding and false expectations made it impossible for them to cope with the hard realities of life — that the rain will fall on the just and the unjust alike. So will the death winds of hurricanes, the quaking of the earth, the random evils of disease and death. Suddenly the ordered, predictable world comes apart and it seems there is no order and no

24. Van Leeuwen, "Enjoying Creation," p. 37.
25. Van Leeuwen, "Enjoying Creation," p. 37.

God behind it. The whole book of Job puts in dramatic form this realization that terrible poverty may come upon even the most righteous person for no visibly good reason. This is chaos, not cosmos.

Biblical wisdom stresses that we cannot predict with certainty that faith will bring material flourishing and delight. Nor may we say with confidence that unrighteousness will always be punished by poverty. In fact, the righteous may "perish in their righteousness [while] there are wicked people who prolong their life in their evil-doing" (7:15). In addition to the book of Job, many of the psalms are soul-bent, lyrical questions sung to God, begging him for an explanation of such injustices and pleading for true justice to come. The book of Ecclesiastes presses the outer boundaries of melancholy to find gladness of heart not through shallow optimism, or positive thinking, but through grim realism. "The heart of the wise is in the house of mourning" (7:4). In this wisdom, the truth of prophetic grieving and Jesus' blessing upon those who mourn, embrace and illuminate one another.

Several "better-than" sayings in Proverbs probe this strange injustice and inspire us not to lose moral courage if (when) we ourselves suffer wrongly:

> Better is a little with righteousness than large income with injustice. (16:8)

> Better is a little with the fear of the Lord than great treasure and trouble with it. Better is a dinner of vegetables where love is than a fatted ox and hatred with it. (15:16-17)

> Better to be poor and walk in integrity than to be crooked in one's ways even though rich. (28:6)

Here is the solemn moment of truth in liberation theology. Circumstances may be so deeply fallen that what should be the sign of good instead marks the presence of evil and vice versa. As in Yeats's famous poem "The Second Coming," all values are turned around and "the falcon cannot hear the falconer." To be righteous leads to ruin, and to be unrighteous brings riches. In such situations God is indeed with the poor and against the rich. He is with the poor, though, not *because* they are poor, but because they have kept their integrity and have suffered for it. They are what the psalms refer to as the *anawim*, the righteous poor, who are God's true people even though they appear to be abandoned and lost. In truth, God has not abandoned the righteous poor. They are his people in a very special sense. Spiritually they are far better off than the unrighteous who are rich. Contexts such as these are the proper ones for saying that God identifies with the poor. In the real world, moral lines are not easily drawn — God identifies neither with the rich nor the poor apart from moral situations in real life.

We draw moral courage from knowing that justice will prevail in the end. Wisdom reminds us what we often lose sight of — that riches cannot save anyone, even the powerful, from death:

The getting of treasures by a lying tongue is a fleeting vapor and a snare of death. (Prov. 21:6)

Treasures gained by wickedness do not profit, but righteousness delivers from death. (10:2)

The truth is that the wicked do not really prosper — not if we understand their lives from beginning to end. They only seem to. Righteousness will prosper and unrighteousness will be ruined. Without fully picturing an afterlife or being specific about the timing of justice, Proverbs envisions a truly just outcome for God's people:

The faithful will abound with blessings, but one who is in a hurry to be rich will not go unpunished. (28:20)

The violence of the wicked will sweep them away because they refuse to do what is just. (21:7)

There is, then, a moral order of cause and effect in God's universe. However, we must understand this order in terms of the long run. Not every evil is punished immediately, nor every good rewarded. The existence of a just moral order is a matter of faith, not immediate cause and effect. God's execution of justice is more narrative art than mechanical science. Like Abraham and Job, we must trust that the Judge of all the earth will do right. The Lord brings justice from painfully long processes of history. He creates his tapestry from endless threads in countless times and places. The God of Scripture is much slower to judge or act than the preachers of either popular or liberation theology are. Nevertheless, wisdom teaches that in the end, "all manner of thing will be well," to cite T. S. Eliot (who was himself quoting Julian of Norwich, the fourteenth-century mystic). Not every time and circumstance will be well, but, in the end, all of time will be well.

Proverbs obviously modifies the popular theology that marks the rich in this life as God's true people (no doubt characteristic of a lot of popular thinking in ancient Israel, too). But it also challenges the more academic habit of identifying them hastily as the poor. Proverbs does not praise or condemn either the poor or the rich as economic classes of people. Nor does it establish a pattern that justifies thinking in simplistic terms one way or the other. Nor does it establish a fixed law of expectations for God's people. If we are faithful, we should not expect to become rich, although we might; nor should we assume that poverty and suffering are always the badge of righteousness, although they sometimes are. In such times we must take heart. Economic life in the fallen world is very complex, and many outcomes are possible. Wisdom is the key.

Wisdom, and a proper vision. For this we do know. God's ideal vision for his people is that coupling of power with compassion:

> Those who mock the poor insult their Maker; those who are glad at calamity will not go unpunished. (Prov. 17:5)

In contrast, the rich person who helps the poor is thereby blessed:

> Whoever is kind to the poor lends to the Lord, and will be repaid in full. (19:17)

> Those who are generous are blessed, for they share their bread with the poor. (22:9)

> One who augments wealth by exorbitant interest gathers it for another who is kind to the poor. (28:8)

The rich person who empowers the poor through the use of financial leverage "lends to the Lord," and is doing the work of the Lord. Such a person is acting in a godly manner, expressing the identity of God the liberator of the oppressed. If it is true to say that God identifies with the righteous poor, it is also true that the righteous rich, who show grace to the poor, identify with God, and God thus identifies with them.

And at one point Proverbs reminds us that either wealth or poverty can lead to evil:

Two things I ask of you; do not deny them from me before I die: Remove far from me falsehood and lying; give me neither poverty nor riches; feed me with the food that I need, or I shall be full, and deny you, and say, "Who is the Lord?" Or I shall be poor, and steal, and profane the name of my God. (30:7-9)

This prayer is rich in wisdom. But it is in my view mistaken, in the larger context of Proverbs (and of the Old Testament as a whole), to make this wise saying into a standard for measuring the morality of a person's lifestyle, as some do.[26] It is a sincere prayer, virtuous, to be sure, in its desire. It is reminiscent of Solomon's prayer for wisdom rather than great riches, expressing the proper humility humans should have before a God who really owes them nothing. It expresses humility before the realities of our sin and weakness as fallen creatures, too. What would we think, after all, of someone whose basic prayer was for great wealth?

As Jesus indicated in the Gospels, the right frame of mind is to presume to receive no more than "our daily bread," and if that is all we get (unlike Israel in the desert), let us be grateful and satisfied. For God has his reasons, and the messianic feast will come in good time, one way or another. But neither this proverb nor the Lord's Prayer gives grounds for the inference that God will not bless us, or others, with considerable fortune — much less that considerable fortune is in and of itself an evil. Solomon did not pray for wisdom because he thought that God could not or would not bless him with great riches had he asked for them. He prayed for wisdom because he knew it was important regardless of whether he had wealth. Nowhere in the book of Job does the main character plead to God for material wealth, but only for restoration of his integrity. God restores his riches anyway. In none of these instances is the modesty of desire anything like a teaching that condemns the condition of affluence in the extreme. To use the text this way is therefore just mistaken.

Thus Proverbs illuminates our vision of economic life in God's moral universe. Our study of this vision in the Old Testament, now at its end, should help broaden and deepen our grasp of things in the New Testament. We are now ready to take this crucial step in our exploration.

---

26. Blomberg, *Neither Poverty Nor Riches.* Blomberg has used this prayer as the keynote for the title of his book, the main moral thesis of which is that this prayer is in fact the model of economic life for affluent people today.

CHAPTER FIVE

The Incarnation and Economic Identity

Is not this the carpenter, the son of Mary?

MARK 6:3

FACING THE "RADICAL JESUS"

Most of us who were brought up in the church learned something about the "person and works" of Jesus Christ. Our tradition teaches that Jesus was both human and God; that he died for our sins; that he was raised from the dead and will come again to judge the world. Also (with some help from picture books), many of us grew up imagining Jesus as a rather harmless person, a kind and gentle man who went around doing good. I recall wondering as a small boy at Easter services how such a person could have had any enemies at all, let alone have something as bad as the crucifixion happen to him. But theologians have recently unearthed some things about Jesus that have been eye-opening and even life-changing to people (like me) who were raised on the "gentle Jesus" of popular church convention.

In his book *Until Justice and Peace Embrace*, Reformed Christian philosopher Nicholas Wolterstorff describes this discovery in autobiographical terms with which many of us will be able to identify:

I have learned of the radical origins of the tradition in which I was reared. Learning of those origins has given me a deepened appreciation of my own identity. It has also produced in me a profound discontent over my tradition's loss of its radicalism.[1]

Liberation theologians especially have shown that the Jesus of the Gospels was revolutionary and dangerous. Indeed, from one point of view, Jesus was a constant threat to the centers of power; he provoked their fury, and they rose up against him.

What was so revolutionary and dangerous about Jesus? To liberation theologians, the whole "Christ event" was like a concentrated form of the exodus. He was the exodus in human form. Jesus Christ identified himself with the poor and powerless of the earth and united with them against the rich and powerful people who oppressed them. Jesus' whole life and all his teachings expressed this revolutionary bond between God and the poor in their struggle against the vast, beastly power of this world. Indeed, Christians need to hear that Jesus unleashed revolution throughout the whole cosmos, in heaven and on earth.[2] This revolution comprehends all of life — our bodies, minds, and souls, the world and its systems. As theologian Abraham Kuyper liked to say, there is not a single square inch of the universe about which Christ does not say, "This is mine." And we do need to hear that Jesus had a special mission to the people whom the world wishes to forget. The Son of the Exodus will not let them be forgotten, and he will not let us forget them without also forgetting him.

But there is still much to debate. In many groups, it is a matter of "theological correctness" that Jesus identified with the poor in a very uncomplicated way. For instance, it passes without question that he was born and grew up in poverty, that his followers were mainly poor people, that together they adopted lives of poverty during their public mission, and that his primary audience was the poor multitudes. Coupled with this picture of his life is a radical interpretation of his teachings. We commonly hear it stressed that Jesus condemned the rich and that he blessed the poor in the very literal terms of economic class.

I have some sympathy with this picture of Jesus and his disposition toward rich and poor. For at least it begins to convey the radical nature of his person and work as a challenge to comfortable, wealthy congregations that

1. Nicholas Wolterstorff, *Until Justice and Peace Embrace* (Grand Rapids: Eerdmans, 1983), p. ix.

2. For a good treatment of the natural antagonism between Christ and the culture of power, see H. Richard Niebuhr, *Christ and Culture* (New York: Harper, 1951), pp. 11-29.

have grown passive. Nevertheless, in the light of the evidence, I have come to think that it greatly oversimplifies the social and economic nature of his life, and thus that it also causes very serious distortions and misjudgments in the Christian ethics that it shapes. For it is not that Christ in his earthly incarnation did not "identify" with the poor; clearly he did. It is just that he also in quite different ways identified with people in other social and economic classes, too. Moreover, the language of being "rich" and "poor" in terms of Jesus' identification is semantically slippery. For as we shall see especially in the next chapter, these terms often extend rather elastically as metaphors to describe spiritual states of affairs as well as (or instead of) material ones. And it is just not accurate to classify Jesus, in the context of his own society, as economically poor. His social and economic standing has to be understood more precisely, as we shall see, and this also needs to be stressed as we construct our framework for Christian spirituality and ethics.

In this first chapter on New Testament narratives, then, we shall consider the social and economic identity of the incarnate Jesus Christ, and also that of his followers. For it is widely understood (I believe correctly) that in this question of Jesus' social and economic identity there arises an identification claim that is very important to how we Christians are to think about economic life on that level. In the next chapter, we shall consider the economic identity of Jesus more narrowly, in the context of his public mission and the manner of life that he adopted in carrying it out. It is also widely accepted that his lifestyle during those years preceding his crucifixion is also in some way normative for all Christians. The deeper questions are about the precise nature of that lifestyle and, then, just how it is normative as a model for Christians.

THE SOCIAL AND ECONOMIC WORLD OF JESUS

Before seeking to comprehend the economic identity of Jesus Christ, we must try to gain an accurate picture of the world in which he existed. Jesus was born into an unstable political climate, in which Israel was an unwilling member of the vast Roman Empire. By all accounts, the young Jesus grew to adulthood in a society that was highly stratified and marked by extremes of wealth and poverty.[3] Recent studies show that Israel had become

3. See Justo L. Gonzalez, *Faith and Wealth: A History of Early Christian Ideas on the Origin, Significance, and Use of Money* (San Francisco: Harper & Row, 1990), pp. 72-75.

a rumbling volcano that might erupt at any moment into violence. Mobs of peasants hungered and thirsted for justice.[4] Riots broke out without warning. The Romans reacted by stationing small armies throughout the land to help the Jewish authorities maintain order. To orthodox Jews this cooperation symbolized the worst possible form of compromise — very like what a Western presence in the Middle East means to certain zealous Arabs today.

The poor of Jesus' Palestine were numerous. Worst off were the thousands of homeless beggars who tried to survive on the streets. Often such people were disabled — blind, lame, riddled with disease, wretched in every physical respect. There were also street children — we do not know how many — orphaned and abandoned to the savaging chaos of life. These multitudes were not without some relief; the "poor tax" (Deut. 14:28ff.) was still in use, meaning that every third year the annual tithe was distributed among the needy. The gleaning laws were also in effect in Jesus' day.[5] Additional aid came from almsgiving, various charities, and a welfare system that grew from the synagogue. This last system may have influenced the early church as described in Acts.[6] Unfortunately, this help was no more than a drop in the bucket. The poorest of the poor were horribly oppressed. As we shall see, the "multitudes" that flocked to Jesus came mainly from this downtrodden mass of suffering people.

A different kind of poverty afflicted the working poor. Among these were day laborers and slaves. The Roman Empire was full of slaves, and there were slaves in Israel, though perhaps fewer than there were in Gentile nations. Most were domestic servants in the wealthiest homes.[7] Jesus' parable of day laborers arriving in the marketplace to wait for work (Matt. 20:1-16) seems an accurate depiction of the situation.[8] Neither group earned much beyond its "daily bread." Day laborers depended entirely on day-to-day contracts. Often they had no real estate or inheritance to fall back on, and, even if they managed to get by, they certainly had little security in their lives. They were poor by any standard.

---

4. See Richard Horsley, *Jesus and the Spiral of Violence* (San Francisco: Harper & Row, 1987).

5. Walter Pilgrim, *Good News to the Poor: Wealth and Poverty in Luke-Acts* (Minneapolis: Augsburg, 1981), p. 45.

6. Pilgrim, *Good News*, p. 45.

7. Pilgrim, *Good News*, p. 43.

8. Pilgrim, *Good News*, p. 43.

Another group of working poor were the so-called *am haaretz*, "the people of the land." Jewish peasants were in some respects the lifeblood of the economy. But research indicates that the system worked against them. In Israel, powerful families used land as a political weapon. This maneuvering naturally benefited the largest landholders and usually hurt the peasants. Sudden land liquidations or controlled changes in the markets could devastate smaller landowners.[9] It was not unusual for desperate peasants to sell what little land they owned to pay off debts. And to be landless in a landed economy was to be poor and powerless. It seems that the jubilee must not have been in force. The entire system, which the Romans had set up to maintain stability, guaranteed a high level of resentment among the people, and the option of joining a patriotic band of robbers or guerrilla fighters (sometimes called zealots) became attractive to more than a few.

Such was the world into which Jesus came preaching and teaching that the kingdom of God was at hand. No wonder so many mistakenly understood him to be speaking of an immediate political revolt against Rome and its collaborators.

At the other extreme were the rich, and in Palestine the rich were very often (though not always) people who had made a bargain with the devil Rome. To pious Jews, these epitomized the unrighteous rich as described in the Old Testament. Traitors to everything sacred, thus they prospered. At the top was the royal family of the despised Herod. His ruthlessness and political cunning was as legendary as it was profitable.[10] One of Herod's favorite ploys was to take land from the people whom he distrusted and give it to proven loyalists. To these belonged the holy priesthood and all the riches that went with it, including revenues from taxation and a corner on all sorts of markets connected with the religious life of the nation.[11] Needless to say, they did not enjoy the love of the people. We will comprehend the New Testament more fully if we understand that financial advantage in Israel often implied direct involvement with political evil and injustice.

Tax collectors, too, rated high on the scale of unrighteousness and social scorn. There were at least three sorts. The most powerful, and most

9. Gonzalez, *Faith and Wealth*, p. 73.

10. Richard Horsley with J. S. Hanson, *Bandits, Prophets, and Messiahs: Popular Movements at the Time of Jesus* (San Francisco: Harper & Row, 1985), pp. 31-34.

11. Horsley and Hanson, *Bandits*, pp. 31-34.

hated, were the publicans. These were large scale tax farmers who were "infamous for their fortune and fraud in the late Republican period of Roman imperialism."[12] They can be pictured as supervisors atop a large pyramid system of toll collectors. In the Roman Empire tax collecting was a kind of multi-layered investment business done under contract with private citizens who agreed to pay the sum of the tax due from conquered territories to the government. They were then free to collect the money from the territories in any way they saw fit, and to do so at a profit.[13] They thus employed a staff of people whose job it was to exact as much money from the people as they could get away with to repay the investment at risk. In charge at the local level of this despised system were "chief tax collectors" such as Zacchaeus in Luke 19:2-9, powerful middlemen who really made the whole system work.[14] Obviously, their economic level was high, but their social status was near the bottom of the scale. Respectable Jewish people naturally hated them. Similar was the situation of the smaller collectors beneath them who set up tollbooths and operated as businesses in smaller localities. Jesus' disciple Levi (or Matthew, as he came to be called) was perhaps one of these third-level collectors.

No doubt some tax collectors were fairer, and hated less, than others.[15] But the New Testament claim that tax collectors were among the most active followers of Jesus, and that one of them even became a member of the Twelve, is truly astonishing if we think that Jesus was essentially a man who identified with the poor and opposed the rich. In fact, some critical scholars find it so unlikely that they judge this tradition about Jesus' behavior to be inauthentic rather than give up their assumptions about Jesus' social and political predilections.[16] (This judgment, of course, raises very complex questions about the nature of historical criticism itself, the depths of which we cannot plumb here. Suffice to say that sociological interpretations of this sort rest on an assumption that the thought and behavior of Jesus and the

12. Horsley, *Jesus and the Spiral of Violence*, p. 212.

13. See John Stambaugh and David Balch, *The Social World of the First Christians* (London: SPCK, 1986), p. 77.

14. See Horsley, *The Spiral of Violence*, pp. 212-13. He contends that the tax collectors mentioned in the New Testament came from this category.

15. See the remarkable encounter between a group of tax collectors and John the Baptist in Luke 3:12-15. The normally rigorist John makes what seems a very modest demand upon them. "Collect no more than is appointed you."

16. So Horsley, *Jesus and the Spiral of Violence*, pp. 212-17.

earliest Christians must conform to what we think we know about patterns in their society, and that they would not have gone against the tide on such issues.[17]) It seems clear, though, that if Jesus did associate as claimed with publicans, then, by inference, judgment that his identification was exclusively with the economically poor is already in doubt. For these tax collectors were among the richest people in Jesus' society (and also among the most nefarious, in terms of their basic vocation). In any event, no one doubts that the polarized political and economic situation made the moral extremes worse. It was difficult to be rich in that environment without being corrupt, and it was a natural path from integrity to rags.

On the other hand, the peasantry was not always on the losing end of things.[18] On a local level, success in the marketplace was naturally related to the quality of one's produce. Sometimes, too, manipulated inflation (price-fixing) by the rich actually created better prices for poorer landowners simply by artificially raising the prices for their commodities.[19] Furthermore, between the extremes of wealth and poverty there was a kind of middle class, for lack of a better term, that was very important. As economic historian Stanley Applebaum shows, ancient Palestine "possessed all the craftsmen, specialized workers and performers of simple manual tasks possessed by any other normal economy of the ancient world."[20] Its economy was strong enough to be differentiated and to support a high degree of specialization. The abundance of crafts and special industries indicates a lively circulation of goods. Rural areas most typically produced pottery, silk, and goods and services connected with the fishing industry (particularly in Galilee).[21] Wine, oil, and perfumes were products of various other communities. Almost all the people's clothing was made in Palestine; commerce surrounding wool was vital to economic movement.

---

17. For a rigorous critique of "sociological" methods of New Testament interpretation, see Bengt Holmberg, *Sociology and the New Testament: An Appraisal* (Minneapolis: Fortress, 1990.)

18. See the massive technical work by S. Safrai and M. Stern, in cooperation with D. Flusser and W. C. van Unnik, eds., *The Jewish People in the First Century: Historical Geography, Political History, Social, Cultural and Religious Life and Institutions,* vol. 2 (Assen, Maastricht: Van Gorcum, 1987), including the informative research essay by Stanley Applebaum, "The Social and Economic Status of the Jews in the Diaspora," pp. 662-65.

19. Applebaum, "The Social and Economic Status of the Jews," pp. 622-25.

20. Applebaum, "The Social and Economic Status of the Jews," pp. 622-25.

21. Applebaum, "The Social and Economic Status of the Jews," pp. 622-25.

Importantly, there were also craftsmen of all kinds throughout Israel. While the majority operated out of Jerusalem and other major cities, many also worked in the smaller towns and villages. The list of what they produced is long: handicrafts, leatherwork, rope, baskets, basalt millstones, special stones for burial, and mason stones for building (perhaps Jesus' trade).[22] There were also metalworkers, bakers (who had organized their own guild), butchers, cheese makers, weavers, wool combers, cobblers, specialists in incense, moneychangers, traders of various kinds, and bankers.[23] The Temple alone supported an economy that employed around twenty thousand people.

THE SOCIAL AND ECONOMIC IDENTITY OF JESUS

This picture of ancient Palestine will serve to sharpen our picture of the social and economic identity of Jesus in the years before he embarked upon his public mission. For one thing, it helps us to see that people in Jesus' own society would not have looked upon him as poor on any level. Now, it is true that Jesus did not enter this world with great power and glory. As Paul wrote, he "emptied himself, taking the form of a slave" (Phil. 2:7). And "though he was rich, yet for your sakes he became poor" (2 Cor. 8:9). There is indeed an awesome lowliness about the entire Incarnation. There is terrible downward movement from divine glory to human form, and in human form a descent through the cross into sufferings we cannot comprehend. As Mary's Magnificat in Luke's Gospel so poignantly expresses the matter, the true Lord of glory is a God who "has scattered the proud," who "has brought down the powerful from their thrones, and lifted up the lowly." He is a God who has "filled the hungry with good things, and sent the rich away empty" (Luke 1:52-53). A young girl from Nazareth with no prestige and a young man who had only enough money

22. It has been suggested that Jesus worked as a "builder" *(tekton)* in stone and masonry rather than as a carpenter in woodworking. The reason for this is that most building in that region was done in brick, adobe, and stone because wood was expensive and in short supply by comparison. See Douglas Oakman, *Jesus and the Economic Question of His Day* (Lewiston, N.Y.: Mellen, 1986), pp. 176-82. Oakman shows that a *tekton* was normally a "jack of all trades" in construction, more like a handyman in our terms. He believes that the village of Nazareth was a guild community, its special craft in all-purpose building.

23. Applebaum, "The Social and Economic Status of the Jews," p. 625.

at the time (perhaps because his wife's pregnancy appeared obviously illegitimate and the dowry was denied by Jewish law) to buy the poorest offering of sacrifice (two doves) to dedicate their son, were the mother and father of the king.

In this sense, there was certainly a poverty about Jesus. Nevertheless, radical Christians lose credibility by overstating the economic lowliness attending his birth. In his discussion of the nativity, Ron Sider appeals to the "insignificance" of Galilee, and stresses that the first visitors in Bethlehem were poor shepherds, and that the flight into Egypt made Jesus a refugee. As a Jewish rabbi, Sider continues, Jesus would have had "no income during his public ministry," and had no home of his own and sent his disciples out "with very little to sustain them."[24] As will be clear, every single one of these claims is stated imprecisely and is therefore misleading as a guide to ethical thought.

The breathtaking spiritual humility and lowliness attending the Incarnation is not an uncomplicated identification with economic poverty on God's part. Poor shepherds indeed attended Jesus' birth, but their visit was followed by that of the wealthy magi. Matthew's Gospel implies that Mary and Joseph had been living in Bethlehem for about two years when these improbable attendants arrived (2:16) and that they had at least the means to procure housing for themselves (2:11). Furthermore, the magi presented the family with precious gifts of gold, frankincense, and myrrh — items that were of no small value in Jesus' day and which certainly would have given the Holy Family some measure of affluence even if they had previously lacked it. These gifts might well have financed the Holy Family's flight into Egypt (I choose to ignore redactional issues and assume the veracity of Matthew's account) and eventual return (itself another exodus of kind). Nowhere does the text suggest that Jesus was a refugee in the sense in which we normally mean the term. And when at last they did go home to Galilee, they did so as residents who were in a position to become established in a family construction business. The narrative of Jesus' early life is thus anything but a straightforward affirmation of literal economic poverty, much less a repudiation of affluence.

Until he was about thirty, it is assumed, Jesus worked in Nazareth — perhaps he even inherited the family business, since there is no mention of

---

24. Ronald J. Sider, *Rich Christians in an Age of Hunger*, 20th Anniversary Revision (Dallas: Word, 1997), p. 49.

Joseph in any narratives of his adult life. At any rate, that is how people identified him; he was known in his hometown as Jesus "the carpenter" (Mark 6:3).[25] For the greater part of his life, then, it seems that Jesus worked at this trade. That is mainly why New Testament scholars Walter Pilgrim and Martin Hengel and others judge that Jesus did not grow up in poverty but belonged to the lower middle class of his day. According to Pilgrim,

> If the tradition that Joseph was a carpenter carries historical veracity, as we have no reason to doubt, then Jesus' family actually belonged to the middle structure of his society, to the small traders and artisans.[26]

Hengel concurs:

> We should note first that Jesus himself did not come from the proletariat of day-laborers and landless tenants, but from the middle class of Galilee, the skilled workers. Like his father, he was an artisan, a *tekton*, a Greek word which means mason, carpenter, cartwright and joiner all rolled up into one (Mark 6:3).[27]

New Testament scholar Craig Blomberg affirms this point, too. He concedes that Jesus would not have been subjected to the grinding poverty that was the burden of so many people in his day.[28] He and others clearly dispel the fairly common notion that Jesus is to be identified with the day laborers, who generally were quite poor.[29] And so the interpretive premise for the argument that Jesus identified with the poor against the rich, at least on the grounds of his own economic background, is greatly weakened, if not refuted.

How well off were Jesus and his family? They were not members of the

---

25. For a thorough treatment of Jesus' vocation see John Paul II, *Laborem Exercens: On Human Work* (Sydney: St. Paul, 1981), pp. 99, 101. See also references in Barry Gordon, *The Economic Problem in Biblical and Patristic Thought* (Leiden: Brill, 1989), p. 47.

26. Pilgrim, *Good News*, p. 46.

27. Martin Hengel, *Property and Riches in the Early Church*, trans. John Bowden (Philadelphia: Fortress, 1974), pp. 26-27. Later traditions say (they are striking for their mundaneness in a context where Christ was worshiped as divine) that he "made yokes and ploughs." On this see the reference to Justin Martyr. There are also reports that Jesus' grandnephews worked a small piece of land toward the end of the first century.

28. Craig Blomberg, *Neither Poverty Nor Riches* (Grand Rapids: Eerdmans, 1999), p. 106.

29. Blomberg, *Neither Poverty Nor Riches*, pp. 106-7.

landed peasantry, as Barry Gordon notes, and thus not subject to poverty typical of that group of Israelites.[30] Of course, we have no detailed ledger of their business, no yearly tax statements, and so on. We know nothing about Jesus' income or personal habits of investment, savings, or charity. All we can say, perhaps, is that a builder's son in Nazareth may not have been rich, but he would have had much to be thankful for compared to the majority of his countrymen.

Furthermore, very recent discoveries have shown that Galilee, where he lived, was by no means the cultural and economic backwater that academic tradition has, until now, supposed it was. This in turn has opened speculation that Jesus may have been a great deal better off in his trade than would have been the norm for builders. The main reason for this is excavation of the site of the ancient capital city of Galilee, Sepphoris.[31] This important city had been destroyed when a rebellion broke out there on the occasion of Herod's death in 4 b.c. His son, Herod Antipas, also a great builder, ordered the entire city rebuilt; he turned it into the "ornament of Galilee" and brought it into the orbit of Roman rule during Jesus' lifetime.[32] This huge stimulus to construction in the immediate vicinity of Nazareth makes plausible, on secure historical grounds, that Jesus' business was unusually prosperous; some have even argued that it probably was.[33] However, as with the use of social pictures (such as what "must" have been the case with Jesus and tax collectors) we must take care that we do not infer too much from historical settings, no matter how secure they are in the evidence. For as Blomberg rightly notes, like the other great Gentile city of the region, Tiberias, there is no mention of Sepphoris at all in the Gospels.[34] There is no description of how Jesus himself related to its flourishing construction industry. We have no way of knowing whether he took part in it or, perhaps for deliberate reasons of purity, did

---

30. Gordon writes in *The Economic Problem*, p. 47, that "the designation of Christ as 'a carpenter' is important in both theological and sociological terms. It indicates amongst other things, that Jesus did not own a part of the Land, and that he was not amongst the poorest of the poor."

31. See the recent book by Richard A. Batey, *Jesus and the Forgotten City* (Grand Rapids: Baker, 1992). Also J. Stambaugh and D. Balch, *The Social World of the First Christians*, esp. pp. 92-94.

32. Stambaugh and Balch, *The Social World of the First Christians*, p. 90.

33. Batey, *Jesus and the Forgotten City*, pp. 65-82.

34. Blomberg, *Neither Poverty Nor Riches*, p. 106.

not.[35] What we do know is that Jesus was not born into and did not grow up in economic poverty.

From the Gospels we also know that he did not live in conditions of social poverty. He may not have been a prince or a member of society's elite. But as a boy Jesus did not grow up, as many children did, homeless and lost on the streets of the inner city.[36] As suggested above, Nazareth was no backwater. Trade routes connected it with the Greek cities of the coastal plain, and it was also linked geographically (by valley) to the Mediterranean Sea. The recent studies that show this region to have been more prosperous than once thought also prove the towns in Jesus' homeland were more sophisticated than we knew. All the cities of Galilee "were Greek-speaking and cosmopolitan, located on busy trade routes connected to Roman administrative centers."[37] This must have made Jesus comparatively well-aware of events taking place both within and outside his nation. And in his immediate environment, moreover, he would have had many enviable advantages. In a larger sense, it is true, he belonged by race and religion to an oppressed people. But on the other hand, within that context, he was the first-born son in a stable two-parent Jewish family with its own home and business. This guaranteed him an education, an inheritance, and many other privileges that most of his contemporaries did not have. He seems to have enjoyed good health, physical strength, possession of a keen intellect, and (until his last days) a good reputation (Luke 2:40). Luke's statement that the young Jesus "increased in divine and human favor" (2:52) comports with our image of him reading the sacred scroll in the synagogue. True, there may have been undertones of suspicion about his origins, as Mark records: "Is this not the carpenter, the son of Mary and brother of James and Joses and Judas and Simon, and are not his sisters here with us?" (6:3). But surely their incredulousness was more due to their mundane familiarity with Jesus than to a long background of ostracism. Hometown carpenters do not quite conform to our image of the ideal messianic king. Nevertheless, in his economic and social conditions, growing up, there was much that others in his day could envy.

---

35. Blomberg, *Neither Poverty Nor Riches,* pp. 106-7.
36. On the hordes of homeless children, see Batey, *Jesus and the Forgotten City.*
37. Stambaugh and Balch, *The Social World of the First Christians,* p. 93.

INCARNATION AND DIVINE IDENTIFICATION

Orthodox Christians believe that Jesus' life was not merely a human event. We believe it was an incarnation — *the* Incarnation, rather — of the divine Son of God in human flesh. If this is true, then (unlike ordinary human beings) his social and economic identity was a matter of deliberate choice and action on his part. In other words, Jesus made the decision beforehand to become just the sort of human being that he was. Among other things, then, liberation theologians are right in stressing that the Incarnation is about divine identification. It is about the kind of human condition and personhood within it that God himself identifies with. I do not mean, of course, to imply that the divine Son of God could not have become some other person, in some considerably different social and economic condition. Who can say, really, what the possible forms of the Incarnation might have been for him? But I do think, with others, that the form it did take implies a very strong identification on God's part with the sort of human personhood that it was.

For one thing, it suggests that there is something right and good about growing up in a healthy environment. If God had used the moral reasoning of some theologians today, Jesus would have been born in the inner city of Jerusalem. He would have grown up among the hordes of beggars, prostitutes, street children, criminals, and worse. He would have been the (probably female) child of a single-parent household. Or he may have been a land-poor peasant, bred on social rage and resentment toward authority and power. Then he would truly and literally have identified himself, in the Incarnation, with the poor. But, contrary to liberation theologians' claims, he did not. Jesus grew up in circumstances that were, to a notable extent, those of some little affluence. They were quite unlike the ones that Israel enjoyed in the Promised Land, to be sure. His life was basic and simple compared to ours, and it is probably easier for moderately successful people in undeveloped nations to appreciate and identify with his experiences. Nevertheless, as we shall see, his circumstances did create the possibility of proper dominion and delight for him, a theme that we shall develop in the context of his public mission.

Thus it would not be true to say that in the Incarnation God did not in any sense identify with the non-poor. We shall later explore Jesus' life, ministry, and teachings, and discuss his commitment to the poor and to such issues as social justice. But for now, we should simply note that there is no moral principle in the specifics of Jesus' Incarnation — at least in what little we can know of his early life — that gives warrant for making an identification with poverty the norm for every good Christian, or even for attributing to it a greater virtue. It seems that the Incarnation leaves the matter of what counts as virtue in our actions of social and economic identification open to quite a variety of possibilities and considerations.

Furthermore, there is a similar point to make about the closely related issues of work and vocation. For it seems that Jesus' chosen (given that we believe in the Incarnation) place in his society as a tradesman reflects very strongly upon the goodness of physicality and physical flourishing in and through the possession of property and by means of creative and productive work. As Greek Orthodox theologian Kenneth Paul Wesche has written, "the Incarnation has to do with redeeming and divinizing the world of materiality."[38] Indeed, the Incarnation is the literal embodiment of the truth that God affirms human existence in its bodily condition. And (remembering the theology of creation we discussed earlier) it is more than just happenstance that Jesus was immersed to an extent in human culture, its commercial system included. The radical or prophetic Gospel of today would be more convincing had Jesus been a landed peasant, never set foot in a city, refused to use Roman coinage, and roundly condemned all businesspeople as traitors to their faith. But he was not, and he did not. Through Jesus' natural involvement in his trade and business, the Incarnation gives divine approval to and redeems human economic culture from all the powers of evil that seek to claim it. Just as the person of Christ as a truly human being redeems our human essence and the essence of creation (the thesis of Wesche's article), it also redeems the essence of human work and business in cultural economic form. Being a builder and a businessman was apparently part of what expressed his true perfection as a human being.

This by extension redeems the notion that Christians may be actively and affirmatively involved in human cultures, even when the extent of their being fallen is considerable. Today quite a few modern Christians are replaying in a limited way the perennial quandary that H. Richard Niebuhr made famous in his book *Christ and Culture*.[39] In the last three decades,

---

38. Kenneth Paul Wesche, "The Patristic Vision of Stewardship," in *The Consuming Passion,* ed. Rodney Clapp (Downers Grove, Ill.: InterVarsity, 1998), p. 119.

39. Niebuhr, *Christ and Culture.*

leading this radical enquiry, Ron Sider has rightly stressed the importance of being aware of structural evil as a phenomenon distinct from evil committed directly by individuals. He has (I believe rightly) stressed that we can sometimes be held morally responsible not just for our own actions, but for the actions embodied by the cultural systems from which we benefit. He has in view the very many instances of corporate injustice for the sake of profit — the sort that proffers material benefits to people who are removed and indifferently insulated from the unjust actions themselves (as the wives of Bashan in Amos).

In our discussion of the prophets, I have already indicated that this broad concept of moral responsibility and guilt by implication, under specific conditions, is quite biblical. But in my earlier book, *Godly Materialism*, I took strong exception to the way Sider stated in a previous edition of his book the conditions for such guilt: "If one is a member of privileged class that profits from structured evil, and if one does nothing to try to change things, he or she stands guilty before God."[40] My main objection to this way of stating the condition was that it makes engaged involvement in modern economic culture morally impossible. For in nearly any ordinary profession or line of work there are bound to be benefits that come (directly or indirectly) from structured evil. This is especially true of modern social economies, which consist of endless networks that are connected in so many ways that we cannot possibly comprehend them all. Some of the structures to which we will be connected are bound to be morally deficient or even evil, and we may not even know (or be able to know) about them. In that instance we would "do nothing to change" the evils, and so, on Sider's condition, we would be "guilty before God." Stated thus, guilt before God would be analogous to Original Sin, for it would become part of the condition of any human being working in the social economy at any level. It seems to me that this entails an Anabaptist view of culture, and that anyone who holds it ought not to promote involvement in the systems of the world, but separation from it.[41]

In his most recent edition of *Rich Christians in an Age of Hunger*, Sider concedes part of my objection, and he grants that one's knowledge of a given evil is indeed essential to accruing moral responsibility for it, and

---

40. Sider, *Rich Christians*, p. 122.

41. A more thorough discussion of this idea can be found in *Godly Materialism* (Downers Grove, Ill.: InterVarsity, 1994), pp. 113-14.

thereby guilt within the context of benefiting from it. He correctly adds the qualification that people exist (Mafia wives, for example) whose not knowing is itself deliberate in a way that makes it similarly immoral. I agree with him that the women of Bashan provide a good case in view.[42] He writes: "Do we sin personally when we participate in an evil system? That depends on our knowledge and response."[43] But what about the structured evil that we both benefit from and do know about? Sider also revises this part of the condition for avoiding guilt by implication. He tempers his earlier requirement that we must "try to change" the evil, writing instead that our obligation is to do "all God wants us to do to correct the injustice."[44] These changes are improvements. For now, at least, people are not held responsible and guilty for failing to correct evils they do not even know about. And, unlike the original requirement, this revised one leaves open the possibility that there may be injustices connected with our vocation that we are in one way or another aware of, but that God calls us to do little or nothing directly to correct them. This sort of limited possibility is tantamount to permission to work in the networks of the world, and so affirming it solves the problem I raised in my original objection. For a satisfactory principle, however, I believe we need to hear a great deal more on how we know which structured evils God calls us to correct and which ones he does not. I believe that the notion of "moral proximity" that I introduced earlier could be of great help in making this needed distinction in our doctrine of Christian vocation. But I must leave that application for another time.

At any rate, Sider also concedes (in part) my second objection, which was that by his standards not even Jesus satisfied the condition for avoiding guilt by implication. After all, it seems that Jesus did benefit from the structures of the Herodian-Roman economy (he used the roads, for instance, and enjoyed the relative peace that it brought), many of whose institutions and policies were morally evil (imperial conquest, tyranny, enslavement, and oppressive taxation being the most obvious areas of moral turpitude). He must have known about these evils (otherwise he was an ignorant fool) and he did nothing directly to change them (nothing the zealots of his day would have acknowledged as social action, anyway). If this

42. Sider, *Rich Christians*, p. 115.
43. Sider, *Rich Christians*, p. 115.
44. Sider, *Rich Christians*, p. 115.

principle is applied, then it follows that in his incarnate life Jesus must have been guilty of sin. But since Jesus was not guilty of any sin (according to orthodox Christian theology), it follows that this principle is false, and that just being in the world under these conditions is not sinful. I agree that there are conditions for guilt by implication, but not these conditions.

Sider now grants that Jesus' unique mission imposed limitations on the scope of his worldly social action, for "as the Jewish Messiah, he was called to live and minister among the Jews of Palestine, not to engage in direct action either to preach the Gospel in Rome or to correct Roman injustice."[45] He suggests that it is not necessarily so for contemporary Christians living in democracies and so forth. But surely Sider does not mean to suggest that God called Jesus to accomplish his mission in a manner that violated universal moral standards. If God called Jesus to a special mission that included his not devoting himself to causes of explicit social and political reform, what reason is there for thinking that God would not do likewise for any Christian, or even millions of them in our day? I can think of none, and thus I see no reason to believe that God does not do so.

In any event, I believe we can all agree that Jesus' entire life, teaching, and work was the spiritual, invisible, but still cosmic overturning of principalities and powers of this world.[46] In this deeper sense — one that almost breaks the bounds of irony — in his death Jesus indeed did do "all that God wanted" him to do about the evil in the dominion of Caesar and the other kingdoms of this world. In that light the words of the promise he made to his disciples ought to be encouragement for Christians now. From the Incarnation and perfection of Christ we learn that one can seek God and the good even in the midst of the social economy of Herod and Rome. If that is so, we ought to think of ourselves as being free to do likewise under the regime of modern democratic techno-capitalism, which, for all its problems, is vastly higher on the moral scale than was the economic culture of Jesus. What he said to his disciples, according to John, has enduring force in our time, "take courage; I have conquered the world!" (John 16:33).

45. Sider, *Rich Christians*, p. 115.

46. For a good discussion of the political dimension of Christ's work, see Richard J. Mouw, *Political Evangelism* (Grand Rapids: Eerdmans, 1973); also John Howard Yoder, *The Politics of Jesus* (Grand Rapids: Eerdmans, 1972).

THE IDENTITY OF JESUS' FOLLOWERS

When Jesus entered the public stage his keynote speech came in the synagogue at Nazareth. There he read the words of Isaiah 61:1-2 and stunned the congregation by applying it to himself: "The Spirit of the Lord is upon me, because he has anointed me to bring good news to the poor" (Luke 4:18). Scholars mostly agree that Jesus envisioned his mission as a cosmic jubilee and ultimate day of release for the poor.[47] Later, when the followers of John the Baptist asked him anxiously if he was indeed the Messiah, he implied that all the signs were visible: "The blind receive their sight, the lame walk, the lepers are cleansed, the deaf hear, the dead are raised, the poor have good news brought to them" (7:22-23).[48]

The statements about "the poor" in these texts raise very difficult and important questions about economic life. As far back as the second century, Celsus used this understanding of Christianity as a critique of its intellectual legitimacy. The assumption that Christianity began as a movement among the rabble and social refuse of society gained credibility in the works of Nietzsche, Marx, and Edward Gibbon. Many theologians in our day believe with them that the original "Jesus movement" arose almost exclusively among the economic poor of his society.[49] But recent evidence has forced scholars to reconsider whether this commonplace, influential

47. See Pilgrim, *Good News,* pp. 64-72.

48. This text is clearly a reference to Isaiah 35, in which the prophet envisions the messianic age as a time when the blind, lame, deaf, and dumb will be released from their oppressions. Notably, Isaiah does not include the poor among those special beneficiaries of the coming kingdom. In Luke, significantly, Jesus has added this group to the list. It seems to be a summary term for "all the above" rather than limited to an economic class of people. On this debate, see Pilgrim, *Good News,* p. 67.

49. Celsus despised Christianity because it made sense only to "the foolish, dishonorable and stupid, and only slaves, women, and little children." He was convinced that Christianity had always been a movement among the lower classes, because Jesus had won his converts from the dregs of society, "tax collectors and sailors." Cited in Wayne Meeks, *The First Urban Christians: The Social World of the Apostle Paul* (New Haven: Yale University Press, 1983), p. 51. In more modern times, Friedrich Nietzsche and Karl Marx have seen this phenomenon as essential to the nature of Christianity itself. Nietzsche scorned Christianity for elevating the "pariah of society" to the top of the world-order and for emasculating the truly great and powerful, dropping them to the bottom of the moral scale. The great historian Edward Gibbon blamed the anti-elitism of Christianity for the eventual collapse of the Roman Empire. In contrast, see the fine discussion by D. Oakman, *Jesus and the Economic Question,* pp. 182-93.

assertion is true. For it seems clear that the social origins of Christianity were much more complex than it suggests they were. In his groundbreaking work *The First Urban Christians*, for instance, historian Wayne Meeks traces the social origins of the first urban Christians to the merchant classes of artisans and tradesmen who flourished in all the main cities. It is very difficult to account for such a strong urban middle-class following so early on if Christianity did indeed begin as essentially a proletarian movement, hostile to the merchant classes. As Meeks states, the supposition that the Pauline churches arose among the poor is groundless, "no matter how congenial it may be to Marxist historians and to those bourgeois writers who tended to romanticize poverty."[50] Quite the contrary, Christianity spread and triumphed in the Roman Empire largely because it penetrated and transformed social systems. It is true that some Christians did live in separation from the rest of society, as we have seen, but the majority did not. Meeks shows that the early congregations in the empire "generally reflected a fair cross-section of urban society."[51]

In fact, Meeks writes that "there is no specific evidence of people who are destitute — such as hired menials and dependent handworkers; the poorest of the poor, peasants, agricultural slaves, and hired agricultural day laborers, are absent."[52] Of course, this does not mean that such were not among the ranks of the early Christians — but it does imply that we should be wary of claims that they were a majority. For our purposes, Meeks's concluding judgment is more important. It is that the typical early Christian was "a free artisan or a small trader . . . [while] the wealthy provided housing, meeting places, and other services for individual Christians and for whole groups. In effect, they filled the roles of patrons."[53] While these findings may not comport with longstanding ideological assumptions, they do follow very naturally from the truths that we have suggested arise from the Incarnation itself.

And while Meeks's work focuses on the Pauline Christian community, the Gospels suggest a similar pattern among Jesus' followers. When we think of them, we should think of three distinct groups.[54] First were the

50. Meeks, *The First Urban Christians*, p. 51.
51. Meeks, *The First Urban Christians*, p. 73.
52. Meeks, *The First Urban Christians*, p. 73.
53. Meeks, *The First Urban Christians*, p. 73.
54. On this distinction of groups, see the useful discussion in Gerd Thiessen, *Sociology of Early Palestinian Christianity* (Philadelphia: Fortress, 1977).

disciples, who left their homes, work, and families to travel with Jesus. They included the Twelve, the Seventy, and select others including Mary Magdalene and other women. The second was a network of sympathizers who "followed" Jesus by staying where they were. Among this group were Mary, Martha, and their brother Lazarus, who lived in Bethany. Third were the multitudes who flocked to Jesus everywhere he went. As we have suggested, this group comprised a wide range of people who were miserable for various reasons. For the most part, these were the literal economic poor but also some wealthy people — tax collectors and prostitutes — whose poverty was spiritual, moral, and social. All were outcasts.

The twelve disciples who traveled with Jesus came from an interesting variety of social and economic backgrounds. We know most about Peter, James, John, and Andrew, who were Galilean fishermen. Sider imagines them as "poor fisherfolk," but his doing so is more than a little misleading. These men were hardly poor by the standards of the time, either in social respect or in economic security. They were good Jews who were self-employed in family businesses. We cannot say exactly how prosperous they were, but, as we saw earlier, research indicates that fishing on the lake in Galilee generated some wealth and a lively commercial industry, mainly because fish was the mainstay of the people's diet there. The Gospels record that these men had their own boats, nets, and even servants. Peter's mother-in-law owned a house in Capernaum that was large enough to serve as home base for Jesus and his disciples.[55] Perhaps most importantly, though, all the Gospels assert that they "left everything" to follow Jesus. This could not have been the act of courage and sacrifice that it apparently was unless what they left behind was considerable enough to make it so. (More on the issue of divestment of property in the next chapter.)

The background of Levi the tax collector is somewhat more complex. His name indicates that he was Jewish, but his profession shows that he had gone to work for the Roman tax system. This would have cost him both moral and social standing among his people — they would have considered him morally poor in a rather repugnant sense. But even if he was nothing more than the third-level manager of a tollbooth, as seems likely,

---

55. I believe that Blomberg somewhat understates their position when he writes in *Neither Poverty Nor Riches*, p. 107, "Zebedee and his sons, John and James, were perhaps better off than many." He fails to mention the description of their equipment and Peter's family by marriage.

he was not poor in material wealth. The Gospels note that he owned a house and that leaving everything behind was a momentous event for him. We know next to nothing about Jesus' other immediate disciples, and so I am not sure why Blomberg thinks that it "is a reasonable assumption that the remaining disciples were ordinary peasants, save perhaps Judas."[56] He really does not indicate why he does. In view of the circumstances of the ones we do know something about, it seems equally reasonable to think that the others came from comparable economic backgrounds. That would at least presuppose a more or less constant pattern of strategy on Jesus' part. But, again, we do not know.

The second group — those who followed Jesus from afar — appears also to have been above average economically. We think of Peter's mother-in-law; of Mary, Martha, and Lazarus; of wealthy men like Joseph of Arimathea and the wealthy women who "provided for [Jesus and his disciples] out of their means" (Luke 8:3). As Meeks says of later Christians, these followers expressed their faith in Jesus by providing funds, bases of operation, and moral support in their towns and communities. Again, we find no stereotype of early Christian poverty in these texts. Martin Hengel has thus written that Jesus' closest followers were not poor, but came mainly from a social and economic background similar to his own — that is, from the middle class of their day.[57] This seems correct. These followers are not prominent in the Gospel narratives, but they must have been extremely important to the entire operation of Jesus' ministry. Their more ordinary sort of discipleship ought to be kept in view as we consider our subject, for their situation parallels that of affluent Christians in our day far more closely than do those of the missionary Twelve and Seventy.

Finally, there were the multitudes that came to hear Jesus and to be healed by him. This group was obviously marked by the severest signs of oppression. Sick, lame, blind, and dumb, they came to him to be healed and to hear his words of wisdom and hope. But even with them we must be careful with our economic terms. For while the majority of them were financially destitute, in later chapters we shall see that not all of them were. Some of the people who came to Jesus in the crowds were financially secure and even rich. The Roman centurion who begged Jesus to heal his servant was wealthy. The chief tax collector, Zacchaeus, was very rich. The

---

56. Blomberg, *Neither Poverty Nor Riches*, p. 107.
57. Hengel, *Property and Riches*, p. 27.

woman (no doubt a former prostitute) who poured a whole bottle of nard on Jesus' hair had money enough. What united them was their deep spiritual poverty. Marginalized in Israelite society for countless reasons, they were the ones to whom Jesus came especially with good news.

New Testament scholar Luke Timothy Johnson provides very strong support for the assertion that the terms "poor" and "rich" in Luke's Gospel are not merely literal but in the prophetic contexts mentioned above deeply metaphorical.[58] "The use of the terms rich and poor," he writes, "go beyond the designation of economic circumstances to express conditions of powerlessness and power."[59] These conditions are not as straightforward as we might expect, for among the poor we find tax collectors and others who were often quite rich in material things. Thus Johnson judges that the "expressions rich and poor function within the story as metaphorical expressions for those rejected and accepted because of their responses to the prophet."[60]

As we will see in detail in the next chapter, Johnson and other scholars believe that Luke's narrative makes use of a literary typology that presents Jesus as a consummate prophet; thus his teachings on wealth distill the principles of prophetic tradition. This interpretation illumines the otherwise murky question of how Jesus could condemn the rich as a class on the one hand and bless the poor on the other, while at the same time affirm certain people who were rich. If Johnson is correct, these terms do not always describe economic circumstances; rather, they indicate positions in relation to God's word and to the corrupt values of the ruling powers of the world: the "poor" are those who need and are receptive to Jesus' message; the "rich" are those who reject it in favor of what the world has to offer (though they need it just as badly). Our discussion of the research on the social identity of Jesus and his disciples indirectly supports this more complex understanding of Luke's semantics and his prophetic narrative themes.

Thus neither the original circumstances of Jesus' life nor the thrust of his initial mission shows a peculiar identification with the economic poor, at least not of the sort that is commonly meant today. If anything, there is

58. Luke Timothy Johnson, *The Literary Function of Possessions in Luke-Acts* (Missoula, Mont.: Scholars, 1977), pp. 132-44.
59. Johnson, *Possessions in Luke-Acts*, p. 140.
60. Johnson, *Possessions in Luke-Acts*, p. 140.

an unromantic and not very spectacular identification with the ordinary, the uncomplicated, the hardworking, the productive, the humble, and the meek. But there is also a predilection for the unpredictable and the extraordinary. The tax collectors, centurions, and whores were rich in goods but abysmally poor in social standing and in moral fiber, and they too were the recipients of the good news. And there is finally that moment of truth in liberation theology — we have seen it throughout the Old Testament, and now we see it in the face of Jesus. It is the eye of the king of this universe upon the innocent ones who suffer most in his world. Their poverty does not ensure their righteousness, but his righteousness ensures that justice will be done for them.

Perhaps it is possible to think of Jesus' life and economic identity thus: he led relatively privileged people into new lives of economic redemption and redemptiveness. As he pulled them out of their safe worlds of social and economic stability, he placed them in contact with the very soul of the suffering world — the poor in economic, social, and spiritual senses. By bringing them together, the rich (in all relevant senses) and the poor (likewise in all relevant senses), he created a new community that was electrified by grace and liberation for everyone in different ways. In a strange way the rich became poor and the poor became rich. At bottom, this was the expression of poverty or lowering of spirit by one group in order to free and empower the spirits of the other one. And the economic expression of this was not some form of leveling or egalitarianism but something very like the order of the exodus people of Israel under the laws of Moses. The rich did not so much enter into economic poverty for the sake of the poor as they did into a new life of economic dynamism, of power born of renewed compassion, and they went on a way that they could never have imagined before Jesus called them to follow him.

CHAPTER SIX

The Radical Jesus as the Lord of Delight

*Foxes have holes, and birds of the air have nests; but the
Son of Man has nowhere to lay his head.*

MATTHEW 8:20

*The Son of Man came eating and drinking, and they say,
"Behold, a glutton and a drunkard, a friend of tax collectors and sinners!"*

MATTHEW 11:19

TWO IDENTITIES OF CHRIST

Jesus left his family, home, and work to begin his fateful public mission at
about the age of thirty. Early on, he called twelve men and a larger mixed
group of others to follow him as disciples. They ate, drank, slept, learned,
and worked together in a common life until Jesus' death by crucifixion.

We have explored the basic social and economic origins of Jesus and
his followers, and we have seen that they came from a broad range of backgrounds. This supports the interpretation that the poor to whom he
brought the blessed good news were not always from the poverty-stricken
classes. In fact, some of them had a great deal of money, such as the chief
tax collector Zacchaeus. As we mentioned briefly in the last chapter, the

term "poor" seems to have been multi-layered, referring most deeply to a disposition of spirit that was receptive to Jesus' proclamation of forgiveness and salvation in the kingdom of God. The same is true of the semantics of being "rich," the ones who were "full now" and already "had their reward." While they normally were affluent in the literal sense (at any rate, there are no explicit instances of Jesus expressing hostility toward people who were literally poor), material wealth was not the essence of their evil; rather, their attitude toward their wealth was symptomatic of a deeper spiritual evil. Their way of being materially affluent was in fact a denial of true delight in the kingdom of God. Jesus' condemnation of these rich — most often the religious and political rulers of Israel — was thus similar in its patterns to the judgments of the prophets in the Old Testament.

This interpretation suggests need for great care in making statements about the kinds of social and economic classes of people whom God is either "for" or "against" in his basic disposition. For it seems that he identified just as intensely with certain relatively affluent people as he did with the literal economic poor. The poor of the kingdom came from all these different groups, and so we might suppose that they can also come from the more affluent classes of our day.

While it is necessary to keep this in mind, there is another very important side to the question of proper economic identity in the Gospels. It is the somewhat complicated matter of what sort of demand Jesus made upon people as the essential condition of discipleship and true faith. The Gospels make it very clear that he did make a demand of that kind, and that it included discipline in the use of wealth. But what sort of discipline was it? And how do its fundamental principles carry over into our advanced economic age?

Getting answers to these questions is anything but straightforward. For, as Luke Timothy Johnson observes, the Gospels do seem to give conflicting messages about the required approach to possessions. "The problem is that the directives seem to be saying different things: they seem to point us in different directions."[1] Indeed, in some instances, as we shall see, it seems that Jesus demanded nearly complete poverty and separation from the world. In fact, this is a powerful theme that rises to very high prominence in the Gospels (Luke in particular). But in other texts, as we

---

1. Luke Timothy Johnson, *Sharing Possessions: Mandate and Symbol of Faith* (Philadelphia: Fortress, 1981), p. 12.

shall also see, it is evident that he required no such thing. On the contrary, in these instances the requirements of discipleship remain consistent with the enjoyment of comparative affluence, and often they do not include separation from the culture at all. Johnson is quite right, then, to warn against the tendency of moral theologians to engage in selective interpretation, and thus to harmonize the texts in favor of one theme or another.

In light of such apparent conflicts, historian Barry Gordon judges that even Luke — the New Testament writer who concerned himself the most with the subject of wealth and morality — "failed to resolve the tensions he experienced concerning discipleship and the economic problem."[2] I respectfully disagree with this judgment, for as my interpretation of key passages suggests, I do believe (as does Johnson) that Luke managed to forge something like an integrated view of Christian faith and wealth. But the fact that a scholar of Gordon's stature could make this statement at the end of his study is indication that, at very least, one should not underestimate the difficulty of working out a unified theology from the Gospels.

The complexity arises primarily from the character of Jesus himself in the narratives. On the one hand they present him as someone who left everything for the sake of the kingdom of God and lived in conditions that seem quite severe in their austerity. In this presentation, Jesus was displaced, sorrowful, and heavy-laden with the burden of this self-imposed way of life. He blessed the poor and was relentless, even at his own peril, in his condemnation of the rich and their lives of prosperity. He was the Son of Man with no place to lay his head. He lacked all feeling for worldly ties of any kind, and he urgently commanded other people to come out of the world, to leave everything and to follow him on his difficult way of faith into God's eternal kingdom. Meanwhile, he pressed on, rejected of men, toward death on the cross.

But on the other side, as it were, there was a Jesus whom Christian moral tradition has largely ignored. He was anything but austere. This Jesus was celebrative, he was the Son of Man who came eating and drinking with his lost people, now found. He lacked all moderation or pious restraint. He celebrated life with such intensity and abandon that it shocked members of the religious establishment. To their wooden souls, his life was embarrassing for the way it broke the constraints of polite moral conven-

2. Barry Gordon, *The Economic Problem in Biblical and Patristic Thought* (Leiden: Brill, 1989), p. 70.

tion. They did not see him as anything like "a man of sorrows, acquainted with grief." Rather, they saw him as shamelessly acquainted with tax collectors, prostitutes, and other sinners. And for all these reasons good people gossiped that he was that wanton son of Deuteronomy, a drunkard and a glutton whose behavior was so destructive of virtue that he should be put to death. But to his disciples and to the multitudes, to be with him was nothing of the kind. His very presence brought the warmth of new life — freedom, camaraderie, peace, good cheer, and a mood of joyous celebration that could not be contained by the old wineskins of tradition. In leaving everything to be with him they got everything back many times over. In fellowship with him, they feasted and flourished as never before.

If we are to have a moral theology of wealth, then, we must take both these images of Jesus and the kind of life that he enjoined upon people into fair account. Furthermore, we must also consider that outer circle of disciples, whom we described in the last chapter. For in most instances, Jesus did not require that they leave their worldly positions — and yet they, too, were his followers. In this chapter, I will seek to offer an interpretation that is faithful to the evidence of all these texts on economic life in the Gospels. And in that light, I shall propose that Luke's Gospel especially provides models that are uniquely helpful to modern Christians living in affluence.

LUKE'S NARRATIVE FOR THE AFFLUENT

The main focus of our discussion in this chapter and the next will be upon the narrative of Luke. For while it is true that all the Gospels acknowledge the great importance of economic life to Christians, none matches Luke's interest in the subject. Indeed, Johnson has shown beyond serious dispute that the subject of possessions operates as a rhetorical topic and theme in Luke, and that it has an immensely important *literary* function in the narrative from beginning to end.[3] Taking off from Johnson's ideas, I will propose more specifically that part of this function was to pose a (for his readers) startling question, and then to answer it in just as astonishing terms. That question was how someone who is rich might (nevertheless) be saved. It is not implausible that Luke would seek to accomplish something

---

3. Luke Timothy Johnson, *The Literary Function of Possessions in Luke-Acts* (Missoula, Mont.: Scholars, 1977).

of that order in his rhetoric. On the contrary, if New Testament scholar Walter Pilgrim's judgment is correct, as I think it is, we might rather expect it. Pilgrim (along with many other scholars) reasons that Luke's "extensive discussion of wealth and poverty is addressed primarily to the rich."[4] If that is true, then Luke's Gospel is the only work in the New Testament with this peculiar focus. It seems, then, that Luke is the most promising source available to modern affluent Christians for finding answers to their particular questions.

I am well aware that the other synoptic evangelists as well as John all offer perspectives on economic life that differ from Luke's, and that in some instances the differences are important enough to note. When useful, I will do so. However (as stated in the introduction to this book), I do not accept the widely held assumption that the differences between the narratives entail theologies, or complete moral views, that are in logical conflict with each other. My assumption (again, strengthened by a particular notion of inspiration) is that on the levels of theology and ethics, the different accounts are on the whole complementary.

For instance, it is true that Luke stresses the physical dimension of the faith while Matthew shows more interest in the spiritual one. But that Matthew (in the Beatitudes) has Jesus blessing "the poor in spirit" (5:3) while Luke has him blessing simply "you who are poor" (6:20) is not by itself evidence enough to warrant judgment that they contradict each other. It is possible that they do, but not logically necessary to think so. Since both propositions could well be true at the same time, it is just as reasonable (more so, given the doctrine of inspiration) to entertain explanations that present their different teachings as complementary. But I will make no effort in this chapter (or the next) to prove that they are, since there is no prima facie reason for the Christian to think that they are not.

In this chapter, then, I will first offer a discussion of the thematic demand of Jesus, in Luke, that his disciples leave everything and then follow him. In the light of critical problems that arise in the interpretation of these "radical" texts, I will then consider the narrative picture of Jesus as the "Lord of Delight." Along the way I will refer to certain groundbreaking works of Lukan scholarship. According to these studies, the Old Testament prophetic tradition is the framework within which the book should be in-

---

4. Walter Pilgrim, *Good News to the Poor: Wealth and Poverty in Luke-Acts* (Minneapolis: Augsburg, 1981), p. 163.

terpreted, and the figure of Moses in Deuteronomy serves as a typological model for Luke's presentation of Jesus.

Furthermore, I will propose that this integrated picture of his person helps deepen our understanding of what leaving everything and following can mean in economic terms. For it seems that, like the semantics of being rich and poor in Luke, this language, too, reaches beyond the literal ranges of ordinary use and extends into the realm of potent metaphor. And so these actions can mean very different things for different people in different circumstances. As evidence, I will appeal to the several instances of disciples who satisfied the requirement by remaining where they were and retaining wealth. And I will make special appeal to Luke's presentation of Zacchaeus as a model of discipleship for wealthy Christians. (Luke presents him in contrast to the respected figure of the rich ruler whom Jesus encounters earlier.) Moreover, I will argue that the Parable of the Pounds, which moral theologians have almost completely ignored, is (nevertheless) the key teaching in Luke for putting the model of Zacchaeus into the larger context of Christian faith and life in the world — and thus a kind of paradigm for Christians living and working in today's economic culture.

THE RADICAL DEMAND

All the synoptic Gospels relate that Jesus called his disciples to leave their families, work, and possessions behind, and to follow him (Mark 2:13-17; Matt. 9:9-13). But Luke alone records, no doubt deliberately for emphasis, that Peter, James, John, and Andrew, and also Levi the tax collector, leave *everything* to follow him (5:28). As Pilgrim notes, this use of the term "everything" *(panta)* is typical of Luke, and its addition obviously conveys his sense of how very radical and daring their break with the past is.[5] Moreover, when others come running, eager to volunteer themselves as disciples, Jesus disabuses them of the notion, cautioning that "foxes have holes, and birds of the air have nests; but the Son of Man has nowhere to lay his head" (9:57-58). He wants them to know that his way is unforgiving and hard, and that once they undertake it there is no turning back — not for anything (9:59-62).

The encounter with the rich young ruler (Luke 18:18-29; Matt. 19:16-22;

5. Pilgrim, *Good News*, pp. 87-88.

Mark 10:17-22) is the most stunning instance of Jesus' severity. The essential details are the same in all three synoptic accounts, and that they all relate it is quite possibly indication of its importance to the memory of early Christians. Luke is alone, however, in identifying the man explicitly as a ruler — a designation that places him socially as well as economically. Furthermore, as Johnson observes, for Luke this clearly means that the encounter is not simply with a rich person. It is rather more deeply an encounter between Jesus and an adversary.[6] The rich ruler is a paragon of worldly success, of the system of values that held sway in Israel. He is thus also the epitome of the rich upon whom Jesus pronounces unexpected prophetic curses in chapter 6. We shall in due course explore the reasons that Johnson and others have given for understanding Luke's narrative of Jesus as a typology of the prophet, and consider how this episode functions as Luke placed it in his larger narrative. But first let us consider the story in detail, and then appreciate how Luke has placed it in his narrative in order to pose a troubling rhetorical question.

The man approaches Jesus with a question. "Good Teacher, what shall I do to inherit eternal life?" As the literary context will make clearer, the question manifests — even culminates — the great theme that Israel's rich have become self-righteous to an extent that merits divine condemnation.[7] But if he is eliciting obligatory affirmation, he picks the wrong rabbi. He finds himself standing there in front of everyone, red faced and burning, as Jesus runs him through a humiliating interrogation. From the start, things go badly. "Why do you call me good?" Jesus asks. "No one is good but God alone." Then (we can imagine a tense moment of silence) he answers the man's question, "You know the commandments." Jesus tersely goes through the familiar checklist, without comment. With no idea that he is about to hang himself, the rich man shoots back, "All these I have observed from my youth." Unfortunately, in his response, he shows his failure to notice the elementary, cruel trick that Jesus plays. For in hastily running off "all" the commandments he has deliberately omitted "You shall not covet." The man thus exposes himself as a very model of that unreflective self-righteousness that Jesus has been condemning among the religious and political authorities all through the Gospel. (More on this point as we go.)

And Jesus refuses to give the man an outlet for saving face. "There is

---

6. Johnson, *Possessions in Luke-Acts*, p. 145.
7. Johnson, *Possessions in Luke-Acts*, p. 145.

still one thing lacking. Sell all that you own and distribute the money to the poor, and you will have treasure in heaven; then come, follow me." The Gospels all record that the man is "sad" when he hears these words, "for he was very rich." And there are no doubt incredulous looks all around when Jesus gives his own interpretation of the encounter. "How hard it is for those who have wealth to enter the kingdom of God! Indeed, it is easier for a camel to go through the eye of a needle than for someone who is rich to enter the kingdom of God."

We must understand, too, that Jesus does not present this to the rich man as an option. He puts it to him as a requirement. Not only this, but (as mystifying as it may be) he puts it down as a requirement for the man's eternal salvation. To inherit eternal life, so it would seem, he must completely divest himself of his possessions, and then he must go physically with Jesus on his way. Furthermore, Jesus' use of the indefinite adverb proves that the problem was not just with this rich man, but with "any" person of wealth. And as Thomas E. Schmidt writes, labored "attempts to shrink the camel (by the claim that Jesus said 'cable' rather than 'camel') or enlarge the needle (by the Medieval legend that there was a small gate in the wall of ancient Jerusalem called 'the needle's eye') are creative, but desperate."[8]

This severity might at first seem to defy all known biblical wisdom. For Jesus implies that the man cannot be righteous before God and rich in possessions at the same time. Rather than liberating the poor from poverty, in an odd reversal of Old Testament thought, it seems that Jesus wants to liberate the rich from their prosperity. How can this be?

It seems that Luke deliberately places this episode as the last in a series of wealth-negative accounts of Jesus in order to elicit just this (for rich people) strange and terrifying possibility. To get the rhetorical force of the question Luke has raised (and to see clearly that he has in fact raised it) through Jesus, we must go back to that series of accounts.

It originates with the calling of the Twelve to leave everything. It comes into focus in chapter 6 with Luke's distinctive narration of Jesus' Sermon on the Plain, in which Jesus pronounces his well-known blessing upon the poor: "Blessed are you who are poor, for yours is the kingdom of God" (6:20). Uniquely in Luke, this verse has a complementary opposite: "But woe to you who are rich, for you have received your consolation" (6:24).

---

8. See Thomas E. Schmidt, "The Hard Sayings of Jesus," in *The Midas Trap*, ed. David Neff (Wheaton, Ill.: Victor, 1990), pp. 17-22.

In chapter 9, the wealth-negative commandment takes new form in the account of Jesus sending forth the Seventy "to proclaim the kingdom of God and to heal" (9:2). He commands them to take nothing with them (a thematic parallel to their leaving everything). They are to take "no staff, nor bag, nor bread, nor money — not even an extra tunic" (9:3). They are simply to have faith that God will provide for them.

In chapter 12, not long after the journey, Jesus uses a dispute between two brothers to drive home a teaching on wealth that is elsewhere presented in the short space of two verses (see, for example, Matthew 6:19-20). These brothers are at odds regarding the estate of their deceased father, and Jesus uses their conflict to set the stage for the Parable of the Rich Fool, which we shall consider in the next chapter. Both this episode and the parable serve as the frame of reference for Jesus' now-famous directives for not worrying about material possessions and security (Luke 12:22-34; Matt. 6:25-34). As Blomberg points out, the heart of this passage is that we should "strive for [God's] kingdom, and these things will be given you as well" (Luke 12:31; Matt. 6:33).[9] Jesus directs his disciples not to worry about food, shelter, or clothing, "for life is more than food, the body more than clothing" (12:23). He advises them to consider the ravens, for "they neither sow nor reap," and the lilies, which "neither toil nor spin" (12:23, 27). He directs them further: "do not seek what you are to eat and what you are to drink, nor be anxious of mind. For all the nations of the world seek these things" (12:29-30). And this leads to the core instruction, just noted, to seek first God's kingdom:

> Sell your possessions, and give alms; make purses for yourselves that do not wear out, an unfailing treasure in heaven, where no thief comes near and no moth destroys. For where your treasure is, there your heart will be also. (12:33-34)

In these texts, it seems that Jesus does enjoin upon them a model of almost complete poverty and withdrawal from the world as a spiritual ideal.

This radical picture of denial as the condition of discipleship becomes more vivid and unmistakably important still in chapter 14, in which Jesus finishes a long discourse on the cost of discipleship with these words: "So therefore, none of you can become my disciple if you do not give up all

9. Craig L. Blomberg, *Neither Poverty Nor Riches: A Biblical Theology of Material Possessions* (Grand Rapids: Eerdmans, 1999), p. 132.

your possessions" (Luke 14:33). So if we were hoping for exceptions to the rule, it would seem that we are disappointed. No one can be a disciple without satisfying this condition of leaving everything.

As we shall see in the next chapter, other similar teachings follow, such as the Parables of the Unjust Manager and the Rich Man and Lazarus (both in Luke 16), so that by the time Jesus (and we) encounter the rich ruler, the condition of faith, and the vexing question it forces us to raise, really has risen to dominance as a theme in Luke. Once again, then, the question is: Can anyone be both wealthy and faithful to God at the same time?

TRADITIONAL INTERPRETATIONS OF THE DEMAND

How are we to interpret these wealth-negative texts? The most obvious, literal explanation is the ascetic one. It is that Jesus did indeed renounce the classical Old Testament vision, and that he believed that simply having possessions (not to mention enjoying them) was to secure spiritual death. However, historic Christianity (even its monastic branches) has wisely understood that this interpretation cannot be true. The main reason is that it makes the material world and its extensions out to be a realm that is inherently evil. The interpretation thus defines our position in that realm (the created order) as an evil state of being. But as is widely understood, it was just this theology that made ancient Gnosticism the heresy that it was, and so very early on caused the church to denounce it.[10]

But if Jesus did not believe that the material world was essentially a realm of evil, again, how are we to interpret his demand in these radical texts? Historic Catholic theology has taught that Jesus' poverty was a voluntary act of supererogation. It was, in other words, a discipline to which he did not have to submit, but did so by choice. The Catholic Church has traditionally understood a good many of the moral directives that he gave as counsels rather than as commandments for every Christian to obey. They set forth a higher discipline and superior path of spirituality and morality than the norm. But they are not required. The church understands monastic poverty to be a virtue of this kind. And so the radical directives

---

10. For an entry-level discussion on Gnosticism and the controversy over it, see Elaine Pagels, *The Gnostic Gospels* (New York: Random, 1981).

we have been considering are, on that understanding, matters of volition and not moral necessity.

Without going into depth on this approach, however, we may give thought to two critical problems that it contains. The one is the assumption that Jesus' demand entailed poverty. We shall see that this assumption is questionable, and I believe that it is in fact false. But the other is that, whatever the demand was, the texts in view make unambiguously (and troublingly) clear that its directives are not voluntary. The theme, as it rises in Luke's narrative, is clearly that no one can be a disciple without obeying its requirements, whoever they are. What is true for the rich man is true for everyone who would be Jesus' disciple.

Historic Protestant theologians have generally rejected this notion of supererogation as unbiblical. They instead link the austere life of Jesus, as well as the demands he placed upon immediate followers, to the unique role that he had to play in redemptive history. Especially in their fundamental critique of monasticism, Protestant thinkers since the time of Luther have affirmed the virtue of Jesus' presumed poverty, but rejected the longstanding counsel that the *imitation* of his economic life is supremely virtuous — more so, say, than being placed in ordinary mundane circumstances. It was Luther who made popular the notion that housewives, farmers, butchers, bakers, and candlestick makers have callings that are just as high as those of professional clerics or monastics.[11]

I agree with the essentials of this approach to the Christian morality of vocation, but in terms of our texts problems persist. There is no doubt, I believe, that the tradition of *imitatio Christi*, admirable as it may be, undervalues the uniqueness of Christ's particular experience and its sufferings. But, on the other hand, the presumption that Jesus was economically poor is (so I believe) false, and the narrative nevertheless makes very clear that the standards Jesus adopted (however differently he practiced them) are the same ones that he demanded of all who would follow him. He directs all his followers to abandon everything in some sense, and then to follow him; confining the demand to one particular moment in history seems therefore improper.

Recent versions of liberation theology understand this last problem and have rightly insisted that all Christians must face the "radical Jesus"

---

11. On classical Protestant understandings of vocation see Lee Hardy, *The Fabric of This World* (Grand Rapids: Eerdmans, 1991).

more directly than we typically have done. But their attempt to make the poverty of Jesus a model for the social and political liberation of the poor seems strained at points, and also confusing. It seems strained because the Gospels, especially in these texts, do not obviously portray Jesus' life as a ministry of liberating the poor. On the contrary, it seems that he blessed the poor in precisely the condition of their poverty.[12] This leads to confusion since to say on the one side that Jesus blessed poverty, but on the other that this blessing is a vision for liberating the poor from just that condition, makes no obvious sense.

Our tradition that Jesus and his disciples adopted lives of blessed poverty thus creates a variety of very serious interpretive problems. Furthermore, the picture of Jesus as the "Lord of Delight" which we have yet to consider has little if any place within these traditional Catholic and Protestant interpretations. Nor, really, does the existence of that outer circle of disciples who did not literally leave everything and follow Jesus but rather retained their working lives and assets. We need a framework of interpretation and theology that somehow takes all these disparate features of the narrative into account. (Or else we are left to accept Barry Gordon's judgment, mentioned above, that there is no way to integrate them, and that Luke, in this sense, failed to give his readers a coherent theology of wealth.) In my view, recent New Testament scholarship can provide that framework. It just happens that theologians have not used this technical narrative work in their social and moral theology. I believe that it can be used thus, and in the next part of this chapter I will seek to do so.

LUKE'S NARRATIVE TYPOLOGY OF THE PROPHET

New Testament ethicist Sondra Ely Wheeler writes the following of Luke: "Much of the time the best indication we have of the author's understanding of, and purposes for, the traditions he hands on are the connections he makes between them and the relations into which he places them."[13] In addition, as she points out, just this sort of "reliance on literary features of

12. Nicholas Wolterstorff's comment that Jesus blessed the poor, but not their condition of poverty, requires much more thorough grounding in these New Testament texts. See *Until Justice and Peace Embrace* (Grand Rapids: Eerdmans, 1983), pp. 76-77.

13. Sondra Ely Wheeler, *Wealth as Peril and Obligation: The New Testament on Possessions* (Grand Rapids: Eerdmans, 1995), p. 58.

the canonical text rather than on historical reconstruction of its sources and setting as a key to interpretation characterizes a number of recent works on Luke/Acts." In other words, Luke's Gospel is more than a sequential account of events. It is history in the form of literary narrative.[14]

Indeed, several important studies on Luke show persuasively that we ought to understand the wealth-negative theme in Luke as narrative typology: the typology of the prophet. On this view, Luke narrates the actions and words of Jesus in a manner that places him squarely in line with the Old Testament prophets and their ideals and teachings. Specifically, Luke identifies Jesus as being a prophet in the Mosaic tradition (Acts 3:22). Like Moses, God raised him up to teach and to guide the people.[15] Luke Johnson joins a sizable (and apparently growing) community of scholars in accepting this typological understanding of Luke, and more than any of them he has developed it in the context of Luke's literary approach to possessions (which we would expect to be a major theme if the typology holds). So it will be very useful to give a condensed summary of his interpretation and arguments.

Johnson grounds his defense of this view largely by means of a convincing study of Moses typology in the book of Acts.[16] With that in mind, he reasonably looks for and finds the same typology in the Gospel of Luke. In fact, Johnson is convinced that this pattern of Jesus as a type of the prophet Moses "shaped the gospel narrative" to a surprisingly great extent.[17] This is true, he thinks, of both Luke's redactional composition (in using Mark and other sources) and his own distinctive presentation (especially the "Lukan" middle chapters, 9–19). Johnson's discussion, of course, is much too elaborate for detailed presentation in this space, but several points of his interpretive argument are essential to the framework needed for the proposals I wish to make about the wealth-negative theme in Luke.

The first point to consider is Luke's use of the journey as a motif.[18] Many prophetic narratives begin thus, with the prophet summoned by God to go forth to the people with his word. The journey is a prominent theme in Luke from the beginning, both in the well-known tradition-

14. Wheeler, *Peril and Obligation*, p. 58, n. 6.
15. Johnson, *Possessions in Luke-Acts*, pp. 65-67.
16. Johnson, *Possessions in Luke-Acts*, pp. 60-78.
17. Johnson, *Possessions in Luke-Acts*, p. 79.
18. Johnson, *Possessions in Luke-Acts*, pp. 105-7.

historical events of Jesus' early life and in the parts of the book considered original to Luke, beginning with the sending of the Seventy in chapters 9 and 10. At this point in the narrative, Johnson observes, everything becomes prophet-like, as Jesus sets himself toward his destiny in the holy city of Jerusalem. We cannot take time and space to point out the linguistic similarities between this part of Luke and similar texts in Ezekiel and other Old Testament prophets. But scholarship has proven that the parallels are much too obvious to be anything but purposeful. As Johnson proposes, they suggest very strongly a prophetic presentation of Jesus. On the way to Jerusalem, "He is prophesying to Israel, and there is a judgment taking place."[19] We add only that the same is true of his immediate disciples' very first mission following Pentecost. Thus that mission, too, is prophetic, and so we best understand the actions in the narrative, including the economic ones, in those terms. (More on this later.)

A second key prophetic theme is the division of the people between those who despise the word of God and are under judgment (though they are the last ones to know it) and those who receive it and repent when they hear it.[20] A very important part of this division is about the rich rulers, scribes, and Pharisees who love their affluent lives more than they love God. They presume that God is with them and that he has rejected everyone else — not just the materially poor, but also the tax collectors and other sinners. In the unfolding drama of the narrative, these religious leaders become a living typology of the rich whom the prophets condemned centuries earlier for similar arrogance and hardness of heart toward the poor and powerless (recall our discussion of Amos). Their hatred of Jesus is directly connected with his conspicuous association with just these sorts of people, and their rejection of him mirrors what their forebears did to the prophets. The reality, though, is a complete reversal of what they believe to be so, and we see this prophetic truth through the character of Jesus.

This literary reference to Jesus and his followers' prophetic heritage provides a framework for the powerful narratives of Luke 9 and 10, in which Jesus sends out the Twelve and the Seventy to proclaim the kingdom of God (whose values, of course, stood in stark contrast to those dominant in Israel at the time). In this dramatic turn of events, his authority is transferred to them, and their power to drive out demons and to heal proves

---

19. Johnson, *Possessions in Luke-Acts,* p. 106.
20. Johnson, *Possessions in Luke-Acts,* pp. 107-11.

it.[21] This part of the narrative is thus not at all to be construed as a teaching on poverty as an ideal or a higher virtue. Nor is it a description of the kind of lifestyle that Jesus ordinarily enjoined. Its placement in the narrative is about the transfer of prophetic power to the disciples, and the unusual austerity Jesus requires is both to teach them the power of God to provide and to vividly enact the truth that they indeed represent a kingdom far different from that of the world.[22] They begin doing the prophetic things that Jesus alone had been doing till then, and this powerful theme returns with Pentecost in the book of Acts. That the directives are temporary becomes clear at the end of the book, in the upper room, when Jesus explains and then revokes them.

> "When I sent you out without a purse, bag or sandals, did you lack anything?" They said, "No, not a thing." He said to them, "But now, the one who has a purse must take it, and likewise a bag. And the one who has no sword must sell his cloak and buy one." (22:35-36)

There is a great deal more to include for a full treatment of just this part of Luke's narrative, but we must go forward with the main thread of our discussion.[23]

The framework of prophetic typology also helps with interpretation of the wealth-negative narratives that begin in chapter 12. If Jesus' reasoning is akin to that of the prophets, it does not follow that in these passages he calls people away from the cosmic good of affluence, which is delight. Rather, he requires them to stand conspicuously apart from a cultural system ruled by people of great corruption. Thematically, he is making something of the same point that he makes in giving his directives to the Seventy. One way to express this is that Jesus directs them not to be rich in a manner that affirms the corrupt and corrupting system and the ways of the people who rule and profit most from it.

In the next chapter, we shall see that the parables of Jesus in Luke that come in sequence after these sayings support the view that his principles were, at bottom, those of a biblical prophet. But furthermore (to the present point), this framework of interpretation helps explain the otherwise baffling

---

21. Johnson, *Possessions in Luke-Acts,* p. 115.

22. Johnson, *Possessions in Luke-Acts* and references, pp. 105, 112-13.

23. See the references in Johnson, *Possessions in Luke-Acts,* to the literature on these texts.

addendum to the wealth-negative demand. Immediately after Jesus' humiliating and vexing pronouncement about the rich ruler, we recall Peter's statement in which he seems to have been angling for reassurance: "And Peter said, 'Look, we have left our homes and followed you'" (18:28). Jesus replies, "Truly I tell you, there is no one who has left house or wife or brothers or parents or children, for the sake of the kingdom of God, who will not get back very much more in this age, and in the age to come eternal life" (18:28-30). This declaration makes quite clear that his directives have not led them into anything like monastic poverty, or poverty in any material sense. If anything, they have resulted quite unexpectedly in material prosperity greater than that which they enjoyed previously while living in the world as they had been doing before Jesus called them. Indeed, Jesus calls the Twelve and his immediate followers into an existence of intense material delight, as the next section will make plain. And we shall see that this, too, is typical of the prophetic narratives, in which the men of God come eating and drinking in a right and sacred way — over and against the rich who do so in a wrong and godless manner. Eating and drinking in the right way is part of the prophet's display of God's condemnation of the present generation. It is to set true delight in opposition to the revelry and evil of the ruling rich. We are now ready to discuss the theme that we considered briefly at the beginning of this chapter. It is the presentation of Jesus as the "Lord of Delight," which we will seek to integrate reasonably into our theology of wealth.

THE LORD OF DELIGHT

The second image of Jesus that comes forth in the Gospel narratives identifies him as someone who by no means renounces the Old Testament vision of delight. Although it seems to an extent hidden in him and needing unveiling, scrutiny reveals that his manner of life during his public mission embodies that messianic vision. It is true that, for a little while, its boldest lines — his dominion, dignity, flourishing, delight, and celebration — become very difficult to discern. But the deeper foundation of that way of suffering that leads him from Bethlehem to Calvary remains the same throughout. If we look closely, we begin to see in him the surgeon's bleeding hands, to recall T. S. Eliot's image, with which God is not denying our dominion as human beings but restoring it from what otherwise would have been a sickness unto death.

154

In responding to the authorities that arrested John the Baptist, Jesus reveals a side of his character that Christian moral theologians have generally not appreciated sufficiently — that is, the deeper presence of joy and celebration in his character. He defends John by pointing out the small-mindedness of his critics' assertion that he "has come eating no bread and drinking no wine," and therefore "has a demon" (7:33). But if they cannot comprehend John's uncompromising wildness and his asceticism, he goes on to say, they are certainly too small of mind and spirit to handle Jesus. For his life, contrary to John's, is one of such intense celebration that the extremes appear dangerous. Unlike John, "the Son of Man has come eating and drinking, and you say, 'Look, a glutton and a drunkard, a friend of tax collectors and sinners!'" (7:34). They think that in Deuteronomy they have found the right typology for understanding the true identity of Jesus (it turns out that they at least have the right book). To be sure, his behavior proves to them that he is a wanton son, that disobedient figure who is so incorrigible and damaging to society that the only recourse is to put him to death. Little do the spiritual authorities see in his eating and drinking fulfillment of the prophets' words and, by extension, God's plan for human flourishing.

A good many scholars make note of the prominent place that feasting and celebration have in the Gospel narratives. As Richard Horsley observes:

> A strikingly distinctive activity of Jesus and his followers was their regular celebration with festive meals, almost certainly a celebration of the presence of the kingdom. A surprising amount of the gospel tradition has to do with feeding, table fellowship, and related teachings, leading to the conclusion that Jesus and his followers were indeed celebrating the presence of the kingdom.[24]

Horsley stresses that "Jesus had a reputation for 'eating and drinking,' one which led opponents to accuse him of associating with people who were indulgently enjoying life rather than observing the Torah."[25] So even though Christian moral theology has not stressed the point, it is evident enough from the narratives that Jesus and his followers lived a celebrative life, one which expressed the reality of the kingdom of God.

24. Richard Horsley, *Jesus and the Spiral of Violence* (San Francisco: Harper & Row, 1987), p. 78.
25. Horsley, *Spiral of Violence*, p. 78.

Apparently the lifestyle is exuberant enough to make the religious authorities wonder (on the occasion of a "great feast" at Levi's house) why Jesus and his disciples do not fast, but instead always seem to be eating and drinking. Jesus responds with a question that is instructive: "Can you make wedding guests fast while the bridegroom is with them?" (Luke 5:34). He then compares his very presence to new wine that simply bursts old wineskins (5:36-39). Indeed, his simile puts the entire tradition of his poverty into the class of "old wineskins," for it does not begin to explain the character we see in Jesus. Horsley gives this literary summary of the theme of his eating and drinking. "God was [in Christ] finally feeding the people with miraculous abundance despite appearances of paucity."[26] It seems that appearances deceive. There was indeed an appearance of poverty about their new existence, and we must say more about this, but they did not live in want of good things. As Pilgrim states, "Luke's portrayal of Jesus' life depicts a person who rejoices in life and accepts the goodness of God's creation, including some of the things that only money can buy."[27]

Several episodes in Jesus' life reveal his role as the Lord of Delight. There is the wedding feast at Cana, where the wine runs out (John 2:1-11). Jesus rescues the situation (at his mother's urging) by turning the six vats of purification water into about 180 gallons of the very best. His very first public miracle, then, the beginning of the things he did to "manifest his glory" (2:11), is simply to preserve a precious moment of celebration and delight for his friends. Then, too, there is that disreputable woman who pours precious nard on him (Mark 14:3; John 12:3). This strange episode seems so thoroughly degenerate that it is the last straw for Judas Iscariot, who chides Jesus' letting her simply waste about a year's worth of income on him. Judas is correct; they certainly could have sold it and given the considerable proceeds to the poor. But Jesus' response — that his passing presence with them is vastly greater and more valuable even than the pressing needs of the poor — does not seem to appease him. For as Mark's narrative makes clear, it is this saying — that "you always have the poor with you, and you can show kindness to them whenever you wish; but you will not always have me" (14:7) — that provokes Judas to betray him. As soon as Jesus has stopped speaking in praise of what this woman had done, Mark relates: "Then Judas Iscariot went to the chief priests in order to be-

26. Horsley, *Spiral of Violence*, p. 179.
27. Pilgrim, *Good News*, p. 124.

tray him" (14:10).[28] Hence, if we are to have an integrated theology of faith and the things of wealth, we must somehow put these apparently conflicting pictures of Jesus and his demands into a coherent form.

How are we to interpret these texts, and how might we see them next to the wealth-negative narratives as part of a larger, coherent whole? In the context of traditional interpretation and moral theology, this is very difficult to do. However, if we understand the narratives, as suggested already, in terms of prophetic tradition, then things begin to fall more coherently into place.

In his book *Lord of the Banquet* David P. Moessner has explored the typology of the prophet in Luke's Gospel to an extent that is unrivalled in the literature on Luke (to my knowledge). The main thesis of Moessner's "literary-critical study" is that the background typology for Jesus in Luke is the exodus and the "calling and fate of Moses in Deuteronomy."[29] In his interpretation the "travel narrative" that is unique to Luke is a kind of "new exodus," led by a "new Moses," who is Jesus the Christ. If this typology is valid, its implications for interpreting Luke's view of the rich, and of wealth, are considerable. For one thing, it provides a strong connection between the vision of life for God's people that Jesus (in Luke) would have had with that of Deuteronomy, which we have already discussed. In that discussion, we noted that having good grounds for this connection with the New Testament would be essential to any attempt at applying the narrative. I believe that Moessner's work does provide those grounds for just that connection.

In the first part of the book Moessner (like Johnson) observes that Luke indeed used the prophetic journey motif to shape the middle section of his Gospel.[30] In the next part he argues (again like Johnson) that Luke presented Jesus in this section as a prophet like Moses, as presented in the book of Deuteronomy.[31] At the core of his argument is Luke's distinctive account of the Transfiguration. Moessner seeks to show that Luke "set forth a fourfold exodus typology of the prophetic calling of Jesus which

---

28. In view of this very clear connection in the narrative of Mark, I do not know why Blomberg judges that we "know nothing about his motives for betraying Jesus." *Neither Poverty Nor Riches,* p. 108.

29. David P. Moessner, *Lord of the Banquet: The Literary and Theological Significance of the Lukan Travel Narrative* (Minneapolis: Fortress, 1989), p. 6.

30. Moessner, *Lord of the Banquet,* pp. 14-44.

31. Moessner, *Lord of the Banquet,* pp. 46-79.

conforms closely to that of Moses in Deuteronomy."[32] The most obvious
parallels between the stories are the glowing of personages on the mountain, the cloud, and the voice of God. In this environment the prophets Eli-
jah and Moses speak with Jesus about his own exodus, which he will perform in Jerusalem (Luke 9:31). Jesus then descends the mountain and, also
like Moses, goes forth followed by those who would reach the Promised
Land. On his way, however, he confronts a perverse and crooked generation, whose perfidy makes necessary his death.[33]

I am not so directly interested in pursuing this broad theory about the
narrative as in the part of prophetic typology that centers on the theme of
eating and drinking as the expression of fullness of life with God in the
land. For it seems that this very prominent theme in the Deuteronomistic
narrative of Moses (and also in the Latter Prophets) helps to explain why
Luke made it so prominent in his narrative of Jesus.

Moessner points out (and we observed earlier in this book) that the
goal of Moses in the teachings of Deuteronomy is "to inherit the blessings
of the covenant to Abraham, Isaac, and Jacob as summed up by 'eating'
and 'rejoicing' before the Lord."[34] The place for this delight is the Promised
Land (in contrast to Egypt and the wilderness), where the people can enjoy
strong drink and wine.[35] The centrality of eating and drinking as the manifestation of loyalty to the covenant, and the kind of existence that follows
from it, is evident in the injunctions for the three great feasts of Israel.
Moessner discusses them in detail and concludes that they express nothing
less than "the consummating point of Israel's peculiar Exodus salvation."[36]

Moses' prophetic journey is in fact to lead the twelve tribes of Israel
into the great banquet of milk and honey that God had set for them in the
land. Unfortunately, the people rebel, and the deepest expression of their
rebellion against God is in their eating and drinking in the wrong way —
the way of indulgence and revelry. For this, as the prophet Amos points
out, God destroys them. Nevertheless, Moses in Deuteronomy looks
ahead to a day "when eating and rejoicing will find its perfect fulfillment."[37] When Moses dies so that the people may enter the land, it is in

32. Moessner, *Lord of the Banquet*, p. 60.
33. Moessner, *Lord of the Banquet*, pp. 66-67.
34. Moessner, *Lord of the Banquet*, p. 264.
35. Moessner, *Lord of the Banquet*, p. 265.
36. Moessner, *Lord of the Banquet*, p. 268.
37. Moessner, *Lord of the Banquet*, p. 272.

the hope of this great restoration and consummation of delight. According to Moessner, in "the Central Section of Luke's Gospel this restoration takes place."[38] Jesus feeds the people in the wilderness — not with manna, but with bread and meat. He gathers the Twelve (a new Israel) to himself on the mountain, and he then goes forth with them and embarks upon a new exodus.[39]

On the way, he gathers households to eat and drink with him as he presses onward toward the sacred city of Jerusalem. But also on the way, "as the Lord of the Banquet, he meets an 'eating and drinking' that is directly contrary to the consummation of the covenant."[40] It is exactly what Moses warned about in Deuteronomy:

> He in fact meets that eating and reveling which matches Moses' description of a hardened people who forget the graciousness of the Lord by neglecting the weightier matters of his commandments, such as the love of God for the poor and justice for the foreigner. It is in the meals with the Pharisees-scribes that this slavery to an unrepentant heart is the most pervasive. At table Jesus confronts the smug security in the blessings of wealth and prestige that the Pharisees-scribes enjoy as the leaders of "this generation" in the land.[41]

This pattern gives shape to the entire journey. Jesus and his followers celebrate the true Feast, while the rulers of Israel, like the rich rulers of Amos's day, eat and drink to their own destruction.

At last, Jesus reaches Jerusalem and chooses the place where he will eat and drink with them for the last time. Moessner understands Luke's account of the Last Supper as, in essence, the consummation of the New Exodus and a foretaste of the Feast that is yet to come. After the ascension and Pentecost, Moessner writes,

> The New Exodus of Deuteronomy 30 has been accomplished! The Prophet like Moses has come. The joy of the feast has now been fulfilled. The covenant to Israel's forebears, their Exodus, and their inheritance in the land — the goal of the entire saving journey history expressed in

---

38. Moessner, *Lord of the Banquet,* p. 272.
39. Moessner, *Lord of the Banquet,* pp. 272-73.
40. Moessner, *Lord of the Banquet,* p. 274.
41. Moessner, *Lord of the Banquet,* p. 274.

eating and rejoicing in the first fruits of the land (Deut. 26:1-11) — after the long journey of Jesus to Jerusalem has now at last been consummated.[42]

In and through his death, like Moses, Jesus has at last led his people into the Promised Land, the full glory of which is yet to come.

We do not have to accept every detail of Moessner's literary analysis to appreciate the plausibility of his larger thesis and its value to our attempt at forging a theology of wealth from Luke. For one thing, it illumines the entire theme of eating and drinking in the narrative as a natural feature of prophetic typology. For another, it provides a literary framework in which to see how the negative and affirmative accounts of enjoyment fit together as a whole. If Jesus' principles were prophetic, we would expect that his condemnation of enjoyments of one sort would be countered, not by ascetic or utilitarian denial, but by enjoyments of the right sort. In this framework, the strong criticisms of the rich in Luke are not at all condemnations of affluence. They follow rather from the assertion of true delight. Like Moses, his mission was not to destroy God's promise to Abraham, but to fulfill it. And in that way he fulfilled the very purpose of God in the beginning. His vision of human existence on his way to Jerusalem was exactly the same as God's in creating heaven and earth in the first place.

This interpretation also helps make sense of what otherwise seems to have been uneven behavior on Jesus' part in what he did or did not require of people who would be disciples. It makes clear that Jesus did not call some to poverty and leave others in their relative prosperity. He rather called them all to take part, in quite different ways, in the material delight of the promise. Under the circumstances, however, delight came with a price. For some, that price was direct involvement in and with the narrative of the prophet, who would be rejected, and their destiny would conform to his. For others, the price was radical redirection of religious and moral life toward the goals of the kingdom as envisioned by Jesus. And for these wealthier Christians this included radical redirection of economic life.

It seems that Luke had just these sorts of Christians in view when he wrote the Gospel. And it seems that he has forced them (and us) to face a question that we would prefer not to face. Can anyone be both affluent and

---

42. Moessner, *Lord of the Banquet*, p. 277.

faithful to God at the same time? Is there a way into God's kingdom that does not require divestment of wealth? Luke has already indicated that there is, but can we be more specific on the patterns of Christian life in conditions of affluence? Along with certain other scholars, I believe that Luke has given the story of Jesus and the chief tax collector Zacchaeus in order to provide a model of discipleship for rich Christians. In the final section of this chapter, then, we shall give this story the detailed attention that we believe it thus deserves.

THE SECOND CIRCLE OF DISCIPLES

In the previous chapter we observed that, in addition to his inner circle of followers, Jesus had a larger network of supporters whom he also counted as disciples. If this is true, then it follows directly that they, too, had met the demand to leave everything and that they, too, followed him. But in fact these disciples did not physically do so, for they remained in their homes with their possessions and jobs and ordinary patterns of life. The sisters Mary and Martha and their brother Lazarus are good examples. It seems that they owned a house in Bethany, near Jerusalem, where Jesus stayed during his travels to that region. We previously considered Peter's mother-in-law, who owned a large house with servants. It seems that her home was the main base of operation for Jesus and the Twelve when they were working in Galilee. We also remember the women "who provided for them out of their means" (Luke 8:3). These women of means apparently traveled with him in Galilee and paid a substantial share of the bills.

In all these instances I believe it is correct to say of them that they left everything in the sense that they directed considerable portions of what they had to Jesus and his mission. And in all but the last instance, they followed him by means of redirected commitment and devotion to him — his person and work gave new meaning and purpose to their possessions. We could well consider other examples, too, such as Joseph of Arimathea, who was rich and followed Jesus from afar (Matt. 27:57; John 9:38; Mark 15:43; Luke 23:50-51). He left everything and followed by providing the humiliated and slain Jesus with a tomb, so that he might at least be laid to rest with dignity.

Furthermore, to finish this major point of our discussion, close scrutiny reveals that not even the inner circle of disciples abandoned their possessions. They indeed left them for a while, but they did not divest themselves of property. For instance, after Jesus' death and resurrection, Peter seems to have brought his boat and nets out of storage and gone back to fishing (John 21).

All these examples give added support to the view we are considering. As Luke Johnson writes:

> The poverty of Jesus is not to be found first in his lack of material possessions, for he and his followers seemed to have received support from others (Luke 8:1-3) and had sufficient funds to help the poor (John 13:29). The poverty of Jesus is to be found first in his faith. It is, properly speaking, a theological poverty.[43]

So we learn from the narrative that the spiritual and moral demand regarding economic life is indeed an existential and religious one, and that very different sorts of people in varying economic circumstances satisfied it in quite different ways. Furthermore, in all of these instances, Jesus called people to follow him in differing forms of Christian material delight.

In fact, the manner in which Jesus built this following into a diverse network of people created a certain cycle of affluence. I do not think that this term is at all inappropriate if used precisely to describe what happened. For the people who remained where they were and followed from afar obviously enjoyed a degree of prosperity, even as they connected it with the mission of Jesus and his immediate disciples. Those, on the other hand, who really left everything and followed Jesus on foot gave up the security they had once enjoyed. But in return, being connected with the network that Jesus was forming, they, too, enjoyed the delights of affluence in and through the good works of supporters. So in leaving everything and following Jesus in these very different respects, everyone gained a new sense of direction and purpose in life, and everyone also benefited from the material goods of the others. I also think that it was something very like the concept of community — perhaps we may call it a new Israel — exemplified in the actions of the church after Pentecost (a main subject of our last chapter).

For most of us, the second circle of disciples provides a much more directly applicable model of economic life than the first one. My assumption

---

43. Johnson, *Sharing Possessions,* p. 77.

in the next subsection is that Luke offers Jesus' encounter with Zacchaeus, the chief tax collector, as a fairly intense and detailed instance of the model he envisioned for the affluent Christians to whom he wrote. For on narrative rhetorical suppositions, it looks like this encounter between Jesus and Zacchaeus is symmetrical in placement to the episode of the rich ruler. It is the very next encounter of its kind that follows, and it is also the last. The remarkable contrasts between Jesus' actions toward the one man and the other suggest the introduction of a powerful dialectic and counter-theme. Indeed, both its position in the narrative and the details of action suggest that this story, too, is a peak in the thematic structure of Luke's writing. In my view, the rhetorical function of this story, then, is in fact to give an answer to the vexing question of Peter in the previous one. Indeed, Jesus had forced him (and us) to wonder anew how a rich person might be saved without ceasing to be rich. In Zacchaeus, Luke gives us a vividly ironic example of how, with God, that might be possible.

THE IMPROBABLE EXAMPLE OF ZACCHAEUS

Of the four Gospel writers, Luke alone relates the remarkable story of Zacchaeus. This is worth noting, for (assuming it was factual, as I do) it suggests that he discerned meaning in this episode that others did not. It is also, I suspect, very important to pay attention to where Luke placed the encounter in his narrative, and how he connected it with other stories in that section of the Gospel. Walter Pilgrim first gave me the idea that this placing was rhetorical and thematic, although Pilgrim's treatment of Luke is more essentially historical and critical in nature. Nevertheless, I completely agree with him in regarding the "story of Zacchaeus as the most important Lukan text on the subject of the right use of possessions."[44] Going further, Pilgrim suggests "that Luke intends this text as the paradigm par excellence for wealthy Christians in his community."[45]

I believe that Luke's placement of the teaching that follows — Jesus' Parable of the Pounds (Luke 19:11-27) — only supports this judgment. Just as Zacchaeus is the last person Jesus encounters and challenges on economic levels, the Parable of the Pounds is the very last connected teaching

---

44. Pilgrim, *Good News,* p. 129.
45. Pilgrim, *Good News,* p. 129.

in the Gospel on the matter of wealth and economic life. And in my view this placement makes that parable a great deal more important to our moral theology than is commonly known. So in the next chapter, on the key parables of Jesus on being rich, I shall return to the story of Zacchaeus and treat it together with the Parable of the Pounds as a unified narrative text.

But as for the story, to this point in Luke, in each and every encounter with wealthy people Jesus has directed them "to leave everything." As stated, the encounter with the rich young ruler is the most intensely radical of them all. It would seem, as the plot unfolds, that the demand of discipleship only gets more rigorous — hence Peter's decisive question. But then comes Zacchaeus, whom Luke introduces in these words: "he was a chief tax collector and was rich" (19:2). The irony is very deep. For unlike the rich ruler, who seemed almost the model of true religion (and his wealth and status only proved it), Zacchaeus is about as deserving of moral condemnation as anyone in those circumstances could be. He is Jewish, but he has sold his birthright for the mess of pottage that is affluence gained by tax gathering.

Luke relates that Zacchaeus strives to see Jesus, and that Jesus picks him out of the large crowd that gathers on that day. The contrast between his responses to the rich ruler and to Zacchaeus is stunning. To this corrupt official Jesus speaks not a word of condemnation, nor does he demand anything of him. Instead, he declares that he will go to Zacchaeus's house and dine with him. This response angers the crowd; they "grumble" that "he has gone to be the guest of one who is a sinner" (19:7). But Jesus is unfazed by their criticisms and goes home with Zacchaeus anyway.

But that is just the beginning of the contrast. Jesus does not initiate the moral discourse and thus establish its terms, as he does with the rich young ruler. Instead, Zacchaeus does. He begins by expressing unsolicited shame for what he has been doing, for he knows very well that he has sinned against God by oppressing and impoverishing God's people. Unlike the rich ruler, there is no trace of self-justification in him, but only a heartfelt desire to make things right. And so he offers that he will repay four times whatever he has taken from the people by fraud. And he adds that he will give half of his possessions to the poor. This is perhaps the sharpest break in the narrative, which till now has made the demand to "leave everything" as unqualified as it could be. Jesus does not make this demand, and Zacchaeus does not offer to meet it. He rather commits himself to begin living justly and, as indication of his good faith, to give back half (not all) of what he has gained by questionable means. Meanwhile, Jesus says not a word, but listens. At the end Jesus simply declares: "Today salvation has come to this house, because he too is a son of Abraham" (19:9).

It seems that Zacchaeus had gone back to the laws of the Old Testament on theft to arrive at these proposed conditions for membership among God's people. The requirement was to put back a minimum of twice the amount stolen, and in worse cases more than twice (Exod. 22:7; 2 Sam. 12:6). So what Zacchaeus did was to apply that code rigorously enough to himself to cover all the possible instances of theft that might have happened under his watch as a supervisor of the tax collection system. Moreover, it is reasonable to presume that he remained in that position, for had he left and followed Jesus we would have expected Luke to mention the fact. It seems rather that Zacchaeus conformed to the moral counsel that John the Baptist gave tax collectors in an earlier episode. His charge to them was not to abandon their business, but to do it honestly and with moral care. In the rigorous context of Luke, we might be surprised at his rendering of John's moderate words to these men: "Collect no more than the amount prescribed for you" (3:13). It seems that what Jesus accepted as sufficient from Zacchaeus was a visibly serious demonstration of a sincere desire to return to the moral principle enshrined in that simple ethic.

It seems to me, also, that there is in this story something more — something greater, even — than just the salvation of a wretched man. It is the redemption of the world, the world of culture, including its morally questionable economic forms. For if a chief tax collector working under the social economy of Herod and Caesar (given what that meant to Jewish religion) can nonetheless be a "son of Abraham," there is surely hope for affluent people in almost all walks of economic life in our time. In this story it is not that a man *is* saved *from* the economics of the world, but that the world is redeemed in and through the salvation and new economics of the man. For now we imagine him to be a greatly powerful influence for good in the entire region that he ruled in his position. It seems reasonable to think that this is exactly the model Luke puts forth to all wealthy Christians, most of whom would not have engaged in occupations anything like as corrupt as the tax system of the day. And it seems right to take Zacchaeus as a model, not to imitate in a literal, slavish way, but to follow in terms of the disposition and principles he displayed. Like him, we can find creative ways to shape our institutions — families, churches, schools, banks, corporations, businesses, and also our larger political system — into instruments of redemptive power. At least we can seek to become agents of such power for good within them. If so, the improbable example of Zacchaeus forever embodies, in cultural form, the ancient truths of the creation, the exodus, the prophets, the books of wisdom, and the Incarnation.

CHAPTER SEVEN

Parables of Affluence

Without a parable he told them nothing.

MATTHEW 13:34

All the Gospels agree that a great deal of Jesus' teaching was on the subject of wealth, and that most of what he taught about it was in the negative. He called his disciples at times to be separated from it, he warned against the deadly dangers it posed to spiritual life, he confronted rich people in the bluntest of terms — and even pronounced curses on them. In his parables, he very often portrayed rich people as empty, desperate, evil, and lost to God. The negative tone of Jesus' teaching on wealth has provoked sweeping judgments such as this one from Jacques Ellul:

> It is the very essence of the whole life of the rich, which is necessarily opposed to God. Apart from the exceptional cases — Abraham, Job and Solomon — there is no righteous rich man, there is no good rich man. Judgment against the rich is always radical.[1]

New Testament scholar Thomas E. Schmidt makes a similar statement: "Every time Jesus offers an opinion about riches, it is negative. Every time he teaches about the use of wealth, he counsels his disciples to give it

---

1. Jacques Ellul, *Money and Power*, trans. LaVonne Neff (Downers Grove, Ill.: InterVarsity, 1984), p. 138.

away."[2] However, we have seen that judgments of this sort greatly oversimplify the matter. For even in Luke's Gospel, which is the most severe of them all toward the rich of Israel, the foundations of Jesus' ethics are not in asceticism or utilitarianism. They are in the vision of God as expressed in and through the prophets. Jesus was the consummate prophet — a Moses figure — in Luke. And this helps to explain how his severe excoriations of the rich in parts of that Gospel fit together with his affirmations of them (under proper conditions) in others.

In this chapter, we are going to continue our exploration of Luke by looking at four parables on wealth that arise at a key stage in the plot development of the distinctive middle narrative of the Gospel. We need not reconsider the points we covered in the previous chapter on the rising economic theme, on the question his narrative raises, and how (in my view) Luke answers it in narrative form. I believe that consideration of these parables in that rhetorically connected context only supports the proposals I have been making on Luke's integrated view of wealth. A careful reading of these parables supports the notion that Luke's frame of reference was deliberately prophetic. It also supports the explanation that Jesus' severe judgments against the rich in the Gospel belong squarely within that theological and ethical tradition. And it strongly supports the proposals I made about Zacchaeus being for Luke a kind of model for wealthy Christians to follow in working out their own faith and life in his generation. Because of the rhetorically crucial placement and interconnection of these parables in the narrative, it seems quite reasonable to think that, taken all together, they constitute a kind of dialectical, narrative thesis that consummates the great economic theme of the writing. Brief comparisons with other texts in Luke that we will not go over in detail (such as the Parable of the Good Samaritan) also support the belief that this is so.

The four parables that we will consider are those of the Rich Fool (Luke 12:13-21), the Dishonest Manager (16:1-9), the Rich Man and Lazarus (16:19-31), and the Pounds (19:11-27). The first three of these parables occur only in Luke, which again indicates his special interest in rich Christians. And Luke alone connects the Parable of the Pounds with the key account of the encounter between Jesus and Zacchaeus. As indicated earlier, I am convinced that this connection makes that parable vastly more important

---

2. Thomas E. Schmidt, "The Hard Sayings of Jesus," in *The Midas Trap*, ed. David Neff (Wheaton, Ill.: Victor, 1990), p. 21.

in its literary function, and to our moral theology, than theologians have generally understood it to be.

THE RICH FOOL (LUKE 12:13-21)

The Parable of the Rich Fool dominates the landscape of Luke's important twelfth chapter. We have already considered Jesus' extensive teaching on wealth there. The parable that Luke connects with his teaching is unusually long, and the detailed explanation of its symbolism suggests its importance to Jesus. It is the occasion for his famous discourse on the lilies and the ravens, and it sets the stage in Luke's Gospel for a series of lessons by Jesus on riches. It seems fair to think that this parable helps to explain both Jesus' response to the two brothers in dispute over their inheritance and the radical directives he gave at that time to his followers.

Jesus gives a brief prelude to the parable by saying to his disciples, in response to the brothers: "Take care! Be on your guard against all kinds of greed; for one's life does not consist in the abundance of possessions" (12:15). He then tells the story of a rich man whose land "produced abundantly." So abundantly, in fact, that he is worried about not having sufficient space to store his crops. His solution is practical: he pulls down his old barns and builds bigger ones. Now, with his grain stored and his finances secure, the man says to himself, "Soul, you have ample goods laid up for many years; relax, eat, drink, be merry" (12:19). But that very night God comes and says to the man, "You fool! This very night your life is being demanded of you. And the things you have prepared, whose will they be?" "So it is," Jesus concludes, "with those who store up treasures for themselves but are not rich toward God" (12:20).

This parable is pretty obviously an ominous warning about the foolishness of covetousness or its twin, greed. But the deeper question is, what was covetous or greedy about the man's behavior? The story challenges hearers to wonder what was so very wrong with his life that God judged him to be no more than a fool and apparently damned him (in keeping with the curse of chapter 6)?

The question of interpretation is, of course, connected thematically with the one we have already faced concerning the radical directives that follow. And we thus already have a frame of reference in the background. It is that of the prophetic voice in Deuteronomy that warns of the spiritual perils of wealth to the wealthy. And this background framework of theological and ethical tradition suggests that the approach of certain writers is not quite on target. Once again, it is necessary to correct the application of Ron Sider, who proposes that the form of greed in this man was his manifest "compulsion to acquire more and more possessions, even though he does not need them."[3] Sider concludes:

> One cannot read the Parable of the Rich Fool without thinking of our own society. We madly multiply sophisticated gadgets, bigger houses, fancier cars, and fashionable clothes — not because such things truly enrich our lives but because we are driven by an obsession for more and more.[4]

The implication (a recurring one in Sider's work) is that things that we do not really need do not enrich our lives, and to desire to have things like fancier cars or fashionable clothes is inherently and obsessively greedy. But as we have observed many times over, this conclusion does not follow from any premise in the prophetic moral literature. In fact, the ethical tradition of that literature quite often contains its denial. There are a good many things that we do not really need, it seems, that indeed do enrich human life and bring it nearer to what God envisions it to be. Nor does the parable give grounds for thinking that Jesus used it to teach an ethics of wealth that was in opposition to the old one. On the contrary, as Luke Johnson has observed, the entire setting and place of this parable at the core of Luke's narrative is that of the consummate Mosaic prophet.[5] Moreover, the man's actions, in the abstract, are not remarkable. In essence, all he did was plan ahead prudently enough so that he could retire. In these actions, the man is more comparable to ordinary men and women who prudently invest in pension plans for those sunset years. Unless we think that economic planning of this kind is inherently and thus always covetous, then the sin of greed and the eternal foolishness of the man are not inherent in his actions, but rather in the deeper and larger spiritual context of those actions.

3. Ronald J. Sider, *Rich Christians in an Age of Hunger,* 20th Anniversary Revision (Dallas: Word, 1997), p. 98.

4. Sider, *Rich Christians,* p. 98.

5. Luke Timothy Johnson, *The Gospel of Luke,* Sacra Pagina Series, vol. 3 (Collegeville, Minn.: Liturgical Press, 1991), p. 201.

The man's sin and his damnable foolishness are rather in his deeper vision of what life is all about, in what it most essentially consists. The evil and damnation follows from his entire vision of human purpose and the spiritual disposition that grows from it. New Testament commentator I. Howard Marshall suggests that the dispute between the brothers, while Jesus does not directly speak to them in return, but instead curtly ignores them, nevertheless provides our point of entry into this parable, and I believe he is right.[6] The brothers have presumably lost their father. In healthy human beings, a father's death has lingering effects — it brings to mind memories going back to childhood, it evokes intense awareness of how fleeting life is, and how passing and relatively unimportant material things are compared to the people in our lives. For, as the soul of someone departs, their wealth remains. It is of no use to them after death. The death of someone as close as a parent puts things in perspective; it impresses upon us as nothing else can what really counts — and what really does not. It clears our minds about what real treasure is and what it is not. But all these brothers worry about, even in this situation, is money. In their craving for financial security they have lost the real treasure of love. They have gained an inheritance and lost their souls.

The brothers are not wrong to want an inheritance. They are wrong to covet it, to make it the end of their existence. And so it is with the rich fool in Jesus' pointed parable. He is not covetous simply because he desires a secure and pleasant retirement, or material things he does not need.[7] He is covetous and foolish because he believes the storage of grain (think IRA's, 401k's, and the rest) solves the problem of his human existence. When his building project is through, he judges that his human project is finished, too. He has arrived. He has it made — or so he believes. His life ends there, with the barns.

Had the story ended with the man's retirement, and no final judgment, we would still sense the foolishness, the tragedy of his existence. There would still be a strange pathos about his merriment. That is because

6. See the commentary on this by I. Howard Marshall, *Commentary on Luke*, The New International Greek Testament Commentary (Grand Rapids: Eerdmans, 1978), p. 521.

7. Commentator Norval Geldenhuys agrees that "In this parable and these pronouncements the Saviour does not condemn the possession of worldly goods as such, but the covetousness and carnal attitude with regard to earthly wealth." *Commentary on the Gospel of Luke*, The New International Commentary on the New Testament (Grand Rapids: Eerdmans, 1951), p. 355.

Jesus pictures him alone, utterly alone — something quite unthinkable for a rich person in that culture. No children run about the house, no wife or friends eat and drink with him. He sits and makes merry all by himself. When he does speak, he speaks to himself. And when God speaks to him, the final question implies that the value of his treasure will perish with him. "Whose will they be?"

The parable sounds an alarm. It awakens us to a hard prophetic truth. Economic life, our manner of "eating and drinking," makes us who we really are, forever. In Luke, Jesus stresses and repeats this truth so many times and in so many ways that it is amazing how seldom we hear it in Christian churches and schools. The rich fool is an eternal fool for he has stored no treasure in heaven. The word is not against solvency. But we must be very sure that our quest for solvency is animated by creative and redemptive love — for God and for the people God gives us for such a little while. Too easily our productive work becomes an end unto itself — an idol — and financial success brings the strange paradox of poverty in our relationships. The parable reminds us that our relationships are the real tests of our success. They are the bottom line. They are the real treasure. They provide the only life of the soul.

The Parable of the Rich Man and Lazarus puts this warning into sharp focus, and places it in a somewhat different light that is also prophetic. Its point is not so much the spiritual one just described, but the classical ethical one we considered in Amos. We might think of these two stories, then, as each drawing out one of the two major prophetic themes in Deuteronomy and elsewhere. The one is the more deeply personal spiritual challenge that comes with being affluent. The other is the moral consequence in society of our not rising successfully to meet it. (And of course these two elements of biblical teaching can operate together only on the assumption that there is indeed a right way to have and to enjoy wealth, just as there is a wrong one.)

THE RICH MAN AND LAZARUS (LUKE 16:19-31)

As we have seen, in the sixteenth chapter of Luke the problem of wealth rises as a distinctive theme. Almost the entire chapter consists of two parables about two men and their wealth. One is the story of the Dishonest Manager (16:1-15), and the other is the tale of the Rich Man and Lazarus

(16:19-31).[8] Luke has pretty obviously linked these two parables together with each other. Commentators have not noted this, but it does seem that Luke presents them as a pair and, in that literary form, links them with the sequence of events that he is narrating on Jesus and wealth. In fact, the relationship of ironic contrast between the two parables is very nearly identical with the one that he has rhetorically crafted between the historical figures of the rich ruler, on the one hand, and Zacchaeus on the other. For in the one parable, a very rich man who seems certain to have the blessing of God is in fact cursed — because of his response to his wealth. In the other, a most improbable character, a scoundrel who seems certain to be rejected by God, is in fact blessed — saved by his right response to his wealth.

In keeping with the larger narrative pattern of Luke-Acts, we will consider the negative example of affluence in the Rich Man and Lazarus first and then offer an interpretation in narrative context. Once we have identified the fundamental moral principles that it enshrines, I will then make some ethical proposals that I believe the parable conveys about being affluent in the wrong way. Afterwards, we will turn to the Parable of the Dishonest Manager, and in the light of its positive principles, we will explore the matter of being affluent in the right way (which turns out to be the background theme in the narrative of Jesus for both stories).

We should begin by noting that this parable directly follows the lesson that Jesus drew from the first one, about the manager. "You cannot serve God and wealth" (16:13). Upon hearing this, the Pharisees mocked Jesus, continuing the theme of their rejection of him and his message about their manner of eating and drinking. "The Pharisees," Luke writes, "who were lovers of money, heard all this, and they ridiculed him" (16:14). We shall return to the rhetorical pattern of prophet typology that this incident extends in just a moment. But it is quite clear that Jesus casts the rich man of the parable as the fictional embodiment of what he judged the Pharisees to be doing. So we should not underestimate the tension and blunt force of the story to its first hearers and readers.

Jesus begins: "There was a rich man who was dressed in purple and

---

8. As Johnson points out, one of several tangled problems in interpreting the Parable of the Dishonest Manager is in determining where it ends. *The Gospel of Luke*, pp. 246-47. It seems to me that verses 10-15 are not part of the parable per se, but they have to be read with the story in order to understand its otherwise murky teaching.

fine linen and who feasted sumptuously every day" (16:19). At his gate lies the poor man Lazarus, whose only comfort in life comes from the dogs that lick his sores. So wretched is he that scraps from the rich man's table are enough to satisfy him. Eventually both the poor man and the rich man die. And here we pause as Jesus makes another strike on the moral universe of his contemporaries, and perhaps our own. He shatters their expectations about the moral destinies of people. There is a great reversal, for when Lazarus dies the angels carry him straightaway to heaven, and to rest in the bosom of none less than Abraham. On the other hand, when the rich man dies, he awakes to the sufferings of torment in Hades, separated by an abyss from paradise. Thus in agony, he pleads with Abraham, begging, "send Lazarus to dip the tip of his finger in water and cool my tongue" (16:24). The irony of reversal is as terrifying as it is complete. The rich man now begs the once-poor Lazarus for a little relief. But Abraham is merciless. To the man he says: "During your lifetime you received your good things, and Lazarus in like manner evil things; but now he is comforted here, and you are in agony" (16:25).

Accepting his own fate, the rich man then implores Abraham at least to send Lazarus to warn his five brothers, "so that they will not also come into this place of torment" (16:28). But Abraham is unmoved. And we must take due note of his reason. "They have Moses and the prophets; they should listen to them" (16:29). But the rich man, failing to grasp the prophetic force of this explanation, persists. Surely if someone returns from the dead, his brothers will listen. But Abraham remains firm. "If they do not listen to Moses and the prophets, neither will they be convinced even if someone rises from the dead" (16:31).

The most obvious and puzzling feature of this parable is the great reversal. Some have suggested the simple, literal reading that God's plan for history is to turn everything upside down. The rich will become poor, and the poor will become rich — in eternal things.[9] But this interpretation grows from what I (with others) have argued is an oversimplified understanding of the Lukan blessings and woes of chapter 6, and of Luke's semantics of wealth and poverty in general. (For one thing, Abraham was himself rich, and so on this interpretation, he would not have been a very good choice to speak for Heaven.) We need not repeat these criticisms in

---

9. See references in Walter Pilgrim, *Good News to the Poor: Wealth and Poverty in Luke-Acts* (Minneapolis: Augsburg, 1981), p. 116, n. 25.

detail. But it will be useful to add that this parable, perhaps more obviously than any other part of Luke's Gospel, manifests the book's prophetic typology, structure, and teaching. As Luke Johnson observes, the parable follows yet another episode in the literary pattern whereby the scribes and Pharisees reject Jesus' prophetic word about wealth.[10] By casting them as he does, Jesus condemns them in the most unflattering terms for their manner of eating and drinking.

A constant theme of the narrative thus far has been that the religious and political rulers self-righteously exclude the poor from their prosperity, even as they chastise and condemn Jesus for associating with them.[11] Jesus defends his own eating and drinking with these people (15:2-31), and he condemns theirs as exclusionary, heartless, and evil. His word to them is the same one that Amos gave to the rich rulers of his day. As Moessner writes, Jesus was saying to them, "They are eating and drinking themselves to Hades."[12]

This prophetic frame of reference, then, strongly favors the interpretation that the rich man's damnation follows not from his enjoyment of good things in excess, but rather from his doing so in the context of ignoring Lazarus. Even his behavior after death — expecting Lazarus to go as his messenger — perhaps does belie "the man's continuing arrogance," as Johnson believes.[13] Even if not, it seems very clear that "there was, in fact, a moral reason for this reversal."[14] Johnson gives this very concise and appropriate summary of the matter:

> The man had not only been rich and extravagant, he had been hard of heart. His wealth had made him insensitive to the Law and the Prophets alike that the covenant demands sharing goods with the poor. The concrete expression of his rejection of the Law was his neglect of the poor man at the gate.[15]

10. Luke Timothy Johnson, *The Literary Function of Possessions in Luke-Acts* (Missoula, Mont.: Scholars, 1977), pp. 140-41.

11. For an extended discussion of this theme in relation to the parable, see David P. Moessner, *Lord of the Banquet: The Literary and Theological Significance of the Lukan Travel Narrative* (Minneapolis: Fortress, 1989), pp. 162-64.

12. Moessner, *Lord of the Banquet,* p. 164. Also Johnson, *The Gospel of Luke,* p. 254.

13. Johnson, *The Gospel of Luke,* p. 256.

14. Johnson, *The Gospel of Luke,* p. 256.

15. Johnson, *The Gospel of Luke,* p. 256.

So far, this understanding of the broad moral principle in the parable seems exactly right. It is simply that of what I earlier called the exodus vision, in which those who have wealth and power must connect their affluence creatively and redemptively with the lives of the poor and powerless.[16]

The broad principle is clear enough, then, and few Christians will deny its truth as biblical teaching. But left as stated, this principle is so broad in scope that it leaves sensitive readers with more questions than answers about their obligations as wealthy Christians in a hungry world. Ron Sider, for instance, applies the parable directly to the matter of world hunger. He implies that the widespread neglect of global poverty by Christians in advanced societies is comparable to the rich man's neglect of Lazarus. "The rich man merely neglected to help. His sin was one of omission. And it sent him to hell."[17] But is that comparison clearly valid? Do affluent Europeans, Canadians, Australians, Japanese, and Americans have obligations to the global poor of the same kind that the rich man in the story had to Lazarus? Likewise, does this parable really teach that every affluent person in one of those societies has a moral obligation of that strong sort to just any poor person who is within technical reach in any of the undeveloped ones? And moreover, is it true (on this parable) that if she or he fails to meet that obligation, the likely outcome is eternal damnation? If so, one fairly clear implication would be that no affluent person in our day would ever have clear enough grounds for eating and drinking with assurance of divine approval. For there would always be one more Lazarus somewhere within reach to help, and so that golf game, or fishing trip, or dinner and movie would almost certainly fall under the headings of purple clothing and sumptuous living — the mortal sins of the rich man.

This improbable implication alone ought to give us pause before applying the parable in loosely and in unqualified form to the vast (and vastly complex) moral field of global hunger. That is so not only because of

---

16. So not to complicate things unnecessarily, I choose to ignore the problem of grounds for the salvation of Lazarus. However, I see no warrant in the parable, or in Luke generally, for the statement by Brian Griffiths that "Lazarus was a man of faith." Brian Griffiths, *The Creation of Wealth* (Downers Grove, Ill.: InterVarsity, 1985), p. 46. Moreover, I also choose to ignore the implications of Jesus' description of Hades as a place of torment for Christian theology. It does seem to reflect a view of the afterlife that was typical in the apocalyptic literature that flourished in the time between the testaments. See Johnson, *The Gospel of Luke*, p. 253.

17. Sider, *Rich Christians*, p. 138.

the apparently crushing weight of obligations that this sort of application generates, but also because of the narrative context itself. As the entire fifteenth chapter makes clear, and as noted, Jesus' moral critique of the Pharisees does not call for radical self-denial on their part, but for getting their eating and drinking right. It calls for eating and drinking in the form of true delight as it was to be in the Promised Land, and as it will be in the messianic kingdom of God. Moessner puts this theological matter very well:

> In 15:3-32 Jesus defends his "eating and drinking" by evoking the very joy of God over the table fellowship of sinners. To the sneers of Pharisees over Jesus' warning to beware the deadening influence of their riches (16:1-9, 10-13), Jesus launches his own offensive in 16:15 by casting them as the rich man of 16:19-31. Repentance is a dead option. They are eating and drinking themselves to Hades (16:9-23). Thus again two houses with two kinds of eating and drinking are pitted against each other.[18]

For this to be possible — even in Jesus' society, where they indeed always had the poor with them — the obligations of wealthy people had to be limited in some merciful way.

But is there any direct support in the parable, or in Luke as a whole, for believing that the obligations of the rich are limited, so that for any rich person there is some definite boundary to the scope of her or his moral obligations? I have already suggested that the obligations of Israel were clearly delimited so that the life that God envisioned in the land would indeed be possible. I referred to this limiting framework as a notion of "proximate obligation," by which the strength of moral obligations on the rich was proportionate to the "moral proximity" of the ones in need. I believe that this principle was basic to the exodus vision and to the social ethics of the prophets. And I believe that something very like it comes through in this parable. Of course, if Luke really did apply the typology of Moses in the exodus in narrating the person and work of Jesus as the work of a true prophet, then this moral logic of the law and the prophets would be expected.

What generates the powerful moral obligations of the rich man in this story? In my view, it is exactly the same element that does so in the Parable

---

18. Moessner, *Lord of the Banquet,* p. 164.

of the Good Samaritan (Luke 10:29-37). The strong obligation-generating power is in the immediate moral proximity of someone in very dire need. What makes the behavior of the rich people in these parables so very hideous and damnable is not that they had wealth, or even that they enjoyed it. It is that they did so, like the rich in Amos, in spiritual obliviousness to grievous human suffering that was as near to them, in the moral sense, as it could be. It was not merely that they neglected "the poor," but that they neglected a *human being* in need directly in front of them. Jesus creates a scene that suggests that Lazarus has taken up a position there, a moral location, and that the rich man passes him by, not once, but every day that he goes through his gate.

In our parable, the rich man even knows Lazarus by name — a Hebrew name, the name of a brother (and wordplay on Abraham's servant of the same name). But as the dogs lick, and as Lazarus scrapes through his garbage outside, the rich man walks right by, unmoved. He goes inside and "sumptuously" eats and drinks. In contrast, the Good Samaritan on the Jericho road cannot pass by the injured person. At risk to himself, and at considerable cost in money, time, and trouble, he does whatever is needed to get the beaten man back on his feet.

The implication clearly is that the rich man has a very strong obligation to help poor Lazarus. For Lazarus is not "the beating crowd." He is not the global poor in the abstract. He is not even the poor of Israel, Jerusalem, or Nazareth. He is Lazarus by the gate. Lazarus occupies what we might think of as genuine "moral space" on the rich man's doorway. It is difficult to put the notion into analytical terms, but the narrative vividly conveys that Lazarus is more to this rich man than just one more beggar among tens of thousands of others like him on the streets. Lazarus has established a residence and "moral location" in the rich man's life, and so his condition becomes important to the rich man's moral life. His narrative identity and place are what give him a proximity to the rich man and that is what makes his eating and drinking so culpable. Not the poor, in the abstract, but *Lazarus* is his test, and he fails.

This interpretation (in the context of Old Testament ethics) suggests that the moral obligations of affluent Christians are strongest where the moral proximity of people in need is greatest. It would also follow that the obligations are weakest where that proximity is least. As I indicated in the introduction, this is not a book of ethics, and so it does not contain detailed case studies and elaborate sets of applications of this moral idea. It is rather a book of theology and thus offers the elementary moral foundations for ethics. And so I will not go into enough detail on this notion of proximity to provide anything like a complete ethical account of its implications. Doing so properly would require an entire book in its own right. But since the notion is very important to the social theology we are forging, I will elaborate it somewhat further — enough so to suggest the direction that an ethical treatment might take.

In the parable, and in the nation of Israel, the notion of proximity is fairly straightforward, since it is essentially national and geographical. In the ancient world, people generally had little contact with those outside their own region, much less with societies in distant parts of the world. Our modern technology has dramatically changed this natural human condition, and it has greatly complicated certain aspects of our lives — including this one. For most any ordinary person living in an advanced society has, by technological means, possible access to almost any other person anywhere in the world. And this means that there is hardly any poor person on earth that any affluent Christian could not help. This revolutionary new and shrunken world of globalism has thus become the primary context for a great deal of radical Christian moral theory.

Now, I believe it is a good thing for Christians to rethink what faith and economic life mean in terms of globalism. But I also think that a good many Christian authors are mistaken at a very fundamental place in their biblical reasoning. For they commonly assume (or so it seems) that just to have technical access to a poor person is, for any rich person, sufficient to produce strong moral obligations — of the sort that the rich man had to Lazarus, or the rulers of Israel to the poor among their own people. This, of course, is a form of reasoning that we would expect to see stressed by defenders of a utilitarian approach to economic ethics. But we have already observed that the ethics of the Old Testament, at least, grew from moral principles that (at key points) deny these utilitarian ones. The main point of conflict between them is on the moral status of enjoyment in contexts where resources might rather be used to help others — somewhere — in need. For in the Old Testament, the narratives, laws, and prophets clearly affirm many instances of enjoyment in just this sort of context. And what makes this affirmation possible, as noted, has to be a limitation that biblical ethics places on the scope of the obligations that the rich people in Israel have to the poor.

I have suggested that the notion of moral proximity illumines the ethics of that limitation. And I am now proposing that the ethics of Jesus in Luke's Gospel were applications of these very same principles. And if so, the mere accessibility of a poor person to a rich one does not entail moral proximity to him or her, and thus does not entail the existence of obligations such as the ones that moral theorists (like Ron Sider) commonly infer that it does. For strong moral obligations to exist (the kind that have consequences like the ones Jesus describes), in addition to mere accessibility, the relationship between persons has to have the qualities of moral proximity. But just what are these qualities? Are we not at this point engaging in the reprehensible, self-serving casuistry of that scribe who evaded Jesus' demands by asking, "Who is my neighbor?" (Luke 10:29)? That is, of course, the danger of this line of argument. However, just this danger is inherent in any affirmation of enjoyment in any context where others within technical access are in need. So it is no different from the danger that God built into Eden, into the promise of blessing to Abraham and his sons, and into the very life of the people in the Promised Land.

It seems that the primary norm for close proximity is one's immediate community of faith and, within it, a matter of one's divine calling. In Israel, greatest proximity was found generally in the nuclear family, then in the extended family, the tribe, and finally the nation of fellow Israelites. As the slavery laws made evident, Israelites had obligations to Gentiles, but these were considerably weaker than to fellow Hebrews. The strong suggestion is that what I am calling moral proximity arises from within one's most nearly ultimate relationships. The principles are thus not at all messianic, for only the Messiah has undertaken the burden of saving the entire world. They are rather societal, and thus quite personal — the more so, the stronger. It seems that the life of Jesus with the Twelve and others comports entirely with these principles (not least his statement about always having the poor with us), as does the Parable of the Rich Man and Lazarus. We will see that the same sort of societal principles operated in the remarkable economic actions that the first Christians took following Pentecost, and also in the fund-raising texts of the Apostle Paul.

They are also vocational, as with the rulers of Israel whom God specially called to care for his people. The same was true of the religious rulers in Jesus' day, whose calling it was to set the poor free from their sins and to bring them into the family of Abraham, but who instead oppressed and crushed them with their legalism and its disposition of arrogance and self-righteous exclusion.

In our complex advanced societies, our societal connections with others often make for a complicated network, and seeking to discern what is morally proximate for us, as well as what is not, can be very difficult to do with confidence. But if we accept the principle, some things do begin to look more straightforward than otherwise. For our immediate relationships — to spouses, children, extended family, very close friends — emerge as the most proximate ones for most of us. The norm would then be to stretch the notion to our immediate Christian congregation, to our local community, state, and nation. In terms of vocation, primary focus will be on the people and various problems that arise within our proper response to it. For the attorney, it will be on her clients and their cases. For the teacher, it will be on her subject matter and students. For the business executive, it will be on market shares, revenues, maintaining employees' loyalty, and so forth.

I am not at all suggesting that globalism generates no obligations, and I will make this point clearer at the end of the book. Nor am I arguing that global issues cannot become morally proximate for Christians in developed societies. In and through vocation, I believe that they indeed can, and that it often happens that God calls certain people to ministries in places that are remote and far away from their natural communities of obligation. And they express something like the intuition of proximity when they say that God has "laid a burden" on them for one group of people or another. But that he does so by no means makes that form of moral calling the norm for everyone else.

This last point suggests that, within the norm, moral proximity will often mean different things to different Christians. The general principle is the same, but it will mean one thing to an unmarried teacher, another to a banker with a large family, and quite another to a professional politician, stay-at-home mother, truck driver, garbage collector, or lonely artist. Moreover, we may each of us have very special senses of proximity that make little or no sense to anyone else. For instance, I grew up in Nebraska on the Great Plains, and for as long as I can remember I have felt a sense of nearness and obligation to the Native Americans who lived on that land before the pioneers came and settled there. My wife and I are modest supporters of tribal colleges on the reservations in South Dakota (just across the state line) and this support expresses a spiritual connection we feel with the history and circumstances of these extraordinary people. On the other hand, I think it would be greatly misguided on our part to go around insisting that everyone else in our vicinity ought to feel the same way. Moreover, it would be very confused and damaging were we to devote as many of our resources to helping Indian students as we do to the support of our own children, or the students we teach in our own classes. For their moral proximity to us is vastly greater than that of the others. I am well aware that there are ethicists, such as Richard Sennett, who regard this way of thinking as "family idolatry."[19] And there are others who think, as John Wesley did, that our obligations to society are equal in weight to the ones we have to family.[20] Nevertheless, our scriptures — and not least Jesus in Luke — encourage us to think, and to live, otherwise.

THE DISHONEST MANAGER (LUKE 16:1-9)

Though Jesus told the Parable of the Dishonest Manager to his disciples, the way Luke presents it makes clear that some Pharisees overheard it, whether they wished to or not.[21] As noted already, they found his conclusion — "You cannot serve God and wealth" (Luke 16:13) — ridiculous. Their mockery, as noted, prompted his telling of the parable we just discussed. That parable, also as noted, seems deliberately placed in a position that is ironically complementary to the one we are about to look at (or vice versa). The parable is notoriously difficult to interpret for several reasons. It is unclear exactly where it ends, the nature of the manager's action is ambiguous, and we have to decide how the moral sayings in verses 9-13 are related to the story in verses 1-8, as well as to the rest of Luke's narrative.[22] In discussing it, however, I have again taken the advice of Luke Johnson:

> The best reading of this section is the one that pays least attention to the technical problems of tradition and redaction (what came from Jesus and what from Luke) and gives careful consideration to the way in which Luke the author has arranged these materials in this place, as well as the consistent themes of his narrative that appear again in this passage.[23]

19. See Pamela D. Couture, *Blessed Are the Poor?* (Nashville: Abingdon, 1991), pp. 110-11.
20. So Couture, in agreement with Wesley, in *Blessed Are the Poor?* pp. 119-34.
21. Johnson, *The Gospel of Luke,* p. 247.
22. Johnson, *The Gospel of Luke,* pp. 246-47.
23. Johnson, *The Gospel of Luke,* p. 247.

On the whole, I agree with the judgment of Pilgrim that this "unique Lukan parable demonstrates in a striking way Luke's concern for the right use of possessions."[24] This conclusion of course supports my own sense that the story links purposefully with the account of Zacchaeus and the Parable of the Pounds that follow it.

Like Zacchaeus, the main character of this story is a disreputable man who redeems himself by creative and redemptive economic means. It begins with these words: "There was a rich man who had a manager" (16:1). When the rich man discovers that the manager is "squandering his property" (we get no further explanation) he fires him. Facing unemployment and eventual poverty, the manager wonders fearfully about his future. "What will I do, now that my master is taking the position away from me? I am not strong enough to dig, and I am ashamed to beg" (16:3). Not one to give up easily, he devises a plan: "I have decided what to do, so that, when I am dismissed as a manager, people may welcome me into their homes" (16:4). With this in mind, he makes his old rounds and allows people to write off portions of their debts — as much as fifty percent. Jesus ends the parable thus: "And his master commended the dishonest manager because he had acted shrewdly; for the children of this age are more shrewd in dealing with their own generation than are the children of light" (16:8).

Following the parable, Jesus gives his now-famous enigmatic teaching:

> And I tell you, make friends for yourselves by means of dishonest wealth, so that when it is gone they may welcome you into the eternal homes. Whoever is faithful in very little is faithful also in much; and he who is dishonest in a very little is also dishonest in much. (16:9-10)

And as if to explain, he exhorts his disciples to ponder this connection: "If then you have not been faithful in the dishonest wealth, who will entrust to you the true riches?" (16:11). And further:

> No slave can serve two masters; for a slave will either hate the one and love the other, or be devoted to the one and despise the other. You cannot serve both God and wealth. (16:13)

And, as noted, this was the point at which the Pharisees could not contain themselves (Luke 16:14).

24. Pilgrim, *Good News*, p. 125.

One of the most puzzling features of this parable has always been Jesus' approval of the manager's dishonesty. Recent scholarship may shine some light on the problem. For it seems that in the ancient world, managers often ran their own businesses on the side. They would loan their own money to clients, so that a portion of the debt was typically owed to them.[25] If Jesus presumed this convention, then the steward's dishonesty was in the dealings (perhaps offering better interest than his employer did, or the like) that got him fired, but not in his actions to cancel the debts. In its favor, presuming this background does indeed make his actions seem remarkably shrewd, which is the point of the story. The prospect of unemployment might have sent him into a panic about solvency, and he well might have called in his debts. But then what? With no income, he would soon have run out of funds, and none of his former debtors would have cared at all to see him in ruin. The moment of anxiety would have launched him into an isolated, friendless existence in poverty. But (and this reading is consistent with the lessons of Luke 12 on anxiety) the manager did not allow fear to get the upper hand. By making the counterintuitive and very brave move of erasing the debts (and thus making himself penniless) he ingeniously created a wealth of friends who would love him and welcome him any time into their homes. On this reading, it makes good sense both that his old master would commend him and also that Jesus would approve the cunning of his actions.

He is thus for us a model of prudence on a cosmic scale, for he used his position of power in a doubly redemptive way. By not falling into self-contained fear, he had faith enough to free himself to liberate others, and so he redeemed himself and them, too. It is a renewed form of the old vision. By opening up in faith and courage to liberate others, rich people in fact set themselves free and find salvation. And there is no indication in the parable (in spite of common opinion on the subject) that this is at all a bad motive. Jesus' words of explanation (and elsewhere, as with the Rich Fool) stress that people with wealth must be very concerned about their own salvation, and that this comes, ironically, through their actions to save others. We make friends with the unrighteous wealth. I do not know if two interlocking meanings are intended, or just one. (Is it the wealth or other people, or both, that we are to befriend?) But what is clear is that, while wealth originates and comes to people in and through very morally complex systems,

25. Pilgrim, *Good News,* and references, p. 126 and n. 5.

its "unrighteousness" does not invalidate its shrewd, creative use by Christians to bring good to the lives of others. The parallel with Zacchaeus's actions is very strong. For it proves that even in quite wicked economic settings wealth can be converted into an ally for the kingdom of God. And if this is so, then how much more so in non-wicked ones!

To strengthen the point, Jesus restates that old prophetic connection between economic life and eternal life. (Considering his sensitivity to the prophetic structure of Luke's narrative as a whole, and especially in this section of the Gospel, I am surprised that Luke Johnson deems this saying an "appendage" that is to an extent "awkward" in its place.[26]) He says to his followers (and the eavesdropping Pharisees) that if they are not "faithful with the dishonest wealth," they should not expect to inherit the "true riches" (16:11). The point of "making friends" with "dishonest wealth," then, is that doing so is essential to being welcomed into "eternal homes." As in the prophets, so it was with Jesus in Luke. Our faithfulness in the realm of money (if and when we have it) is a measure of our faithfulness to God.

Furthermore, the norm for being faithful in this parable is anything but unworldly. As mentioned, it does include a disposition of freedom from anxiety, courage, and trust, in opposition to covetousness and the cowardice that it veils. But as with Zacchaeus, it also has to do with converting the dark, oppressive powers of the world system ("dishonest wealth") into powers for creation and redemption. And as with the Rich Man and Lazarus, the notion of proximity rises. The steward's moment of moral trial, testing, and triumph was framed by the small boundaries of his job as a money manager. The larger world system, full though it may be of dishonest wealth, fades into the background. Nothing remotely like the rigorous "principle of guilt by implication in fallen structures" comes into play. The real world of moral life is the little group of people who are locked in the grip of debt and entirely at his mercy. When people are drowning, you do not waste time analyzing the pollution levels of the water. What really matters is that the conniving steward brought a brand new life and integrity to that depressed little world. Almost in spite of himself (Adam Smith would be proud) his courageous, creative action converted it into a community of redemption for everyone. How much more integrity and life should the children of light bring to their worlds?

---

26. Johnson, *Sharing Possessions: Mandate and Symbol of Faith* (Philadelphia: Fortress, 1981), p. 17.

In my view this parable links with the story of Zacchaeus in Luke's narrative to put forward a kind of Christianity that is very aggressive within the economic culture. It is a Christianity that affirms Christian involvement, even in economic settings that are dishonest, that is, not exactly pure in nature. For if one has enough power within them, as these two characters obviously did, and if one knows the score, as they also clearly did, then the potential for doing good is very great indeed. To put it in more contemporary terms, the model of Christianity that emerges in the last parts of Luke's original narrative on wealth is world-affirmative and world-transformative, and not in the least a mandate of withdrawal and separation. Perhaps no text in the New Testament serves this model more clearly and powerfully than the Parable of the Pounds as placed and narrated by Luke.

THE POUNDS (LUKE 19:11-27)

To cite Luke Johnson again, "The usual interpretation of this parable takes it as an allegory that is only incidentally connected to the Lukan narrative."[27] On this view, it is a fairly disconnected teaching on the end times, and on holding out in faith until Christ returns. I strongly agree with his judgment that this interpretation quite mistakenly ignores the place of the parable in Luke and, also, the particular shape that Luke gives it. "It is better, therefore, to take the parable as an integral part of Luke's literary work."[28] Indeed, it seems best to understand it — as the other parables in Luke — "as an authorial commentary on the narrative."[29] It comes at the climax of that narrative — enhancing its importance to the interpretation of the whole. And with it Luke "provides the reader with a parable that serves to interpret that larger story."[30] Since that story is largely about Christian economic faith and life, it seems that certain very influential Christian writers on the subject have missed an extremely important point, and have thus invited very serious deficiencies into their accounts of a Christian "view" of wealth and poverty.[31] In this last part of the chapter, I

27. Johnson, *The Gospel of Luke*, p. 293.
28. Johnson, *The Gospel of Luke*, p. 294.
29. Johnson, *The Gospel of Luke*, p. 294.
30. Johnson, *The Gospel of Luke*, p. 294.
31. For instance, Ron Sider, remarkably, fails to include any discussion of this text at all in *Rich Christians*. Since he does not offer an explanation for this strange omission, I will not

shall offer an interpretation of this parable in the context of Luke's placement and distinctive shaping of it, and then I will suggest how we might integrate its teachings into a larger theology of wealth for affluent Christians (as I believe the parable itself does).

As we have proposed, the story of Zacchaeus (Jesus' last encounter with a rich person) brings a gracious resolution of the dreadful tension that Luke (through Jesus) had created for his wealthy Christian readers. The way into the kingdom for Zacchaeus was not poverty, or even withdrawal from his home and line of work. Salvation comes to his house through creative and redemptive uses of his economic power. From its placement immediately after, it is pretty obvious that Luke presents the Parable of the Pounds as an interpretation of that astonishing part of his narrative. And if so, given what we have proposed as the significance of that part of the narrative, Luke places this parable as a commentary on the entire theme of wealth for Christians. As I will also propose (with others), the parable has a broader purpose and function still, which is, together with the example of Zacchaeus, to give a model for how Christians are to understand life in the world until Christ's promised return. For it seems that, by the time Luke wrote his Gospel, the hope that his return would be imminent had passed, and that a new generation was facing the question of what Christian faith and practice ought to be in what was emerging as "the long run."

The immediate connection is clear, as Luke inserts the remark, "As they heard these things" (about the salvation of Zacchaeus) "he proceeded to tell them a parable" (Luke 19:11). The Parable of the Pounds thus reaffirms and expands the lessons of Zacchaeus's story. But the broader and larger eschatological connection is clear, too, as Luke explains that Jesus told the story "because he was near Jerusalem, and because they supposed that the kingdom of God was to appear immediately" (19:11). Part of Luke's distinctive purpose (Matthew gives no such context) was to bring home to his readers that this expectation was improper. Luke wished to press the point that Jesus himself had taught that there would be a time "between the times" — that is, the time during which the kingdom comes, but is not

---

speculate on why he has done so. But if my reading of the parable is even marginally correct, the implications for his entire theological view of our subject are fairly devastating. Moreover, perhaps the most prominent of all the liberation theologians, Gustavo Gutiérrez, in his famous pioneering theological work, *A Theology of Liberation* (Maryknoll, N.Y.: Orbis, 1973), also fails to include an interpretation of this parable.

yet consummated in its fullness. In this indeterminate meantime the servants of the king must live in faith and do his work until he finally comes. The parable thus gives Luke's last vision of what faithfulness means, and of course (as with the previous texts) it is centered on faithfulness in economic life on the parts of Christians entrusted with material wealth and power. It is, as it were, prophetic theology placed in the new form of Christian eschatology.

So begins the story: "A nobleman went into a distant country to get royal power for himself and then return" (19:12). This nobleman gives each of his ten servants a pound to trade with until he comes back.[32] When he returns, he asks each servant to give an account of what they have done. The first servant has turned his pound into ten. In words that seem deliberately to connect the story with the Parable of the Dishonest Manager, the master commends him, saying, "Well done, good slave! Because you have been trustworthy in a very small thing, take charge of ten cities" (19:17).[33] The second servant has converted his pound into five, and so the master gives him rule over five cities. But the third servant has hidden his pound in a piece of cloth. He excuses himself, saying, "I wrapped it in a piece of cloth, for I was afraid of you, because you are a harsh man; you take up what you did not deposit, and reap what you did not sow" (19:20-21). At this the nobleman is enraged and so condemns the man out of his own mouth: "You knew, did you, that I was a harsh man, taking up what I did not deposit and reaping what I did not sow? Why then did you not put my money into the bank? Then when I returned, I could have collected it with interest" (19:22-23).

The royal man then instructs the other servants to take the man's pound and to give it to the man who has ten. Sensing their incredulity, Jesus explains the hard truth. "I tell you, to all those who have, more will be given; but from those who have nothing, even what they have will be taken away" (19:26). As if this is not severe enough, the master then commands

32. Besides the rhetorical context, there are differences of detail between this Parable of the Pounds and Matthew's Parable of the Talents (25:14-30). Matthew has only three servants, whereas Luke has ten. Matthew's servants each receive large sums of money for investment, whereas Luke's receive only about three months' wages "to trade with."

33. Luke Johnson rightly notes the connection between the language of this parable and that of the Parable of the Dishonest Manager, and thus with its teaching "that the followers of Jesus are expected to use their possessions in a creative way." Johnson, *Sharing Possessions*, p. 18.

his servants to bring his enemies before him, those "who did not want me to be king over them" (19:27), and has them slain in his presence.

The parable delivers another blow to our predictable moral universe. Seeming to demolish the Old Testament vision, the "radical Jesus" had come cursing the rich and blessing the poor. But we have learned that he did not come to destroy Moses and the prophets. He came to fulfill them in the new age of his own coming. The Parable of the Pounds is the last act in this creative drama that has descended from strength to weakness, and now rises back again to strength. We have, in a sense, been taken into the death and resurrection of material affluence as a cosmic good.

There is not much in Christian theology today that honors God as a warrior-king, or that honors the courage of godly people in the marketplace. But this is a parable of power and the enlargement of dominion through wealth. It is a parable that honors the fearsome courage and strength of a warrior and king, who will not stop until his realm is enlarged over all the earth. It is a parable that honors the strength and courage of his servants who are fruitful in the worldly realms of power. It is a parable that honors the *enlargement* of people who would become stronger, and would make their master stronger, through the creation of wealth. And it is also a parable of dire warning against a spirit of timidity and fruitlessness in our response to the world. It takes us back, through Christ, into something more profound even than the social ethics of the prophet. It goes to the very foundations of their message, which is the creation itself, and the existence of dominion and delight that God envisioned for human beings.

The two praiseworthy servants create a most interesting picture of faithfulness. More to the point, they create a most provocative image of the master whom they serve. Although he is away for most of it, his spirit dominates the whole parable. He is a powerful figure, a man of fierce enlargement. This, I believe, is the right metaphor for understanding and applying the whole story. Unlike Zacchaeus and the Dishonest Manager (or the negative lessons of Lazarus and the Rich Man), virtue for the two servants is not connected with an obligation to empower the poor. It is rather about their obligation to enter the world and, by means of trade and investment, to enlarge the master's power and dominion within it while he is away. I am not proposing that this broad mandate is in conflict with the narrower redemptive one. On the contrary, Luke has made clear that we accomplish the one in and through the other — at least in part. But the larger eschatological message to wealthy believers just is that our king has gone to take a kingdom, and this defines the spirit in which they have to serve him. To represent his character in the world, then, they (we) must be the sorts of people that a warrior-king can identify with, be proud of, and approve at the end. In the "small" matter of money, they have proved themselves worthy of greatness.

But then there is also the servant who has failed. We are familiar with Jesus' many warnings about the dangers of wealth, the perils of "success." With this character, however, Jesus sounds a very different alarm, one that is missing from moral theology today. He warns against being so conscious of our master's severity that we retreat, withdraw from the world, and thus render our economic lives fruitless. The servant's excuse sounds pious. For it appeals to the demanding, austere quality of the master.[34] But in truth he is a coward who cannot take the stresses of responsibility in the world. The true servant of a warrior-king cannot be a coward. A little heartburn and fatigue will not stop him from putting on the armor every morning, going to the office, and doing his best to win the day in his small world. Most men, and increasing numbers of professional women, will understand this immediately. The economic world is a battlefield, and it takes wit, bravery, and a strong will that is loath to retreat, much less surrender. The moral leadership of the church does not understand this very well. In my whole life I have never once heard (nor heard of) a sermon on the dangers of cowardice in the business world, much less on the virtues of bravery competing within it. But the parable (in its context) is a strong warning against those who would erode the strong, aggressive, competitive spirit of behavior (particularly economic behavior) among Christians who believe that their king has given them pounds to trade until he comes. Let us beware lest we find ourselves feebly wrapping our pounds in pieces of cloth, covering lives of fear and escapism with pious excuses about God's indifference to the things of the world, and his severity toward those who work within it.

Quite obviously, Jesus did not pronounce an unqualified blessing upon economic gain. His life and teachings all demonstrate the conditions for godliness that must exist before our gains become true enlargement of

---

34. Marshall suggests that the meaning of the servant's statement, "You take what you did not deposit, and reap what you did not sow," suggests that the servant thought, even were he to make money, the nobleman would take it from him anyway. See *Commentary on Luke*, pp. 706-7.

his kingdom, before they become fruitfulness. However, if those conditions have been recreated, then the creative, productive economic life becomes something that is absolutely true to our humanity and to the identity of God. For people who have good reason to believe that God has blessed and entrusted them with wealth and the ability to create it, creative and productive economic living is both a mandate and a blessing. They should view it as good, and so should the moral leadership of the church. There comes a time in the lives of such people when agonizing over imagined guilt and the Lord's displeasure drags on into nothing more than glorified diffidence and sanctimonious fear. Having done what they can to satisfy the conditions, committing themselves to lives of servant-dominion, professional people must begin to cultivate a spirituality of royal confidence in the goodness of their calling. Jesus tells us to be brave.

This reaches all the way back to the mandate and blessing at creation: "Be fruitful, and multiply, fill the earth and subdue it." After all the requisite qualifications have been made, that is essentially what human life is all about. The parable again blesses fruitfulness in the economic realm.[35] That this is so comes through in the system of rewards that the parable presents. It strongly suggests a connection between faithful enlargement of one's economic position (properly done, of course) in this life and greater enlargement in the life to come. This is the twist on the connection between economic life and eternal life that we found in the Wisdom books, and more enigmatically in the instance of the Dishonest Manager.

Furthermore, as noted, this interpretation suggests a view of life in the culture, including economic life, that gives it considerably more importance and value than we might think it has. Most people, even professional people, feel they are ultimately insignificant, that their work does not really matter in any ultimate way. At most they may see their work as a means to an end, but not as something that is in itself good. The Parable of the Pounds, however, dignifies the "small kingdom," and its small queen or king. It suggests that the real treasure of human history is hidden in ordinary people enlarging realms that hardly seem great. C. S. Lewis once wrote that a common charwoman carrying out her duties in faith may well be changed, in the kingdom of God, into a creature of such glory that we

---

35. As Brian Griffiths states, "It is difficult not to broaden the lesson of the parable so that its meaning extends to all the resources which we have been given." *The Creation of Wealth*, p. 48.

would be tempted to worship her. The message, I believe, is to enlarge and to dignify whatever realm God has given us. We should go about our work with royal pride and dignity.

The essence of life is not in the quantity and visibility of our dominion, but in its quality. This only the nobleman truly knows and judges, and he will reward our labors as only he can. By his grace there is eternal glory buried within the passing smallness of our lives. The teacher, the doctor, the lawyer, the insurance salesperson, the small motel manager, the fry cook, the owner of the toy store, the professional athlete, the school janitor, the film actor, the hardware merchant, the corporate executive, the college administrator — great or small — all have pounds to trade with royal grace, purpose, and effect. Such servants befit the warrior and king of the universe whom they serve. And the parable leads us to trust that what we do in the small matters of unrighteous wealth, provided we do it in keeping with faith in the King, reaches in some indescribable way into eternity, and gives shape to the homes and dominion we will have in the age to come.

CHAPTER EIGHT

Narratives of Wealth in the Early Church

They would sell their possessions and goods.

ACTS 2:45

In this chapter we shall explore key New Testament narratives and teaching on economic life in the book of Acts, in the writings of the Apostle Paul, and in the epistle of James. It seems natural to begin with Acts, since doing so will enable us to resume our study of Luke's thematic treatment of the topic. Furthermore, the early narratives of Acts are among the most important and controversial in the history of Christian thinking on wealth and possessions. And they are very important to any theology of wealth.

Luke relates the extraordinary action that the first Christians took, following Pentecost. As with the exodus and the Incarnation, the outpouring of Pentecost was no mere spiritual event. For, as if in a single narrative breath, Luke relates that about three thousand people repented, devoted themselves to the apostles' teaching and breaking of bread, and that "all who believed were together and had all things in common; they would sell their possessions and goods and distribute the proceeds to all, as any had need" (Acts 2:44-45). This visible display of new life sealed their words with the stamp of truth, and so Luke lets us know that "day by day the Lord added to their number those who were being saved" (2:47). A bit later on (for reasons we will consider), Luke repeats his description in more detail, writing that they were "of one heart and soul, and no one claimed private ownership of any possessions, but everything they owned was held in common" (4:32). Luke narrates that the outcome of this behavior was that "With great power the apostles gave their testimony to the resurrection of the Lord Jesus, and great grace was upon them all. There was not a needy person among them" (Acts 4:33). He explains that "as many as owned lands or houses sold them and brought the proceeds of what was sold. They laid it at the apostles' feet, and it was distributed to each as any had need" (Acts 4:34-35).

As church historian Justo Gonzalez has written, these are "two of the most debated passages in Acts."[1] The most fundamental issue is whether the described actions ever really happened at all. Some scholars have proposed that Luke must have presented a kind of "idyllic fiction" as a picture of what things would look like in the ideal church.[2] I have no doubt that Luke Johnson is correct in his thesis that Luke has indeed used wealth symbolically in Luke-Acts, and also that Luke described the Jerusalem community in somewhat general and idealized terms.[3] The books of Luke and Acts are, after all, a single work of literary, narrative art, and not a merely straightforward record of events in history.[4] And as Johnson also observes, this view of the text makes the matter of its "historical basis" a very complicated one.[5] On the other hand, I take very seriously Luke's explicit claim to have gathered and written "an orderly account" that grew from the testimonies of eyewitnesses whom Luke, "after investigating everything carefully," judged to be trustworthy sources of the truth (Luke 1:1-4). It seems best to think that Luke presented his descriptions of economic life in Jerusalem as rhetorically carved summaries of real events. And it seems that he gave these summaries the very sort of symbolic, theological literary function and purpose that (as we shall see) Johnson ascribes to them. That rhetorical technique is continuous with what I have proposed (with others) that Luke used in his Gospel. As with narrative in the Gospel of Jesus, in

---

1. Justo L. Gonzalez, *Faith and Wealth: A History of Early Christian Ideas on the Origin, Significance, and Use of Money* (San Francisco: Harper & Row, 1990), p. 79.

2. Gonzalez, *Faith and Wealth*, p. 80. Note his criticisms of Luke Johnson's view, which he takes to be of this kind.

3. Also see Craig L. Blomberg, *Neither Poverty Nor Riches: A Biblical Theology of Material Possessions* (Grand Rapids: Eerdmans, 1999), p. 160.

4. See the discussion of Luke-Acts as narrative in Luke Timothy Johnson, *The Literary Function of Possessions in Luke-Acts* (Missoula, Mont.: Scholars, 1977), pp. 1-28.

5. Johnson, *Possessions in Luke-Acts*, p. 5.

Acts Luke uses his material on the church to narrate both affirmative and negative examples of economic life among the people of God.

At any rate, the secondary issue of debate is an exegetical and interpretive one. Aside from its historical reference, intense debates also exist over precisely what sort of economic arrangement Luke describes. In ancient theology the church understood it (as with the life of Christ) as the literal framework for the order of monastic life and its ideal of poverty.[6] Mainline Protestant theologians, such as Luther, Zwingli, and Calvin, also interpreted the arrangement as one of divestment, but of course they repudiated this literal application (as they did monasticism) and explained it as unrepeatable history with enduring spiritual meaning for Christians.[7] The Anabaptists also understood it this way, but they sought to rebuild the entire church along the communal economic lines they believed that Luke set forth in Acts.[8]

In more recent times worldwide debates on preferred social and economic systems have amplified controversies over the interpretation of these summaries in Acts. In prosecuting their larger case against capitalism, certain Christian writers have appealed to Luke's summaries. Art Gish, for instance, writes that in these texts "private property is abolished," and thus judges that "as Christians we need to make a complete break with the capitalist economy."[9] In his view, the book of Acts is manifestly clear in teaching that "Capitalism stands opposed to *koinonia*."[10] As an alternative, he favors small Christian counter-communities, offering as an example the New Covenant Fellowship (of which he is a member), a communal vegetable farm using "a minimum of machinery, most of the work being done by hand." Community members are committed to the virtue of a kind of "poverty" that is based in "the logic of the Incarnation" and that leads to "simple living."[11] Other writers affirm his judgment that the narratives in Acts promote divestment of property, but they apply the purported principle in terms of state socialism.[12]

In the main body of this discussion I shall explain in detail why I do not

6. Johnson, *Possessions in Luke-Acts,* p. 1.

7. Johnson, *Possessions in Luke-Acts,* pp. 1-2.

8. Johnson, *Possessions in Luke-Acts,* p. 2.

9. Art Gish, "Decentralist Economics," in *Wealth and Poverty: Four Christian Views,* ed. Robert Clouse (Downers Grove, Ill.: InterVarsity, 1984), p. 139.

10. Gish, "Decentralist Economics," p. 151.

11. Gish, "Decentralist Economics," p. 151.

12. John Gladwin, "Centralist Economics," in *Wealth and Poverty,* ed. Clouse, pp. 181-97.

accept this communalistic interpretation. I am in agreement with those interpreters (probably the majority of recent commentators) who judge that Luke
does not describe the abolition of personal property, but rather gives creative
new and distinctly Christian meaning to the idea of property. I will give the
specific supporting arguments for this view in that part of the chapter, and so
will not go into them now. But the core of the inductive part of the argument
is grammatical — Luke's use of the imperfect rather than the aorist tense of
the verbs referring to the economic actions works against a description of divestment on a principle of property abolition. Moreover, the deductive part
of the argument is thematic. For if Luke's ethics indeed grew from the ethical
traditions of the prophets, then the divestment view is implausible, to say the
least. There are also historical reasons for rejecting that view.

This last comment brings us to the third problem with Luke's two
summaries. It is the hermeneutical problem. Whatever we think Luke's assertions are, it is not obvious how the actions he describes apply to Christians in following generations under new Christian and cultural circumstances. Moreover, on some readings, such as the divestment one, it is not
obvious that Luke presents a model at all, or that what he presents is at all
binding in a moral way upon believers outside of that first community in
Jerusalem. Quite a few scholars accept the divestment view exegetically but
judge hermeneutically that the practice of the Jerusalem church was a one-
time affair. Historian Barry Gordon, for instance, judges that the Jerusalem
experiment of divestment was a splendid failure, and that it was thus a
good lesson on how *not* to order communities. For once the little church
left the protecting refuge of property, all it took was a stretch of bad
weather to devastate and impoverish them.[13] Other authors have gone so
far as to accuse the Jerusalem leadership of gross incompetence in financial
matters, and thus deem them counter-examples of how to go about ar-
ranging the economics of societies of any kind.[14] In support of this judgment they appeal to evidence that outside Jerusalem Christians indeed did
not follow that original apostolic plan. On that evidence, which Gordon
summarizes at length, he offers the conclusion "the Jerusalem case was a
unique one."[15] And the research of social historian Wayne Meeks offers

---

13. Barry Gordon, *The Economic Problem in Biblical and Patristic Thought* (Leiden:
Brill, 1989), p. 79.

14. J. A. Zeisler, *Christian Asceticism* (Grand Rapids: Eerdmans, 1973), p. 110.

15. Gordon, *Economic Problem*, p. 81.

very good reasons for seeing the economic arrangements of the first urban churches as quite creative and diverse in form.[16] It seems that the primary influence of the Jerusalem model was, as noted, upon early Christian monasticism, but not on mainstream Christian ethics.[17]

There are several issues to sort out in this context. As to the larger hermeneutical question, I find it implausible that Luke presented these summaries as mere histories and not as thematic models for Christian ethics. This reading is completely alien to everything that we have considered in our scrutiny of Luke's purpose and methods as an author. As will be clear, it seems very obvious that Luke develops the use of his summaries as models later in Acts when he poses the figure of Barnabas, on the one hand, against the negative characters of Ananias and his wife Sapphira (Acts 4:36–5:11). This counter-pairing (reminiscent of similar devices that Luke employed in the Gospel — recall the rich man and Zacchaeus) cannot work without the presentation of the earlier summaries as models of some kind. But furthermore, the divestment interpretation, rigid and alien to biblical tradition as it is, makes the use of it as a model very difficult, if not impossible, for the Christian. Since I do not accept this exegetical reading, however, I do not inherit the special hermeneutical difficulties that come with it. On the view that the descriptive summaries in Acts are highly stylistic examples that enshrine revivified prophetic ideals for God's people, we may discern conceptually between those ideals and the one-time economic strategy in which Jerusalem Christians elected to apply them. And on this distinction, the fact that early Christians outside Jerusalem did not use this same strategy does not entail that they ignored the ideals enshrined within it. On this analysis, the diversity of strategies may well be evidence to support the judgment that Luke did present his descriptions as models. I believe that close scrutiny of those churches' actions in fact does bear this judgment out, as I will show in the sections on Paul's writings and James.

So in sum, in reference to the three major problems that come up with the interpretation of these key texts I presume (1) that Luke gives highly stylized and morally thematic accounts of events that really did happen, (2) that what happened was not the abolition of property, but a creative

16. Wayne Meeks, *The First Urban Christians: The Social World of the Apostle Paul* (New Haven: Yale University Press, 1983).

17. Gonzalez, *Faith and Wealth*.

approach to property, and (3) that this approach embodied ideals that are normative for all Christians. It remains to show now in more detail what that creative approach was, what its ideals were, and how they might apply to Christian economic life in our time.

RETHINKING PROPERTY

The remarkable story of Barnabas, Ananias, and Sapphira gives the most detailed impression of the mechanisms, and it clearly reveals that the system respected personal freedom and control over property. This was not a model of decapitalization or disinvestment, but something else. In this story of economic good and evil, reminding readers perhaps on purpose of the similar story of Achan in Joshua,[18] Luke presents Barnabas as a godly man who "sold a field that belonged to him, then brought the money, and laid it at the apostles' feet" (Acts 4:37). This action of Barnabas obviously exemplifies what the most admirable wealthy people were doing in Luke's account. (It also introduces him into the narrative as a righteous man, later to be teamed with Paul in the great missionary sections of the book.) It is worth noting that in the previous verses his emergence in this light is connected with a clear allusion to Deuteronomy 15:4-5, in which the Year of Release presents this ideal for the people in the Promised Land: "There will be no one in need among you" (v. 4). As Luke Johnson writes, "Luke portrays the believing community as the faithful Israel which enjoys the blessing of God on the land."[19] To me Johnson's judgment (as usual) seems right, in contrast to the widespread view that Luke's summaries stemmed from a philosophical ideal of friendship, as in Plato and Aristotle.[20] We should not underestimate the extent to which Luke has exodus theology and ethics in the background — especially as we begin making theological deductions of our own. In the sharing of goods the people became a true Israel, and in his action Barnabas proved himself to be a true Israelite in the spirit of Moses.

The ideal behavior of Barnabas is thus a stark frame of reference for the

18. See F. F. Bruce, *The Book of Acts,* The New International Commentary on the New Testament (Grand Rapids: Eerdmans, 1953), p. 110.

19. Johnson, *Possessions in Luke-Acts,* p. 200.

20. See Robert C. Tannehill, *The Narrative Unity of Luke-Acts: A Literary Interpretation* (Minneapolis: Fortress, 1990), p. 45.

contrary actions of Ananias and Sapphira. They pretend to follow the example of Barnabas and others. They, too, sell a piece of property and present the money to the apostles. But Luke relates of the husband that "with his wife's knowledge, he kept back some of the proceeds, and brought only a part and laid it at the apostles' feet" (5:1-2). The contrast is dramatic, and it heightens as Peter (prophetically) sees through their conspiracy and confronts Ananias. He asks him why Satan has filled his heart "to lie to the Holy Spirit and to keep back part of the proceeds of the land" (5:3). Peter's reason for judging their action inexcusable reveals details of the economic strategy that we would otherwise not get from Luke's more concise descriptions. "While it remained unsold, did it not remain your own? And after it was sold, were not the proceeds at your disposal?" (5:4). In Peter's line of argument we thus learn that earlier statements about having all things in common did not mean abolishing private property at all or even setting up communal mechanisms of ownership. On the contrary, the entire moral critique that Peter makes of Ananias presupposes a very strong notion of ownership on his part. He was under no obligation to sell the land in the first place — because it was *his* land. And even after he did sell it, the proceeds remained at his disposal, in trust to distribute as *he* deemed right. As scholar F. F. Bruce puts it, "No compulsion had been laid on Ananias to sell his property."[21]

The affirmation of ownership in this story is so strong that New Testament scholar Jouette Bassler judges it simply to be in conflict with what Luke had just written.[22] At least her premises are correct. Luke does make a strong affirmation of property rights. And she is also correct to say that "it is also surprising to find the general summaries so quickly contradicted."[23] Indeed, if that were so, it would be quite a surprise to readers of Luke, as disciplined as he was in his rhetoric and presentation of facts and normative themes. However, I believe the more reasonable inference from the passage is that what Luke contradicts is her interpretation of the summaries in these chapters and, on the assumption that Luke was tolerably aware of his own deeper convictions about such things, her interpretation is mistaken, and the correct reading of the summaries is consistent with the affirmation of property in this story.

---

21. Bruce, *The Book of Acts,* p. 113.

22. Jouette Bassler, *God and Mammon: Asking for Money in the New Testament* (Nashville: Abingdon, 1991), p. 126.

23. Bassler, *God and Mammon,* p. 126.

At any rate, the sin of Ananias and Sapphira was clearly not that they withheld property, but that they lied "to the Holy Spirit" about doing so. The outcome of the story — Peter pronounces divine judgment and they drop dead on the spot — is entirely consistent with the prophetic theme, and with the warning of Deuteronomy (against the background of Eden) that on that day, as Moses promised, "you shall surely perish" (Deut. 8:20). It also sustains Luke's theme of conflict and devious opposition to the new thing that God is doing in the world. Even as his new church has just begun, like the creation when it was finished, devilish powers seek to destroy it from within — through a man and woman. As the story flows onward, more obvious powers will arise to destroy it from without. But they, too, personified by Saul of Tarsus, will be thwarted and even, as in his case, turned around for good.

But even Ron Sider concedes that the church in Acts "did not insist on absolute economic equality. Nor did they abolish private property."[24] For quite aside from the story just discussed, the grammar of Luke's description certainly supports his assertion. As writers often point out, Luke's unusual use of the imperfect tense of the verbs, instead of the expected aorist, warrants a picture of ongoing strategic liquidation, as needs arose, and not one of divestment all at once.[25] As Pilgrim judges, "What Luke has in mind is not a total selling of all one's possessions at one time and then living off the proceeds from that moment on, but a continual selling and sharing as the needs emerged or as the treasury became low."[26]

Furthermore (and lastly on this point), there are partly deductive reasons for believing that Luke did not describe the elimination of property. At bottom, this follows from the assumption that Luke was narrating the fulfillment of prophetic spiritual and moral tradition, and certainly not its denial. The allusion to the Promised Land in Acts 4:34 is but an explicit indicator of this literary frame in Luke-Acts, as we have seen. So in this New Israel the people now used their wealth in a manner that was true to the liberating vision of the exodus. And if so, the ideals of this vision must have endured in some form. Moreover, I very much suspect that what endures is not just an affirmation of property, but also (in some form) an affirmation of the dominion and delight which was its human purpose. In

24. Ronald J. Sider, *Rich Christians in an Age of Hunger,* 20th Anniversary Revision (Dallas: Word, 1997), p. 90.

25. See Gonzalez, among others, on this point. *Faith and Wealth,* pp. 82-83.

26. Pilgrim, *Good News to the Poor: Wealth and Poverty in Luke-Acts* (Minneapolis: Augsburg, 1981), p. 151.

the next subsection I will seek to show that this is so, and that the moral ideals of Luke's summaries support an ethics of affluence that is more in keeping with Old Tradition than with modern utilitarianism.

RETHINKING THE ETHICS OF PROPERTY

It is fairly common to read in Christian moral literature that the ideals of Luke's summaries in Acts are those that we associate with utilitarian ethics. As previously noted, I am using this term in the limited sense that to attain the good in economic life requires putting one's resources to the best use possible. And in this way of thinking, "best use" means meeting the greatest need that one is able to meet without doing harm to oneself or others. In practice, this approach makes it very difficult to imagine circumstances in real life where it would not be immoral (much less morally good) to enjoy some portion of one's affluence. For in our shrunken world of globalism, there are never circumstances in which no needy people are within our technical reach to help them.

I have already argued that, even if we grant that this approach to ethics may be coherent, its core principle is not in accord with the ethics of the Old Testament, nor with that of Jesus in Luke's Gospel. And if that is true, then it seems pretty certain that it does not comport with the ethics that Luke describes in Acts. For it seems that he upholds the Jerusalem approach as a model of Old Testament, prophetic tradition in a new messianic form. Nevertheless, certain Christian writers discern principles in these narratives that are very like those of utilitarianism. It is the view that affluent Christians are morally obliged to bring their standard of living down to extremely low levels in order to help liberate the desperately poor of the world from extreme poverty.

Liberation theologian Gustavo Gutiérrez approves the moral reasoning of widely cited ethicist Jean Du Pont:

> If goods are held in common, it is not therefore in order to become poor for love of an ideal of poverty; rather it is so that there will be no more poor. The ideal pursued is, once again, charity, a true love for the poor.[27]

27. Gustavo Gutiérrez, *A Theology of Liberation: History, Politics and Salvation*, trans. and ed. Sister Caridad Inda and John Eagleson (Maryknoll, N.Y.: Orbis, 1973), p. 301.

I presume that Du Pont (with Gutiérrez) has used the term "poor" in two distinct senses in this statement, and thus that it is not obviously incoherent. For an ungracious reading would have him making claims that entail, first, that poverty is a good and then second, that it is an evil. It seems that the "poverty" that affluent Christians are obliged to live in is not the same as the "poverty" from which they are to liberate the poor. So the message is not that the affluent should become impoverished in that extreme way, but that they (we) must trim their (our) commonplace lifestyle to the extent that considerable excesses are now devoted instead to people in greater need.

This is also the message of North American writer Ron Sider, leader of the "simpler living" movement among radical evangelical Christians, mainly in the United States. Sider does not advocate that rich Christians should live in poverty, but he does advocate (as we have seen) an ethics that places a very strong obligation upon them to reduce their enjoyments. My complaint (as noted) is that his principle for doing so seems to leave no clear moral room for any enjoyments at all. I do not see how his occasional assertions that "some enjoyments" are good can be consistent with the driving principle of his ethics. For a great many of his moral directives seem to embody the core principle of utilitarianism.

At any rate, Luke's descriptions of the Jerusalem church are a very crucial place in Scripture for this kind of argument about the ethics of Christian lifestyle. And so we must briefly consider their reasons for interpreting Luke that way. The backbone of the case for Christian "poverty" of the sort advocated by Gutiérrez or (to say the same thing) the "simpler living" that Sider promotes is Luke's statement that they distributed the proceeds "as any had need" (Acts 2:45). As stated this description certainly makes it sound like they applied straightforward utilitarian principles. Sider infers from Luke's description that "They simply gave until the needs were met."[28] Furthermore, he extends the principle, which he calls "economic *koinonia*," to cover the ethics of affluent Christians in their relationships with poor Christians and non-Christians around the world. In this application Sider appeals to the so-called Great Collection of Paul (which ironically was for the Jerusalem church that was by that time poor).[29] I will come back to Paul's fundraising later in this chapter,

28. Sider, *Rich Christians*, p. 81.
29. Sider, *Rich Christians*, pp. 83-89.

and I will register my objections to this use of Paul's texts (for the Great Collection had very different purposes than the actions of the Jerusalem Christians). But first, I wish to offer an interpretation of Luke's summaries in Acts that is more clearly in keeping with the enduring theology and ethics of biblical tradition.

First, as Sider himself concedes, Luke's descriptions are incomplete. (This is a sure sign of the rhetorical shaping and idealizing of the scene.) For in reality it seems clear enough that not all who had homes did sell them:

> "No one said that any of the things which he possessed was his own." That does not mean that everyone donated everything. Later in Acts we read that John Mark's mother, Mary, still owned her house (12:12). Additional passages indicate that others retained some private property.[30]

So the situation behind the literary scenes was more complex than we might think. Luke relates, for instance, in thematic terms, that Barnabas sold a field and laid the entire proceeds at the apostles' feet (unlike Ananias and Sapphira). But this narrative scene gives us no intellectual right to infer that Barnabas sold all his property, or even that he ceased to be well off in comparison with average Israelites. So while Luke's scenes convey a great deal of information about the strategy that affluent members of the community employed in order to help the poorer members, they give us practically no information about how these actions affected their standard of living. No clear utilitarian principle emerges, nor even a principle of voluntary poverty or simpler living.

In my view the principle is that of the exodus placed in prophetic and boldly messianic terms. In reference to interpreters who have sought to build ethics of Christian communalism on these passages, Luke Johnson makes this very severe judgment: "The scriptural basis for the community of possessions as the ideal way for Christians to share goods is slender, superficial, selective, and suspect."[31] The main reasons (as noted) are linked with failure to grasp the carved, symbolic rhetoric of the narrative. I believe the same judgment, for the same sort of reason, applies to interpreters like Sider who seek to build an ethics of simpler living from them.

A second feature of the narrative also weighs against utilitarian sorts of

---

30. Sider, *Rich Christians*, p. 81.

31. Luke Timothy Johnson, *Sharing Possessions: Mandate and Symbol of Faith* (Philadelphia: Fortress, 1981), p. 131.

readings. Gutiérrez, Sider, and others ignore that Luke has given consider-able effort to showing that the strong moral obligations of the rich to the poor were confined to the new Christian community. That Luke has deliber-ately done so is yet another indication of his purpose, which was to narrate the birth of a New Israel — the true Israel — in the context of a new exodus. We do not need to rehearse the points on moral proximity that we consid-ered in the chapter on the exodus, and then again in our discussion on Jesus' teachings and parables. Nevertheless, that same sort of exodus thinking seems to operate in Luke's understanding of the new community of Jesus Christ and the Holy Spirit. In his scenes there is not a trace of interest evident in society on the outside. That, of course, does not imply that Luke had no such interest, or that Christians today ought not to have it. But what it does seem to imply is that the very strong moral obligations we have in view do not exist generally (as they do in utilitarian ethics) but only under special conditions. That is to say, they do not exist between just any rich person and just any poor person, but only between rich and poor persons who are re-lated by means of faith in the true God, and now in Jesus Christ. So I believe it is improper and heavy-handed for writers to use Luke's descriptions of ac-tion in this setting as moral paradigms for the actions that affluent people must take on behalf of poor people anywhere and everywhere.

Of course we need paradigms for the radically new and complex cir-cumstances that have come with globalism, but I do not think we can get them from Luke's thematic scenes in Acts. We must get them rather from a more complex analysis of economic development in the context of Chris-tian commitment to the proposition that all human beings — Christian or not — are creatures made in the image and likeness of God.

But there is one last feature of Luke's summaries that has bearing on this discussion. It is Luke's vivid picture of the new community in constant celebration and delight. He stresses that the first gatherings were more like feasts than like some of our contemporary somber services. In breaking bread they mirrored the banquets of Deuteronomy as filtered through the eating and drinking the disciples had enjoyed with Jesus. In the *koinonia* of these very first Christians, it seems that they adumbrated in the present the messianic banquet that was yet to come. This feature of their gatherings also supports thinking that the ideals Luke upholds for Christians are those of the exodus in Christian form. They are ideals in which the people embody God's vision of human dominion and delight and the virtues of humility and compassion that follow from it.

JAMES AND THE GREAT ECONOMIC CRISIS

In the decade or so that followed Pentecost the church in Jerusalem had become ravaged by persecution and poverty. The letters of James and Paul both reflect this changed situation. The epistle of James may very well be the earliest Christian writing now in existence. The tradition also may be true that its author was the brother of Jesus, chief elder of the community in Jerusalem.[32] The interpretation of James that I offer, however, does not depend in any direct way upon these historical judgments (although I happen to accept them).

In the recent past, under the dominating influence of form critics like Martin Dibelius, scholars generally believed that James was a loose collection of sayings, and that it contained no coherent structure or theology.[33] This opinion has changed considerably as commentators have identified a deliberate literary structure and theology.[34] There is good reason to think that the main readership of James was economically poor, and that the trials and sufferings he describes are in part due to their poverty. Moreover, his message is decidedly negative toward certain wealthy people that he has in view, as it is toward the significance of material things in general.

In fact, for this reason there is considerable opinion in scholarship that James (like Luke, it is believed) condemned the rich and favored a model of divestment and poverty for Christians.[35] As Barry Gordon writes, "The writer of James gives the strongest impressions that this [divestment] is the only wise course for a Christian with assets."[36] Obviously written to exhort poor Christians, James indeed contains a profound critique of the rich. First, very like Jesus, he makes relative the importance of wealth. Riches are fleeting, they do not bring happiness, and so poverty is not the worst possible condition to be in (1:9-10). Like Jesus (recall the rich fool), James blasts those who think commerce and trade will bring them real security (4:13). The rich should "weep and wail" for the miseries that will come upon them (5:1). Like Jesus, James blesses the poor Christians, for God has chosen them — those who are "poor in the world" — to be "rich in faith and to be heirs of the kingdom" (2:5). Meanwhile, like the prophets and

---

32. Blomberg, *Neither Poverty Nor Riches*, p. 147.
33. Blomberg, *Neither Poverty Nor Riches*, p. 148.
34. Blomberg, *Neither Poverty Nor Riches*, p. 148.
35. See references to this view in Gordon, *Economic Problem*, pp. 59-60.
36. Gordon, *Economic Problem*, p. 60.

wisdom of old, he censures the rich for living evil economic lives. They have "dishonored the poor" through oppression by dragging poor Christians into court (2:6).

Nevertheless, it is not immediately obvious that James's statements support the conclusions drawn by Gordon and others. For if New Testament scholar Craig Blomberg is correct, "the rich" in James 1:10 are Christians. And if so, then James envisioned the possibility, but not a general mandate, of divestment.[37] But even if not, it hardly follows that James equated being rich with being in an unchristian condition. Perhaps the rich whom God would soon bring low, and who would disappear like a flower in the field, are comparable to the unrighteous rich of the Psalms and books of wisdom. James could well have been referring to the powerful ruling classes in Jerusalem who persecuted and impoverished the vulnerable little community of Christians. That judgment would place James squarely in line with the prophetic and wisdom traditions of Israel, and there is a longstanding opinion in scholarship that this is exactly where James belongs. Luke Johnson judges that "the New Testament letter of James continues the witness of the Law, Prophets and Writings to the church of Jesus Christ."[38]

The teachings of James certainly comport with this view of his assumptions. He rounds off his opening section with a statement that he then develops in the rest of the epistle. "Religion that is pure and undefiled before God, the Father, is this: to care for the widows and orphans in their distress, and to keep oneself unstained by the world" (James 1:27). Placed in the context of the moral vision of the prophets and the literature of wisdom, a reading emerges that centers on the use of wealth, not on the inherent evil of having possessions. Riches are evil on the conditions that people make them absolute ends of life, and especially when they become an altar on which to sacrifice the poor. When that happens (as Proverbs and Jesus promised), it is better to remain poor than rich, for when people are rich in that evil manner, God will inevitably destroy them (5:1-7). And it is better to be patient and to endure like the prophets (5:10) and like Job (5:11).

But none of this implies that James denies the possibility and goodness of riches in a context of faith and righteous action. We conclude that

---

37. Blomberg, *Neither Poverty Nor Riches,* p. 150.
38. Luke Timothy Johnson, *Sharing Possessions,* p. 100.

James stands as a prophetic warning to the rich and thus as a powerful document of advocacy for the poor. Less a manifesto of social transformation, it is more a peculiar source of encouragement to the poor in their suffering.

PAUL AND THE GREAT COLLECTION

The Apostle Paul also wrote, albeit sparingly, on Christian economic life. The background for his teaching was mainly the disastrous situation of crisis in Jerusalem. During the peak years of his work as an apostle (from about A.D. 48 to 56), Paul worked intensely to collect money for "the poor among the saints at Jerusalem" (Rom. 15:26).[39] He mentions this collection in several of his letters.[40] Considering the importance that Paul attaches to this mission, and also the stress on economic themes in Luke-Acts, it is very odd that Luke fails to mention either the poverty of the Jerusalem church or Paul's Great Collection. It is particularly mystifying since, in Galatians, Paul relates how they agreed at the Council of Jerusalem to launch this effort.[41] Furthermore, if Ron Sider's interpretation of the collection is sound — that it exemplified the ideals presented by Luke in Acts for a general Christian ethics — then we would expect Luke to have narrated it in that way. But he did not, and I would think that this weighs against that interpretation and application of Paul's teaching.

At any rate, the most important text in Paul for our discussion is in his second epistle to the Corinthians, especially chapters 8 and 9. The importance of the collection to Paul is very evident from both the amount of space he devotes to it in the letter and from the sophisticated quality of theological argument in his appeal. He begins by grounding it in the narrative of Jesus' life: "For you know the generous act of our Lord Jesus Christ, that though he was rich, yet for your sakes he became poor, so that by his poverty you might become rich" (8:9). Paul appeals to a principle of equitability or fairness in

---

39. See Bassler, *God and Mammon*, pp. 89-116.

40. Acts 15 and Galatians 2 recount how the agreement to perform such duties was struck at the Jerusalem Council of A.D. 48. This makes it even more difficult to explain Luke's omission of it from the narrative of Acts. Paul writes of it in 2 Corinthians 8 and 9 as well as in the cited reference to Romans 15.

41. On this problem see Gordon, *Economic Problem*, p. 78. Also Johnson, *Possessions in Luke-Acts*, pp. 32-36; and 219-20.

terms that sound very like those of liberation theologians and defenders of simpler living: "I do not mean that there should be relief for others and pressures on you, but it is a question of fair balance between your present abundance and their need, so that their abundance might be for your need, in order that there might be a fair balance" (8:13-14). He then cites the story in Exodus (16:18) of God providing manna for his people in the wilderness: "As it is written, 'The one who had much did not have too much, and the one who had little did not have too little'" (8:15).

Paul completes his appeal by stressing its voluntary nature (even though he seems rhetorically to have put it in the form of an implied command). "Each of you must give as you have made up your mind, not reluctantly or under compulsion, for God loves a cheerful giver" (9:7). He reminds the Corinthians that "God is able to provide you with every blessing in abundance, so that by always having enough of everything you may share abundantly in every good work" (9:8-9).

As we have seen, Sider, Blomberg, and others believe that these texts from Paul are strongly normative for general Christian ethics, and the ethics they draw from them are decidedly utilitarian, in the context of the manna. There are two claims here. Oddly, I believe that the second one is (in a qualified sense) true. I believe that Paul did teach in these passages that the Corinthians could choose to submit out of grace to an ethics of the utilitarian sort. But I do not believe that Paul taught (implicitly or explicitly) in these passages that this ethics is normative for all Christians in all times and circumstances. I discern no clear grounds in them for the first part of Blomberg's statement: "So many principles for Christian giving can be derived from these chapters that we must proceed extremely slowly through this text."[42] On the contrary, there are good reasons — both exegetical and historical — for thinking that Paul advanced this ethics as both provisional and exceptional in response to an emergency and grave crisis in the early development of Christianity as a faith.

As for historical and contextual reasons, various scholars point out that Paul was not here collecting for world relief, or even for the world church. The collection was exclusively for the church in Jerusalem during its critical moment. Bassler observes that Paul's main concern was not even the economic poverty of Christians in Jerusalem.[43] Her argument

---

42. Blomberg, *Neither Poverty Nor Riches*, p. 191.
43. Bassler, *God and Mammon*, pp. 92-96; Johnson, *Sharing Possessions*, pp. 112-13.

seems to me irresistible. For if we begin with the question of why Paul undertook this collection for Jerusalem alone, the answer cannot be that this was the way he believed the churches should react in the event that poverty struck one church or another. In this passage Paul begins by noting that the Macedonian church was poor, too, but he made no appeal to collect for them. In fact, he appealed to them to give to the church in Jerusalem. Why?[44] "It was thus clearly not on economic grounds alone that the collection was destined for the Jerusalem church."[45]

Paul's primary concern was rather with the connection between Israel and the emerging Gentile church. It was with repairing the broken relationship between the older covenant and the newer one, to promote the salvation of his own people, and to preserve the basic traditions needed for Christianity to be a genuine messianic faith, the true form of Judaism that Paul believed it was.[46] The time in Christian history was unique and precarious, and the bond between Jew and Gentile in the formative years was essential to its validity as a faith. These circumstances were thus exceptional, and Paul's emergency measure in response to the crisis was clearly provisional.

Paul's unusual appeal to the exodus narrative of the manna supports this judgment. Sider takes from it an example for economic life in all circumstances where poverty exists. Of the Israelites who hoarded more for themselves than they needed for the day, he writes that they were "greedy souls," who "apparently tried to gather more than they could use."[47] The insinuation clearly is that when people in our day keep for themselves more than they can use they, too, thereby commit the grave sin of greed. Craig Blomberg likewise judges that Paul's use of the manna narrative is paradigmatic. He interprets it to enshrine a universal principle of "relative equality" among Christians, one that shows "that there are extremes of wealth and poverty which are intolerable in the Christian community."[48] He thus proposes that affluent Christians endorse a graduated tithe in keeping with Paul's vision of equality, which requires "closing the gap between rich and poor in the body of Christ."[49]

---

44. Bassler, *God and Mammon*, p. 92.
45. Bassler, *God and Mammon*, p. 92.
46. Bassler, *God and Mammon*, p. 94.
47. Sider, *Rich Christians*, p. 87.
48. Blomberg, *Neither Poverty Nor Riches*, p. 194.
49. Blomberg, *Neither Poverty Nor Riches*, p. 195.

But we have seen that in the exodus narrative the diet of manna and the rules that God affixed to it (taking no more than a day's ration) were temporary and probationary. The time in the wilderness eating manna under the one-day rule was a test of Israel's faith, and a prelude to entry into the land flowing with milk and honey. It is intriguing that Paul begins his appeal to the Corinthians by declaring "I am testing the genuineness of your love" (2 Cor. 8:8). And this dire emergency over the fate of Jewish Christianity, and the relationship between old and new covenants, called for similarly exceptional, drastic remedial action. Even the poor Macedonians have rallied to the cause. And it is also interesting that Paul continues his argument by shifting from the language of self-sacrifice to that of abundance. If they act as he hopes they will, Paul promises, God will bless them and they will be "enriched in every way for your great generosity" (2 Cor. 9:10-11). This statement suggests that Paul envisioned their sacrifice as temporary and, while the enrichment was not just that of material blessings, it certainly included them. In the end, then, their delight would be greater for their sacrifice.

But furthermore, Paul makes it very clear that these actions are quite optional. Now, if he built his appeal on universal moral standards for all times and circumstances, response to them could not have been optional. For the directives that followed would have been moral commandments, and commands require obedience. But Paul does not put his appeal in the form of a command, and so the measures he encourages the Corinthians to take could not have grown from universal moral standards for ethics. The form of Paul's appeal was rather that of exhortation and strong preference on his part that they join with him in his effort. But there is no moral commandment to do so. This seems to be an instance of the supererogation that we discussed earlier. One is free to do it, and it would be good to do it, but one is under no moral obligation. So if the actions he advised them to take in this emergency were utilitarian, they were neither morally necessary nor permanent.

In summary, Paul responds to a special economic crisis with a most creative and powerful economic use of Christ's Incarnation and life. Just as the God of the exodus used his might to liberate and empower Israel, so did that God's Son give of himself for our sake — that we might become rich. If Christians may for a time be deprived of their abundance, like Israel in the desert, the point and purpose holds fast to the vision of flourishing for everyone.

Being Affluent in a World of Poverty

What happens in the next twenty years with the 2.8 billion
people whose average income is 2$ a day or less will say a
lot about the moral quality of our generation's Christians
— and our generation of human beings.

MICHAEL NOVAK[1]

In this book I have offered a theological vision for Christians seeking to
live with integrity in a culture of capitalism. Contrary to widespread opinion, it seems that there is a distinctly Christian way to be affluent. In the
first chapter I sought to identify the workings of modern high-tech capitalism — its spirit and ethos — and to show that there are no obvious
grounds for believing that Christian faith and life cannot be integrated
into an active economic involvement in the culture of capitalism. In fact,
as I argued in that chapter, there are good grounds for thinking that they
can be. For the culture of modern capitalism (distinct from older versions)
is unusually suited to the expression of Christian virtues. Furthermore, in
the following chapters I have argued that the biblical narrative gives forth a
constructive, coherent vision for rich people of faith, and that this vision
consists of both affirmation and challenge. The affirmation grows from

---

1. "The Ethical Challenges of Global Capitalism" (transcript of a debate between Ron
Sider and Michael Novak), *Discernment* 8, no. 1 (winter 2001): 2-5.

creation itself, on the view that God designed human beings for conditions of material delight. The challenge grows from the narratives of redemption in a fallen world, and it is to embody the character of God as revealed in the exodus, exile, Incarnation, and Pentecost.

As part of this argument, I have observed that in the key biblical narratives of society and social morality, the strongest relevant obligations of rich people are confined to their relevant defining communities — in terms of both society and unique vocation. I inferred from this limitation that a principle of proximate obligation exists in the morality of economic life, and that this makes possible the remarkably strong affirmation of material delight in those texts (especially in the Old Testament), even in a fallen world where a great many people live in poverty. This notion raises serious doubts about certain moral theories in our time. It especially raises doubts about the moral reasoning that Christian writers commonly apply to the ethics of world poverty. I argued that the notion of proximate obligation makes it doubtful that globalism alone (that is, our technical connectedness with people around the world) generates the theologically strong obligations for people in affluent societies that these writers claim it does. I do not deny that affluent people in the West have obligations of some kind to the global poor, but only that they normally do not have obligations of this theologically ultimate and prophetic kind, as is so commonly argued.

I have not yet indicated in any depth or detail what obligations rich Christians have in this global context. I have suggested that there is something quite personal about the discernment involved with knowing what they are. And I suggested that most often it may be a matter of special divine communication and calling, the work of the Holy Spirit "laying a burden" on the heart for some cause or other in a distant place. In broad terms, then, I believe that the narratives of Scripture help us to keep our sense of obligation from messianic distortion, and in the right perspective.

But I also believe that certain recent works in global economic theory can illumine the moral dimension of economic life for wealthy Christians. I have come to believe that the economic framework for most Christian moral theory on this issue is woefully inadequate to its task, and that most Christians who are concerned about global poverty think about it in fundamentally wrong economic terms. This leads almost inevitably to fundamentally (if sincere) wrong ways of thinking about the morality of global wealth and poverty. As stated earlier, for the most part the economic theories that have been most influential on Christian moral theology are the ones that have grown either from Marx or Weber. And (as also noted) both these powerful systems of economic theory are antiquated in the extreme. Indeed, the new things of modernity have not only burst the wine skins of Christian tradition. They have also "scattered the proud" in things economic, and theorists are groping madly to find fresh unifying accounts of what is happening in economic life.

There is today no Marx or Weber to tower above everyone else. But there are rising stars. And among this new constellation of lights is Peruvian economist Hernando de Soto. De Soto has recently written a book that a good many experts judge to be a work of seminal genius. Its provocative title is *The Mystery of Capital: Why Capitalism Triumphs in the West and Fails Everywhere Else.*[2] In this epilogue, I am going to complement the theology of this book by offering a summary of de Soto's argument. At the end, I will make several modest proposals on how I think it may illumine Christian spiritual and moral thinking on global poverty.

GLOBAL POVERTY AND THE "MYSTERY OF CAPITAL"

Hernando de Soto is president of the Institute for Liberty and Democracy, which has its headquarters in Peru. *Time* magazine named him one of the five leading Latin American innovators of the twentieth century, and as advisor to Peru's president, he masterminded its recent economic reforms.[3] The major premise of his argument (which he supports throughout the book) is that almost everyone has misunderstood what capital is. Most people think of it as a synonym for property, or money, or the means of production. De Soto explains that none of these concepts defines the "mystery of capital." In the context of vast real-world study of economies, crossing continents and spanning more than a decade, he explains that these are mere "assets." And the mysterious truth is that the poor nations have more than enough assets to be successful.

Indeed, the statistics he gives on the net worth of the world's poor will

2. Hernando de Soto, *The Mystery of Capital: Why Capitalism Triumphs in the West and Fails Everywhere Else* (New York: Basic, 2000).

3. This biographical information comes from the book's cover panel.

be eye opening to most readers. Contrary to almost everything we read in economic theology, de Soto makes this stunning claim: "most of the poor already possess the assets they need to make a success of capitalism."[4] The value of savings alone among the poor of the world "is, in fact, immense — forty times all the foreign aid received throughout the world since 1945."[5] To bring the point home:

> In Egypt, for instance, the wealth that the poor have accumulated is worth fifty times as much as the sum of all direct foreign investment ever recorded there, including the Suez Canal and the Aswan Dam. In Haiti, the poorest nation in Latin America, the total assets of the poor are more than one hundred fifty times greater than all the foreign investment received since Haiti's independence from France in 1804. *If the United States were to hike its foreign aid budget to the level recommended by the United Nations — 0.7 percent of national income — it would take the richest country on earth more than 150 years to transfer to the world's poor resources equal to those they already possess.*[6]

According to his numbers, the total value of all the *real estate* owned either formally or informally by the world's poor is in fact 9.3 trillion dollars — about twice the total circulating money supply in the U.S.[7] The problem, then, is (contrary to almost all common opinion) not that these nations lack wealth. It is rather that they hold it in what de Soto calls defective forms.[8] Their assets are dead and they must be brought to life. For assets do not become capital until this happens, and therein lies the "mystery" of which de Soto speaks.

De Soto's "work boot" research, trudging into places where no government official or Western economist had ever been, convinces him that the key is formal property law. One thing poor nations all have in common is that they lack integrated systems of property law to validate real property by binding representation (something people in advanced nations take so much for granted that they hardly are aware of its powerful effects). De Soto's argument (which he supports from a great variety of angles) is as

4. De Soto, *The Mystery of Capital,* p. 5.
5. De Soto, *The Mystery of Capital,* p. 5.
6. De Soto, *The Mystery of Capital,* p. 5 (italics mine).
7. De Soto, *The Mystery of Capital,* p. 5.
8. De Soto, *The Mystery of Capital,* p. 6.

simple as it is ingenious. The representation of assets in this form is what enables societies to create capital from them and to prosper. "This is the mystery of capital."[9]

De Soto compares this conversion process to an electrical system with a power source, a network of wired connections, and outlets available everywhere to people. In this picture, capital is the invisible power of the electricity to move in currents wherever and in what degrees people want it to.[10] In real terms, the capital of the wealthy nations is the power of their assets to change into moveable shapes, like business and home loans, investments, wages, taxes, securities, and so forth. In short, capital is not the stuff people have. It is the invisible connections that must be in place before the stuff can become electrified with the power to be and to create wealth. For no matter how many resources a people have (and most poor nations have a lot), or how hard they may try to make things work (and people in the Third World work hard), without formal property representation the system cannot work.

Indeed, de Soto seeks to show that the economies of Europe and the United States did not really work either until the chaotic state of their formal property law was put into coherent shape. But once it was put in order (which did not happen overnight), their economies took off. Europe has a similar history to that of the United States, only worse in its confusion and in the time it took for integrated systems for banking, investing, representing, taxing, regulating, and so forth to at last emerge.[11]

"The formal property system is capital's hydroelectric plant. This is the place where capital is born."[12] In de Soto's extraordinary analysis, then, so long as nations lack this integrated legal (and political) framework, capitalism in their societies will look like it does now. The standard is what French historian Braudel called the bell jar. At its inception capitalism in the West looked very like capitalism does today in many parts of the world. Inside the bell jar lives a small, privileged elite. Outside the jar lives the rest of society in relative degrees of poverty.[13] Because of this, de Soto warns, capitalism is rapidly losing support in most places where hopes were once high, but are no more.

9. De Soto, *The Mystery of Capital*, p. 6.
10. De Soto, *The Mystery of Capital*, pp. 44-45
11. De Soto, *The Mystery of Capital*, pp. 105-51.
12. De Soto, *The Mystery of Capital*, p. 47.
13. De Soto, *The Mystery of Capital*, pp. 66-67.

While de Soto is by his own admission no great defender of capitalism, as some might suspect, and is somewhat downcast about the future of capitalism in certain places, he also believes that the solution to the mystery is as straightforward as it could be. "All" that has to be done is to create integrated and stable formal systems of property law, and the rest will fall into place. But how does de Soto's compelling work illumine the way that we wealthy Christians ought to think spiritually and morally about global poverty? I want to finish this addendum by identifying three key points of his analysis that lead to creative, fresh, and badly needed new perspectives in Christian thought.

THE MYSTERY OF CAPITAL AND CHRISTIAN MORAL THEOLOGY

The first point is that concerned people in the developed nations have to change the way they have been conditioned to think about conditions in the Third World:

> The words "international poverty" too easily bring to mind images of destitute beggars sleeping on the curbs of Calcutta and hungry African children starving on the sand. These scenes are of course real, and millions of our fellow human beings demand and deserve our help. Nevertheless, the grimmest picture of the Third World is not the most accurate. Worse, it draws attention away from the arduous achievements of those small entrepreneurs who have triumphed over every imaginable obstacle to create the greater part of the wealth of their society. A truer image would depict a man and a woman who have painstakingly saved to construct a house for themselves and their children and who are creating enterprises where nobody imagined they could be built. I resent the characterization of such heroic entrepreneurs as contributors to the problem of global poverty. They are not the problem. *They are the solution.*[14]

A second point follows from the first one. It is that the problem of poverty in these nations is not primarily external, but internal — it is the legal and political disintegration and chaos in the realm of property rights. And from this a third: neither is the solution to poverty in these places external

14. De Soto, *The Mystery of Capital*, pp. 36-37.

— it is rather to solve the mystery on the inside "of how assets are transformed into live capital."[15]

All three points raise serious criticisms of the standard Christian moral writings on global poverty. They suggest that the picture these writers give of global poverty is as patronizing as it is economically mistaken in the first place. They suggest also that the guilt and sense of responsibility they lay upon people living in the prosperous countries is essentially misplaced. And, likewise, these points suggest that many of the "solutions" they propose — reforming international policies of trade, expanding foreign aid, and especially reducing consumption at home (simpler living) are at bottom as misguided as they are well-meaning. If de Soto's analysis is correct (as a good number of experts in development believe he is), then it invalidates a great deal of what has become the almost unquestioned approach to world poverty among theologians in the First World.

For instance, in a recent lecture Ron Sider presents the lack of capital (as he uses the term) available to the poor as a consequence of how "market economies" are operating — in "damnable defiance of the biblical God of justice."[16] Instead, he argues, the authorities (we suppose) in these economies (whichever ones they are) must execute a "redistribution of effective access to capital."[17] He declares that to do otherwise is "straightforward disobedience to biblical teaching."[18]

But what exactly is it that Sider is urging us to do, lest we forsake our faith? In the first place, the nations we all have in view do not have market systems in anything like the form envisioned by Adam Smith or advocated by contemporary defenders of modern capitalism. If they did, there would not be such widespread poverty. Secondly, access to capital is not something that people can just redistribute (as, say, parcels of land). For in these nations, on de Soto's definition, there is no capital, but only dead assets. And if there were, there would be no need to redistribute access to it. One feature of real capital, like electricity in a properly wired grid system, is that it just is available. As Novak points out in direct response to Sider's proposal, "Capital is not something that you can have access to, like fruit on a tree. You have to invent it or discover it."[19] What the poor need, Novak

15. De Soto, *The Mystery of Capital,* p. 37.
16. "Ethical Challenges," p. 2.
17. "Ethical Challenges," pp. 2-3.
18. "Ethical Challenges," p. 3.
19. "Ethical Challenges," p. 5.

points out, is a legal and political environment in which they have access to credit, and to better education, so that they can create capital.[20]

What this implies regarding the moral involvement of those Westerners who wish to help is unclear, but it at very least gets the problem and solution into sharp focus. And of course it does place the greater weight of the moral burden where it belongs — upon the leaders in those nations who have a legal hydroelectric plant first to build before anything else of deep significance can happen for their people. Meanwhile, I suppose that one of the best things we outsiders can do is maintain the health and power of our own plant and, thus, provide a good model and also resources that insiders can take for inspiration and means in the elimination of poverty and the liberation of the poor from its deathly grip. I have no idea how doing so is even marginally possible on a model of reduced consumption of "non-necessities," however — at least not in this world.

But furthermore, as a Peruvian, de Soto stresses throughout the book that neither the success of the wealthy nations nor the poverty of the undeveloped ones is due to special qualities among those peoples. Contrary to what we may believe about ourselves, we are not smarter and more hardworking than our poor neighbors. On the contrary, he movingly observes how people in the Third World work so hard for their smallish gains as to be heroic. The difference is not in the people, but in the systems that serve the people (or do not do so). In the United States an ordinary teenager, lacking all maturity, insight, or any remarkable skill at anything, can slide a credit card into a gas pump slot and draw immediately on the magical mystery of capital. His parents take for granted that they can have a mortgage, or loan on their business, that will enable them to convert what they have into the capital they need to secure, among many other things, the requisite four years in college. This, of course, gives the unwitting teenager vast power compared with his counterparts in the Third World, many of whom are more serious, smarter, and better human beings than he. So his position of privilege is not something he earned, for the formal legal system governing property (of which he has not a clue) has saved him from poverty and made him rich by sheer *grace.*

There are of course grave dangers in this situation. Affluent people may become oblivious to the grace that creates their circumstances in the first place. They may thus become arrogant and even hard toward the suf-

20. "Ethical Challenges," p. 5.

fering of others. They may say to themselves in a great variety of ways that they have "made this wealth by their own hand," as Deuteronomy has it. And they may become ruined, lacking strength of character in every sense of the term. But nor is the great good fortune of these people in any clear way a moral injustice, as ethicist John Rawls suggests it is.[21] Their success may be undeserved, but surely there is nothing immoral about our teenager's privileged position in the world, or others like him. It is just his good luck (or fortune) to be in the right place and time.

Dinesh D'Souza puts this matter of good luck very well. On the whole, the people who are wealthy have indeed done a lot to create their fortunes.[22] And the ones who have just lucked out — won the lottery, so to speak, by choosing their parents well — do not for that reason lose their moral rights to what they have. Unless there are other deciding moral factors involved, they no more lose their right to have it than someone who finds a hundred dollar bill on the sidewalk loses her right to it.[23]

But at the same time, two people in Haiti who wish to save and to procure land for some purpose must go through so many bureaucratic steps that the process takes, on average, *nineteen years.* And even then there is no legal assurance that the title is theirs.[24] That does not give them any direct right to part or all of what the teenager has, but it most assuredly makes them deserving of his (our) heartfelt compassion. What actions should follow from compassion, however, are unclear, since they will depend on a great variety of circumstances that we cannot very well know ahead of time. It is clear, however, that any actions not directed at this formal legal problem will be of very little enduring help.

The final point, then, is that de Soto teaches us what we already should know from our scriptures and traditions. Prosperity does require hard work. But at bottom, it really is a matter of grace, and not works. It is a gift, lest we forget it. And the poverty of people worldwide (and sometimes even at home) is almost always more a matter of bondage and bad fortune than deliberate choice. It requires from us who are wealthy a spirit of compassion, full of respect for that condition and the people trapped within it. It would be good to see de Soto's ideas integrated into Western moral the-

21. See Dinesh D'Souza, *The Virtue of Prosperity: Finding Values in an Age of Techno-Affluence* (New York: Free Press, 2000), pp. 100-103, on Rawls's argument.

22. D'Souza, *The Virtue of Prosperity,* pp. 87-99.

23. D'Souza, *The Virtue of Prosperity,* p. 101.

24. De Soto, *The Mystery of Capital,* p. 21.

ology on the subject of global poverty. For his work encourages thought-fulness on the part of affluent Christians, guiding us lest our compassion be misplaced.

Bibliography

Abraham, William J. *Divine Revelation and the Limits of Historical Criticism.* Oxford: Oxford University Press, 1982.

—————. *The Divine Inspiration of Holy Scripture.* Oxford: Oxford University Press, 1981.

Applebaum, Stanley. "The Social and Economic Status of the Jews in the Diaspora." In S. Safrai and M. Stern, *The Jewish People in the First Century: Historical Geography, Political History, Social, Cultural and Religious Life and Institutions.* Vol. 2, pp. 662-65. Edited by D. Flusser and W. C. van Unnik. Assen, Maastricht: Van Gorcum, 1987.

Augustine. *In Psalmos.* Edited by J.-P. Migne. Patrologiae Cursus Completus, Series Latina. Paris: Garnier, 1834.

Barth, Karl. *Church Dogmatics.* Vol. II/1. Edited and translated by Geoffrey W. Bromiley. Edinburgh: T&T Clark, 1957.

—————. *Church Dogmatics.* Vol. III/1. Edited and translated by Geoffrey W. Bromiley. Edinburgh: T&T Clark, 1958.

—————. *Church Dogmatics,* III/2. Edited and translated by Geoffrey W. Bromiley. Edinburgh: T&T Clark, 1960.

Bassler, Jouette. *God and Mammon: Asking for Money in the New Testament.* Nashville: Abingdon, 1991.

Batey, Richard A. *Jesus and the Forgotten City.* Grand Rapids: Baker, 1992.

Bavinck, Herman. *The Doctrine of God.* Translated by William Hendriksen. Grand Rapids: Baker, 1977.

Bellah, Robert. *Habits of the Heart.* New York: Harper, 1985.

Blomberg, Craig L. *Neither Poverty Nor Riches: A Biblical Theology of Material Possessions.* Grand Rapids: Eerdmans, 1999.

Bly, Robert. *Iron John.* New York: Vintage, 1990.

Braaten, Carl, and Robert Jenson. *Christian Dogmatics.* Philadelphia: Fortress, 1984.

Bright, John. *The Kingdom of God.* Nashville: Abingdon, 1953.

Brokaw, Tom. *The Greatest Generation.* New York: Random House, 1998.

Bruce, F. F. *The Book of Acts.* The New International Commentary on the New Testament. Grand Rapids: Eerdmans, 1953.

Brueggemann, Walter. *The Prophetic Imagination.* Philadelphia: Fortress, 1978.

Brunner, Emil. *The Christian Doctrine of God.* Translated by Olive Wyon. Philadelphia: Westminster, 1949.

Calvin, John. *Institutes of the Christian Religion.* Edited by John T. McNeill and translated by Ford Lewis Battles. Library of Christian Classics. Philadelphia: Westminister, 1960.

Carroll R., Mark Daniel. *Contexts for Amos: Prophetic Poetics in Latin American Perspective.* Sheffield: Sheffield Academic, 1992.

Childs, Brevard S. *The Book of Exodus.* Philadelphia: Westminster, 1974.

————. *Introduction to the Old Testament as Scripture.* Philadelphia: Fortress, 1979.

Chilton, David. *Productive Christians in an Age of Guilt Manipulators.* Tyler, Tex.: Institute for Christian Economics, 1981.

Clark, Malcolm. "The Legal Background to the Yahwist's Use of 'Good and Evil' in Genesis 2–3." *Journal of Biblical Theology* 88 (Sept. 1969): 266-78.

Clines, David J. A. "The Image of God in Man." *Tyndale Bulletin* 19 (1968): 53-103.

Cooper, John. *Body, Soul, and Life Everlasting.* Grand Rapids: Eerdmans, 1989.

"The Cornwall Declaration on Environmental Stewardship." *Religion and Liberty* 10, no. 2 (March and April 2000): 9-11.

Couture, Pamela D. *Blessed Are the Poor?* Nashville: Abingdon, 1991.

de Soto, Hernando. *The Mystery of Capital: Why Capitalism Triumphs in the West and Fails Everywhere Else.* New York: Basic, 2000.

D'Souza, Dinesh. *The Virtue of Prosperity: Finding Values in an Age of Techno-Affluence.* New York: Free Press, 2000.

Ellul, Jacques. *Money and Power.* Translated by LaVonne Neff. Downers Grove, Ill.: InterVarsity, 1984.

Eskridge, Larry, and Mark A. Noll, eds. *More Money, More Ministry: Money and Evangelicals in Recent North American History.* Grand Rapids: Eerdmans, 2000.

"The Ethical Challenges of Global Capitalism." Transcript of a debate between Ron Sider and Michael Novak. *Discernment* 8, no. 1 (winter 2001): 2-5.

Frankfort, Henri. *The Intellectual Adventure of Ancient Man*. Chicago: University of Chicago Press, 1977.

Gay, Craig M. *With Liberty and Justice for Whom? The Recent Evangelical Debate Over Capitalism*. Grand Rapids: Eerdmans, 1991.

Geldenhuys, Norval. *Commentary on the Gospel of Luke*. The New International Commentary on the New Testament. Grand Rapids: Eerdmans, 1951.

Gish, Art. "Decentralist Economics." In *Wealth and Poverty: Four Christian Views*, edited by Robert Clouse. Downers Grove, Ill.: InterVarsity, 1984.

Gladwin, John. "Centralist Economics." In *Wealth and Poverty: Four Christian Views*, edited by Robert Clouse. Downers Grove, Ill.: InterVarsity, 1984.

Gonzalez, Justo L. *Faith and Wealth: A History of Early Christian Ideas on the Origin, Significance, and Use of Money*. San Francisco: Harper & Row, 1990.

Gordon, Barry. *The Economic Problem in Biblical and Patristic Thought*. Leiden: Brill, 1989.

Gottwald, Norman K. "The Exodus as Event and Process: A Test Case in the Biblical Grounding of Liberation Theology." In *The Future of Liberation Theology*, edited by M. Ellis and O. Maduro. Maryknoll, N.Y.: Orbis, 1989.

Green, Robert, ed. *Protestantism and Capitalism: The Weber Thesis and Its Critics*. Boston: Heath, 1959.

Griffiths, Brian. *The Creation of Wealth*. Downers Grove, Ill.: InterVarsity, 1985.

Gutiérrez, Gustavo. *A Theology of Liberation*. Translated and edited by Sister Caridad Inda and John Eagleson. Maryknoll, N.Y.: Orbis, 1973.

Hardy, Lee. *The Fabric of This World*. Grand Rapids: Eerdmans, 1991.

Hartley, John. *Word Biblical Commentary: Leviticus*. Dallas: Word, 1992.

Hasel, Gerhard. "The Polemical Nature of the Genesis Cosmology." *Evangelical Quarterly* 46 (1974): 81-102.

Hauerwas, Stanley. "Christian Schooling or Making Students Dysfunctional?" In *Sanctify Them in the Truth: Holiness Exemplified*, pp. 219-26. Nashville: Abingdon, 1998.

Hauerwas, Stanley, and L. Gregory Jones, eds. *Why Narrative? Readings in Narrative Theology*. Grand Rapids: Eerdmans, 1989.

Hawkin, Paul, Amory Lovins, and Hunter Lovins. *Natural Capitalism*. Boston: Little, Brown, 2000.

Heidel, Alexander, trans. and ed. *The Babylonian Genesis*. 2nd ed. Chicago: University of Chicago Press, 1963.

Hengel, Martin. *Property and Riches in the Early Church*. Translated by John Bowden. Philadelphia: Fortress, 1974.

Holmberg, Bengt. *Sociology and the New Testament: An Appraisal.* Minneapolis: Fortress, 1990.

Horsley, Richard. *Jesus and the Spiral of Violence.* San Francisco: Harper & Row, 1987.

Horsley, Richard, with J. S. Hanson. *Bandits, Prophets, and Messiahs: Popular Movements at the Time of Jesus.* San Francisco: Harper & Row, 1985.

Hubbard, Robert. "The Go'el in Ancient Israel: Theological Reflections on an Israelite Institution." *Bulletin for Biblical Research* 1 (1991): 3-19.

Huber, Peter. *Hard Green.* New York: Basic, 1999.

John Paul II. *On the Hundredth Anniversary of "Rerum Novarum."* Boston: St. Paul, 1991.

————. *Laborem Exercens: On Human Work.* Sydney: St. Paul, 1981.

Johnson, Luke Timothy. *The Literary Function of Possessions in Luke-Acts.* Missoula, Mont.: Scholars, 1977.

————. *Sharing Possessions: Mandate and Symbol of Faith.* Philadelphia: Fortress, 1981.

————. *The Gospel of Luke.* Sacra Pagina, vol. 3. Collegeville, Minn.: Liturgical, 1991).

Kaufmann, Yehezkel. *The Religion of Israel* (Chicago: University of Chicago Press, 1960).

Landes, George. "Creation and Liberation." In *Creation in the Old Testament,* edited by Bernhard W. Anderson, pp. 135-51. Philadelphia: Fortress, 1984.

Lay Commission on Catholic Social Teaching and the U.S. Economy. *Toward the Future: Catholic Social Thought and the U.S. Economy.* North Tarrytown, N.Y., 1984.

Leo XIII. *Rerum Novarum.* Vatican City: Democrazia Christiana, Direzione Nazionale, Dipartmento Formazione, 1991.

Levine, Baruch A. *The JPS Torah Commentary: Leviticus.* Philadelphia: Jewish Publication Society, 1989.

Limburg, James. *The Prophets and the Powerless.* Atlanta: John Knox, 1977.

Luther, Martin. "An Appeal to the Ruling Class." Translated and edited by John Dillenberger in *Martin Luther.* Garden City: Doubleday/Anchor, 1961.

Marshall, I. Howard. *Commentary on Luke.* The New International Greek Testament Commentary. Grand Rapids: Eerdmans, 1978.

McNeill, John T. *The History and Character of Calvinism.* New York: Oxford University Press, 1954.

Meeks, Wayne. *The First Urban Christians: The Social World of the Apostle Paul.* New Haven: Yale University Press, 1983.

Middleton, J. Richard. "The Liberating Image? Interpreting the Imago Dei in Context." *The Christian Scholars Review* 24, no. 1 (Sept. 1994): 8-25.

Bibliography

Moessner, David P. *Lord of the Banquet: The Literary and Theological Significance of the Lukan Travel Narrative.* Minneapolis: Fortress, 1989.

Mott, Stephen. *Biblical Ethics and Social Change.* Oxford: Oxford University Press, 1981.

Mouw, Richard J. *Political Evangelism.* Grand Rapids: Eerdmans, 1973.

Nash, James. *Loving Nature.* Nashville: Abingdon, 1991.

Neuhaus, Richard John. *Doing Well and Doing Good: The Challenge to the Christian Capitalist.* New York: Doubleday, 1992.

Niebuhr, H. Richard. *Christ and Culture.* New York: Harper, 1951.

North, Robert, S.J. *Sociology of the Jubilee.* Rome: Pontifico Istituto Biblico, 1954.

Novak, Michael. *The Spirit of Democratic Capitalism.* New York: Simon & Schuster, 1982.

———. *Will It Liberate? Questions about Liberation Theology.* New York: Paulist, 1986.

Oakman, Douglas. *Jesus and the Economic Question of His Day.* Lewiston, N.Y.: Mellen, 1986.

Pagels, Elaine. *The Gnostic Gospels.* New York: Random, 1981.

Payne, J. Barton. *The Theology of the Older Testament.* Grand Rapids: Zondervan, 1962.

Pilgrim, Walter. *Good News to the Poor: Wealth and Poverty in Luke-Acts.* Minneapolis: Augsburg, 1981.

Plantinga, Alvin. *Warranted Christian Belief.* Oxford: Oxford University Press, 2000.

Robinson, Joan. *Freedom and Necessity.* New York: Pantheon, 1970.

Royal, Robert. *The Virgin and the Dynamo: Use and Abuse of Religion in Environmental Debates.* Grand Rapids: Eerdmans, 1999.

Safrai, S., and M. Stern. *The Jewish People in the First Century: Historical Geography, Political History, Social, Cultural and Religious Life and Institutions.* Vol. 2. Edited by D. Flusser and W. C. van Unnik. Assen, Maastricht: Van Gorcum, 1987.

Schmidt, Thomas E. "The Hard Sayings of Jesus." In *The Midas Trap,* edited by David Neff. Wheaton, Ill.: Victor, 1990.

Schneider, John. "Can Protestants Let the Trees Do the Talking?" *Religion and Liberty* 10, no. 2 (March and April 2000): 5-7.

———. *Godly Materialism.* Downers Grove, Ill.: InterVarsity, 1994.

Shakespeare, William. *King Lear* (1605).

Sider, Ronald J. *Rich Christians in an Age of Hunger: Moving from Affluence to Generosity.* 20th Anniversary Revision. Dallas: Word, 1997.

Stackhouse, Max. *Public Theology and Political Economy: Christian Steward-ship in Modern Society* (Lanham, Md.: University Press of America, 1991).

Stackhouse, Max L., and Dennis P. McCann. "A Postcommunist Manifesto: Public Theology after the Collapse of Socialism." In *On Moral Business: Classical and Contemporary Resources for Ethics in Economic Life,* ed. Max L. Stackhouse, Dennis P. McCann, and Shirley Roels, pp. 949-54. Grand Rapids: Eerdmans, 1995.

Stambaugh, John, and David Balch. *The Social World of the First Christians.* London: SPCK, 1986.

Swinburne, Richard. *The Coherence of Theism.* Oxford: Clarendon, 1977.

Tannehill, Robert C. *The Narrative Unity of Luke-Acts: A Literary Interpreta-tion.* Minneapolis: Fortress, 1990.

Thiessen, Gerd. *Sociology of Early Palestinian Christianity.* Philadelphia: For-tress, 1977.

Trible, Phyllis. *God and the Rhetoric of Sexuality.* Philadelphia: Fortress, 1978.

Van Inwagen, Peter. "Critical Studies of the New Testament and the User of the New Testament." In *God, Knowledge and Mystery: Essays in Philosophical Theology.* Ithaca: Cornell University Press, 1995.

Van Leeuwen, Raymond C. "Enjoying Creation — Within Limits." In *The Mi-das Trap,* edited by David Neff. Wheaton, Ill.: Victor, 1990.

————. "Wealth and Poverty: System and Contradiction in Proverbs." Paper presented at the Religion and Theology Department Colloquium at Cal-vin College, Grand Rapids, Mich., 1990, and at the Society of Biblical Literature, New Orleans, La., November 1990.

von Rad, Gerhard. *Genesis.* Translated by John Marks. Philadelphia: Westmin-ster, 1972.

————. *Old Testament Theology.* Vol. 2. Translated by D. M. G. Stalker. New York: Harper & Row, 1965.

Walden, Mark, and Frank Cougar. "The Human Consequences of a Consumer Society." *Green Cross* 2, no. 2 (summer 1996): 13-15.

Weber, Max. *The Protestant Ethic and the Spirit of Capitalism.* Translated by Talcott Parsons. New York: Scribners, 1958.

Wesche, Kenneth Paul. "The Patristic Vision of Stewardship." In *The Con-suming Passion,* edited by Rodney Clapp. Downers Grove, Ill.: Inter-Varsity, 1998.

Wheeler, Sondra Ely. *Wealth as Peril and Obligation: The New Testament on Possessions.* Grand Rapids: Eerdmans, 1995.

White, Lynn Jr. "The Historical Roots of Our Ecological Crisis." *Science* 155 (March 1967): 12-26.

Bibliography

Will, George F. *Suddenly: The American Idea Abroad and at Home 1986-1990*. New York: Free Press, 1990.

Wolterstorff, Nicholas. *Until Justice and Peace Embrace*. Grand Rapids: Eerdmans, 1983.

Wuthnow, Robert, ed. *Rethinking Materialism: Perspectives on the Spiritual Dimension of Economic Behavior*. Grand Rapids: Eerdmans, 1995.

Yoder, John Howard. *The Politics of Jesus*. Grand Rapids: Eerdmans, 1972.

Zeisler, J. A. *Christian Asceticism*. Grand Rapids: Eerdmans, 1973.

Index of Names

Abraham, William J., 6n.3, 9
Applebaum, Stanley, 122
Augustine, 26-27, 31

Balch, D., 126n.31
Barth, Karl, 44, 47n.8, 51n.15, 57n.28
Bassler, Jouette, 199, 207n.39, 208-9
Batey, Richard A., 126n.31
Bavinck, Herman, 51n.15
Bell, Daniel, 37, 39, 40n.73
Bellah, Robert, 42n.3
Benjamin, Walter, 38
Bennett, William, 37
Berry, Wendell, 20, 37, 75
Blomberg, Craig L., 42n.2, 60n.31, 67n.5,
    69-70, 81, 84, 86, 92n.5, 102-3, 109n.22,
    115n.26, 125, 126, 135n.55, 136, 147,
    157n.28, 194n.3, 206, 208, 209
Braaten, Carl, 47n.8
Bright, John, 53n.18
Brokaw, Tom, 18
Bruce, F. F., 198n.18, 199
Brueggemann, Walter, 95n.8
Brunner, Emil, 51n.15
Buffett, Warren, 75
Burkett, Larry, 29

Calvin, John, 27, 195

Capone, Al, 22
Carpenter, Joel A., 29n.50
Carroll R., Mark Daniel, 95n.8, 105n.20
Celsus, 133
Childs, Brevard S., 69n.7, 77n.16, 92
Chilton, David, 80n.21
Clark, Malcolm, 62
Clines, David J. A., 48n.12
Cooper, John, 57n.27
Cougar, Frank, 54-55
Couture, Pamela D., 182nn.19, 20

De Soto, Hernando, 213-20
Dibelius, Martin, 205
D'Souza, Dinesh, 4, 20-22, 30, 33, 34, 38-
    40, 55-56, 219
Du Pont, Jean, 201-2

Eberly, Don, 37
Edwards, Jonathan, 28
Eliot, T. S., 41, 113-14, 154
Ellul, Jacques, 167
Eskridge, Larry, 29nn.48,50

Feuerbach, Ludwig, 90
Frankfort, Henri, 44n.4, 46n.7

Galileo, 19

Index of Names

Gates, Bill, 20, 30, 75, 100, 102
Gay, Craig M., 23n.34, 25nn.38,39
Geldenhuys, Norval, 171n.7
Gibbon, Edward, 133
Gish, Art, 195
Gladwin, John, 79n.20
Gonzalez, Justo, 26n.41, 118n.3, 194, 200n.25
Gordon, Barry, 26n.41, 42n.2, 78n.19, 81n.23, 125n.25, 126, 141, 150, 196, 205, 207n.41
Gottwald, Norman K., 66n.3
Griffiths, Brian, 31n.55, 176n.16, 191n.35
Gutiérrez, Gustavo, 66, 82, 187n.31, 201-2, 204

Hall, Peter Dobkin, 28n.46
Hardy, Lee, 149n.11
Hartley, John, 82n.27, 86-87
Hasel, Gerhard, 59n.29
Hauerwas, Stanley, 22, 32, 36
Hawkin, Paul, 54
Hengel, Martin, 125, 136
Heston, Charlton, 65
Hitler, Adolf, 18
Holmberg, Bengt, 122n.17
Horsley, Richard, 119n.4, 121n.14, 155, 156
Hubbard, Robert, 85
Huber, Peter, 56
Hyma, Albert, 27

James, William, 61
Jefferson, Thomas, 57, 87
Jenson, Robert, 47n.8
John Paul II, Pope, 15-16, 125n.25
Johnson, Luke Timothy, 137, 140, 141, 142, 145, 151-53, 157, 162, 170, 173n.8, 175, 176n.16, 182, 185, 186, 188n.33, 194, 203, 206, 207n.41
Julian of Norwich, 114
Justin Martyr, 125n.27

Kaufmann, Yehezkel, 65, 78n.18
Keller, Catherine, 52

Keynes, John Maynard, 16
Kuyper, Abraham, 117

Landes, George, 41n.1
Leo XIII, Pope, 13, 16
Levine, Baruch A., 82n.27
Lewis, C. S., 191-92
Limburg, James, 76n.15, 92n.2
Lippmann, Walter, 32
Locke, John, 87
Lovins, Amory, 54
Lovins, Hunter, 54
Luther, Martin, 27, 195

McCann, Dennis P., 17n.14
McFague, Sally, 52
MacIntyre, Alasdair, 22
Marcos, Ferdinand, 97
Marcos, Imelda, 43, 97
Marshall, I. Howard, 171, 190n.34
Marx, Karl, 2, 16, 20, 57, 133, 213
Meeks, Wayne, 134, 136, 196-97
Middleton, J. Richard, 47, 52n.16, 59
Moessner, David P., 157-60, 175, 177
Mother Teresa, 30
Mott, Stephen, 90n.1, 108n.21
Mouw, Richard J., 132n.46

Nash, James, 45n.6
Neuhaus, Richard John, 14n.4, 16n.8, 17n.14
Niebuhr, H. Richard, 9, 13-14, 117n.2, 129
Nietzsche, Friedrich, 57
Noll, Mark, 29n.50
North, Robert, 79n.20, 84, 86
Novak, Michael, 1, 2, 4, 13, 16-17, 19-20, 23, 39, 211, 217-18

Oakman, Douglas, 123n.22, 133n.49

Pagels, Elaine, 148n.10
Pilgrim, Walter, 125, 133nn.47,48, 143, 144, 156, 163, 174n.9, 183, 200
Plantinga, Alvin, 6n.3

Index of Scripture References